TERROR, FORCE AND STATES

To Harriet

Terror, Force and States

The Path from Modernity

Rosemary H.T. O'Kane

Department of Politics
University of Keele

Edward Elgar
Cheltenham, UK • Brookfield, US

Published by
Edward Elgar Publishing Limited
8 Lansdown Place
Cheltenham
Glos GL50 2HU
UK

Edward Elgar Publishing Company
Old Post Road
Brookfield
Vermont 05036
US

British Library Cataloguing in Publication Data
O'Kane, Rosemary H.T.
  Terror, Force and States: Path from
  Modernity
  I. Title
  321.9

Library of Congress Cataloguing in Publication Data
O'Kane, Rosemary H.T.
  Terror, force, and states : the path from modernity / Rosemary
H.T. O'Kane.
      p.   cm.
  Includes bibliographical references and index.
  1. Totalitarianism.   2. State-sponsored terrorism.   I. Title.
JC481.039   1996
320.5'3'0904—dc20   95–34568
                                                            CIP

ISBN 1 85278 694 9

Typeset by Manton Typesetters, 5–7 Eastfield Road, Louth, Lincolnshire LN11 7AJ, UK
Printed and bound in Great Britain by Biddles Ltd, Guildford and King's Lynn

Contents

Acknowledgements

While writing this book I found it hard at times to think of anything other than its concerns. I benefited doubly, therefore, from the Keele Research Award which relieved me of normal teaching and administrative duties, for it afforded me not only the uninterrupted opportunity to work but also more peace of mind. I am grateful to the Politics Department at Keele, particularly for accommodating my leave. I am especially indebted to Brian Doherty in whose capable hands the Political Sociology courses were run in my absence and negotiated through the perilous change to modularization. I would also like to thank Margaret Canovan for inspiring my interest in Hannah Arendt's work which proved so central to both my concerns and my understanding. I am also doubly indebted to Kim Johnson and Maureen Groppe for typing the manuscript. Not only did they smile through my seemingly endless changes, but they had to face the subject matter without warning. Kim's move from Keele is a great loss and I am exceedingly grateful to Maureen for stepping into the breach. As always, I am also indebted to my family, Les and Harriet Rosenthal, just for being there. Again, I am grateful to Edward Elgar who gave me not only the opportunity but also the freedom to write this book.

Rosemary H.T. O'Kane
Keele

Introduction

The theory presented here aims to explain the nature and causes of states – or rather, in agreement with Arendt, 'so-called' states – where terror rules. The theory runs against the common view of states defined in terms of their monopoly of the means of coercion and renders the normal tools of political science inappropriate and, therefore, misleading when applied to terror governments.

The potential for developing a theory of terror regimes grew from a familiarity with the debates surrounding the subject of totalitarianism. These ideas were fed by my research into *coups d'état* and military regimes and, later, by my investigations into revolutionary reigns of terror. Together these areas of research served to draw attention to the peculiarities shared by Germany under Hitler and the Soviet Union under Stalin, whether compared with 'normal states' or with states in abnormal times. Events in Eastern Europe in 1989 for most commentators drew interest away from totalitarianism towards the 'end of history'. From a position of interest in military regimes and reigns of terror as a stage of revolution, witness to the absence of concentration camps in Eastern Europe seemed to sharpen their significance. Against the usual tendency in the literature to blur totalitarian theories as one, the crucial differences between Arendt's and Friedrich and Brzezinski's view were brought into stark relief. As totalitarianism ended in Eastern Europe it was Friedrich and Brzezinski's totalitarianism which had collapsed, not Arendt's. The benefits of *glasnost*, in yielding access to new information on Stalin's rule, also afforded possibilities for new understanding. Informed by the existing theories and the potential for fresh comparison of the classic cases, the opportunity was opened for the generation of a new explanation of terror regimes.

The theory of the nature and causes of terror regimes offered here is generated in outline, in Part I, through critical assessment of existing conceptualizations and explanations. It begins in Chapter 1 with a critical assessment of the existing views on power and the role of coercion in states. The view of force as a form of power (domination) is rejected as, too, is the view of the monopoly of coercion as the essence of the state. Terror is differentiated both from power and force, and repressive governments and terror governments are distinguished conceptually.

In Chapter 2, the most recent and influential theory of the Holocaust, that proposed by Bauman which relates modern genocide to modernity, is critically examined in the light of the works of Beetham and Weber. Two of the important themes of the new theory, secrecy and the relevance of economic crisis, are developed. Most importantly, the value of Weber's ideas on substantive rationality is demonstrated; these ideas give rise to the development of the notion of 'substantive irrationality' which forms the crux of the explanation of terror regimes offered here.

Returning to earlier approaches, in Chapter 3 the classic theories of totalitarianism are examined and compared, in the light of Bauman's theory. In this process, the importance of modernity as explanation for the rule of terror is challenged further and the crucial distinction between totalitarian dictatorship and totalitarian regime, offered by Arendt, is developed. As illustration, Italy under Mussolini is shown to classify as a totalitarian dictatorship but not a totalitarian regime, and the importance of the distinction made between terror and force is confirmed.

In Chapter 4, Arendt's proposed origins of totalitarianism are explained and through critique of her position the outline of a new theory is developed which stresses both the importance of socioeconomic preconditions of terror regimes and the importance of the leader's immovable conviction in the economic utility of forced labour. Separated from totalitarian dictatorships, which are based on substantive rationality, the proposition is formulated that totalitarian regimes are based on substantive irrationality, severed, that is, from the anchor of the market and based not on plans but on wild schemes.

In Part II, this tentative theory forms the framework for detailed investigation of the classic cases, Stalin's Russia and Nazi Germany. The Soviet case is deliberately tackled first, both because it is the case for which fresh evidence has only recently been made available and because Arendt's theory, which inspires the arguments here, is based on Nazi Germany rather than Stalin's Russia. Russia under Stalin is covered in Chapters 5 and 6, Hitler's Germany in Chapters 7 and 8. In each case the chapters are divided to reflect the break between totalitarian dictatorship and terror as government which occurred in 1930 and 1938 respectively. In turn, the cases serve to refine the theory developed in outline in Part I. To ensure that differences as well as similarities between the cases are brought to light, each case is examined independently through the available historical research. The analyses of the two cases are structured through the tentative theory but are not constrained by it. For example, racialism is shown to play a crucial part in Nazi Germany but does not feature in the case of Stalin's Russia and neither is it claimed that something else played a similar role.

In Part III, Pol Pot's Cambodia is examined as a test case for the value of the theory, now fleshed out through the two classic case studies, as generalization. Examples of terror systems in more primitive societies are also brought in for comparison. Lessons are drawn for terror regimes in general. The methodology employed, part deductive and part inductive, is theoretically informed comparative analysis. The lack of available cases, their rarity being an intrinsic part of the argument, is supplemented by the consideration of existing generalizations.

Though the cases may be limited, the propositions generated contain broad lessons for modern societies and governments. Contrary to the currently popular view, the lessons drawn suggest that totalitarianism, modern genocide, is not intrinsically related to modernity. Where terror rules, it is irrationality, not rationality, that features. Above all, it is the economic rationality of modern society, most particularly in respect of the labour market, which acts as the barrier to terror's rule.

PART I

THE THEORIES

1 Power, force, violence, terror and government

The study of modern politics concentrates on governments in peaceful times – established governments. In theory, in pluralist democracies power is diffuse and an important role of government is to enable groups to put forward opinions and then to draw these opinions into the political system. Modern political systems are portrayed in terms of reconciling differences, encouraging participation and responding to demands. The government may have ideas of its own but it puts such ideas forward as policies to be debated, negotiated through bargaining and compromise. In this approach, analysis of pressure groups, parties and government formation takes place within a framework of the policy process. The 'state' is neutral and taken to be synonymous with 'bureaucracy' which is itself perceived as the servant of the democratic process. Policies are not viewed as imposed; no force or domination is involved in the analysis of 'modern government'. When the police and the military feature it is their control by citizens which is stressed.[1]

In this predominant approach to politics, with democracies characterized by their openness and freedom of association, violent regimes, such as dictatorships, can be contrasted with modern government, and totalitarianism can be portrayed as the political type furthest from democracy. In this view democratic government, a reflection of public opinion institutionalized through competing political parties, stands at the furthest extreme from the monolithic totalitarian state. As a form of government, the word 'state' is reserved for undemocratic political regimes to imply the absence of representation, a domination of government over people which does not seek to take citizens' interests into account and under totalitarianism seeks to destroy conflicting opinions altogether.

State and government: contrary views
There are, however, other approaches where the distinctions between democracies and totalitarian regimes are more blurred. In these analyses of modern governments, viewed as liberal or bourgeois rather than pluralist democracies, political institutions are approached in the light of domination, force placed at the heart of the modern state. In Marx's analysis of 'bourgeois democracy', the state in capitalist societies serves only the interests of the owners of the means of production and acts, therefore, in direct conflict with the interests of the proletariat. (See, for example, Feuer, 1969, chs 1 and 5.)

3

In Michels's (1962) analysis political organizations will inevitably become oligarchical, with leaders, whether of parties, pressure groups or govern- ments themselves, using these organizations to further their own interests over those whom they were elected to represent. In Weber's (1964) analysis, modern legal–rational government is leadership democracy with politicians winning support from the electorate for policies which the leaders have instigated and in which, without the counterweight of strong political leaders, bureaucracy pursues its own organizational interests.

Later theories have drawn democracies closer to totalitarian imagery. Ques- tioning the reality of democracy in the USA, Mills (1956) drew attention to the unelected power of the military and big business after World War II. On Mills's analysis, a 'power élite' existed in which top politicians, along with top military and top business personnel, used their organizational positions to pursue their common interests. Mills also argued that in the USA a mass society was emerging, with a significant proportion of the population's opin- ions going unrepresented because of the 'mass media of distraction'. True opinion-forming publics essential to the pluralist tradition, in Mills's view, were being undermined. Mills also contended that parties, in particular, and pluralist groups, in general, operated only within the 'middle levels of power' between the 'emergent mass society' and the 'power élite'. Significantly, the inclusion of the top military in the power élite drew direct attention to the proximity of force to everyday politics. The lack of true representation and the emergent mass society also challenged the polarized view of western democracies and totalitarian governments. Recognizing the importance of mixed economies in Western Europe, theories of corporatism were developed to reflect the political importance of certain unelected economic groups, in particular big business, but also trade unions. (For a general discussion of these various theories see King, 1986, pp. 115–40.)

An upsurge of interest in comparative history also led to a refocusing on 'the state'. Skocpol (1979) argued through a comparative study of the French, Russian and Chinese revolutions that states acted autonomously. Finegold and Skocpol (1984) expanded this position in a study of the New Deal. In a further essay, Skocpol (1985, p. 7) poignantly stated that 'social scientists are now willing to offer state-centred explanations, not just of totalitarian coun- tries and late industrialisers, but of Britain and the United States themselves'. Tilly (1985), drawing from the lessons of European history, confirmed the importance of war-making to state-making, found in Skocpol (1979), and argued that European states 'began with the effort to monopolise the means of violence within a delimited territory adjacent to a power holder's base' (Tilly, 1985, p. 172).

From a wider analysis of states, ancient and modern, western and Asian, Mann (1984) also argues for a view of 'autonomous state power' in which the monopoly of violence is an essential part. Mann offers two 'dimensions' of 'state power', argued to be found in all states, which combine to form four 'ideal types' of states – feudal, imperial, bureaucratic and authoritarian (according to whether the dimensions are high or low). These dimensions are 'despotic power', which is power by the state élite itself *over* civil society, and 'infrastructural co-ordination', which is 'the power of the state to penetrate and centrally co-ordinate the activities of civil society' (Mann, 1984, p. 190). So, western liberal democracies (classified as 'bureaucratic') are low on despotic power and high on infrastructural coordination and Nazi Germany and the Soviet Union (classified as authoritarian) are high on both despotic power and infrastructural coordination .

With a particular focus on surveillance and the increased capacity for violence offered by twentieth century techniques and means of warfare, Giddens (1981, p. 190; 1985, p. 121) defines the nation-state as 'a set of institutional forms of governance maintaining an administrative monopoly over a territory with demarcated boundaries (borders), its rule being sanctioned by law and direct control of the means of internal and external violence'. In this formulation, totalitarianism is a 'potentiality' of all modern states through 'the consolidated political power generated by a merging of developed techniques of surveillance and the technology of industrialized war' (ibid., p. 295).

Weber and Marx: coercion and the state
This importance of the monopoly of violence as a basic feature of the state, whether traditional or modern, is central to Weber's view. Agreeing with Trotsky's declaration that 'Every state is founded on force' Weber, in his much quoted formulation, defines the state as 'a human community that (successfully) claims the monopoly of the legitimate use of physical force within a given territory'. Weber explains, 'of course, force is certainly not the normal or the only means of the state – nobody says that – but force is a means specific to the state'. He reaffirms this, 'specifically, at the present time, the right to use physical force is ascribed to other institutions or individuals only to the extent to which the state permits it. The state is considered the sole source of the right to use violence.' Again, 'Like the political institutions historically preceding it, the state is a relation of men dominating men, a relation supported by means of legitimate (i.e. considered to be legitimate) violence.' (For the above quotations see Gerth and Mills, 1970, p. 78.)

Walter (1972, p. 50) stresses that what Weber is talking about is violence. In the original German Weber uses the word *Gewalt*, meaning either force or violence, only when quoting Trotsky but consistently throughout this passage on the state he uses *Gewaltsamkeit*, unequivocally 'violence', at each point, eight times in all. (This is supported in the most recent translation, Lassmann and Speirs, 1994.) Because the state is the 'sole source of the right to use violence', Weber argues that 'politics' for us means 'striving to share power or striving to influence the distribution of power either among states or among groups within a state' (Gerth and Mills, 1970, p. 78). Power is something for which those 'active in politics strive' and its special attribute is that with it comes the right to use violence (ibid.).

Whilst Marx's opposition to 'bourgeois democracy' stands in sharp contrast with Weber's defence of liberal (plebiscitary) democracy, in Marx's analysis, as in Weber's, coercion plays a crucial role in the capitalist state. For Marx (1973, p. 205), 'state power' is embodied in its coercive structures, the police, army, courts and bureaucracy, with the police the state's 'ultimate expression'. In the communist society, the one-class society, in theory lacking conflict of interest, these coercive functions of the state can for the first time, logically disappear. Similarly, Engels (1969, p. 522) distinguishes between 'the political state' with its machinery for the coercion of people, and the 'simple administrative functions of watching over the true interests of society'. In the Marxist view of the communist society, the latter will remain and the former will 'wither away'.[2]

Failure to anticipate Stalinist Russia and to distinguish between the capitalist systems in Nazi Germany and, for example, New Deal America are problems for the Marxist analysis. Yet these themes of class domination and conflict of interest in capitalist societies are found in all later Marxist analyses of the state. For example, defining power within the context of class conflict, Poulantzas (1986, p. 145) views power in the following terms: 'the capacity of one class to realize its own interests through its practice is in *opposition* to the capacity and interests of other classes. This determines a *specific* relation of *domination* and *subordination* of class practices, which is exactly characterized as a relation of power'.

Whilst all these analyses, whether of 'government' or 'state', differ from each other in part, what they share is a view of power in capitalist societies, whether approached as bourgeois, liberal or pluralist democracy, as power *over* others, involving conflict and domination. This view of power as domination aligned with force also predominates in the literature on the concept of power.

The definition of power
Russell defined power as 'the production of intended effects'. He adds, 'Naked power is usually military and may take the form either of internal tyranny or of foreign conquest' (Russell, 1986, p. 21). This is echoed in Bierstedt (1950, p. 733) for whom 'force is manifest power' and Goldman (1986, p. 157) for whom 'the central idea in the concept of power is connected with getting what one wants. An all powerful dictator is one whose every desire

for state policy becomes the policy of the state'. Weber views power as 'the probability that an actor in a social relationship will be in a position to carry out his will despite resistance, regardless of the basis on which this probability rests' (Weber, 1964, p. 152). Influenced by Weber, but concerned to measure power within a decision-making framework, Dahl (1957) defines power as 'A has power over B to the extent that he can get B to do something that B would not otherwise do'. Power for Dahl is relational; it is exercised over others, against resistance, and it can be observed. So, even in the benevolent pluralist view of democratic government force and power are blended together.

Bachrach and Baratz: power and force
Bachrach and Baratz object to the prevalent pluralist view of power and argue that force and power are distinct phenomena which, if merged conceptually, lead to a misconceived notion of power. Their argument centres on compliance: 'As we see it, the essential difference between power and force is simply that in a power relationship one party obtains another's compliance, while in a situation involving force one's objectives must be achieved, if at all, in the face of other's *non* compliance' (Bachrach and Baratz, 1970, p. 27). The point is that in Bachrach and Baratz's view there is an essential difference between having the power to get someone to comply with a demand or request, such as handing over money, and forcing a person to surrender their money by knocking them to the ground and grabbing their purse. In the latter case, though the money may have been obtained, compliance or agreement has clearly not been gained. Furthermore, where the victim is shot in the back to achieve the same outcome, they point out that force is entirely non-relational, something which power can never be.

Bachrach and Baratz further argue that manipulation is an aspect not of power but of force, exactly because compliance is not involved. 'For, once the subject is in the grip of the manipulator, he has no choice as to course of action' (Bachrach and Baratz, 1970, p. 28). In their view, then, neither force, nor the 'sub-concept' manipulation, is relational. They also note that the 'major defect' of Russell's definition of power as 'intended effects' is that such effects can be produced through the exercise of either force or power (ibid., p. 27, fn. 2).

Russell's 'naked force' is anything but the extreme form of power for Bachrach and Baratz. Such force is employed when A lacks power to get B's compliance, 'the actual application of sanctions is an admission of defeat by the would-be user of power' (Bachrach and Baratz, 1970, p. 28). If threat of sanctions works, however, they argue that power is being exercised. Though past use of force can be the basis upon which future threats are made to work, actual use of force, they argue, can undermine power. It can reorder values (as in Nazi-occupied countries where, after the experience of violence, the value of freedom took precedence over life) and when experience of force proves less than feared it can encourage non-compliance (as a naughty child, deprived of a loved toy, finds it possible to manage quite well without it). Threats of sanctions never carried out, they argue, will also undermine power.

While for Bachrach and Baratz power and force in the practice of politics may be intertwined, conceptually they are quite distinct. The exercise of force is the actual use of sanctions. The exercise of power does not involve the actual use of sanctions, but power depends upon potential sanctions. The exercise of influence does not involve this threat (ibid., p. 30).

Lukes: power and manipulation

Bachrach and Baratz's view of power has been criticized by Lukes (1974, pp. 16–20) for not moving far enough away from the Dahlian view of the exercise of power as the conscious decision-making of individuals within the political arena over actual conflicts of values. In place of Bachrach and Baratz's view of power as obtaining compliance through the threat to use sanctions, Lukes defines the concept of power as 'A exercises power over B when A affects B in a manner contrary to B's interests' (ibid., p. 34). Importantly, these interests are not necessarily consciously perceived by B. This adaptation seems instinctively right, for in addition to Bachrach and Baratz's consideration of 'non-decisions', Lukes's 'interests' include situations where there are no overt grievances because the powerful have been so successful in achieving 'a false or manipulated consensus' (ibid., p. 24). Bachrach and Baratz's view of the 'other face of power', which operates to prevent issues getting on to the political agenda and therefore into the open decision-making arena, Lukes acknowledges to be a great improvement on Dahl's 'one-dimensional' view. Nevertheless, Lukes argues that Bachrach and Baratz remain too much within a measurable decision-making framework with Bs always being aware of their 'true' interests.

To arrive at this critical position, however, Lukes is obliged to cloud the distinction between power, force and its 'sub-concept', manipulation. Claiming confusion in Bachrach and Baratz's argument, Lukes (1974, p. 17) argues as follows:

> Bachrach and Baratz use the term 'power' in two distinct senses. On the one hand, they use it in a general way to refer to all forms of successful control by A over B. Indeed, they develop a whole typology (which is of great interest) of forms of such control – forms which they see as types of power in either of its two faces. On the other hand, they label one of these types 'power' – namely, the securing of compliance through the threat of sanctions. In expounding their position, we can, however, easily eliminate this confusion by continuing to speak of the first sense as 'power', and by speaking of the second as 'coercion'.

Their typology of 'power', then, embraces coercion, influence, authority, force and manipulation.

Now while it may be admitted that Bachrach and Baratz's discussion of the use and threat of use of force and its effects on power is not entirely satisfactory because they give only examples of what has happened rather than laying down a clear basis upon which to predict what will happen, they are absolutely clear that force is not power because force is the actual use of sanctions in the face of non-compliance. They are unshakeable on this claimed importance of the compliance–non-compliance distinction. If Lukes's 'manipulated consensus' exists with people unaware of their 'true' interests then the relationship between the dominant and subjugated is closer to the case of the mugged victim in the face of non-compliance, rather than compliant surrender. Where Lukes sees power being exercised over people who have been deprived of the knowledge of their true interests and therefore deprived of choice itself, Bachrach and Baratz see manipulation, the sub-concept of force.

Lukes is aware of this problem of the difference between power and force, for he devotes considerable time to the two theorists – Parsons and Arendt – who deviate from the predominant view of power as something carried out over others.[3] Indeed, in a very short book, fully 10 per cent of its content is devoted to these theorists.

Parsons conceptualizes power in terms of the pursuit of collective goals and argues that the 'threat of coercive measures, or of compulsion, without legitimation or justification, should not, properly, be called the use of power at all' (Parsons, 1963, quoted in Lukes, 1974, pp. 27–8). Parsons departs from the norm, Lukes argues, because the definition is required to fit within Parsons's theory of social integration which is based on value consensus. Lukes then criticizes Parsons because 'By definitional fiat, phenomena of coercion, exploitation, manipulation and so on cease to be phenomena of power – and in consequence disappear from the theoretical landscape' (ibid., p. 29). In support of this criticism, Lukes (1974, p. 30) cites Giddens (1968, p. 265) who argues, first, that 'sectional interests' are often served by the decisions made by those in political office and second, that the 'most radical conflicts in society stem from struggles for power'. Both of these cases, Giddens argues, are ruled out as phenomena of 'power' by Parsons's view of power as the property of a system with collective goals.

Giddens's view of power is one which stresses the importance of resources and the domination which results from the structured inequalities of those resources. (See Giddens, 1981, p. 51.) Giddens accepts Foucault's (1979) view that power is not inherently repressive but argues that Parsons 'does not sufficiently emphasise that power is a double-edged phenomenon: that repression and coercion are prominent features of the operation of power'. Giddens (1968) also objects that the move to a view of power as a 'system property' permits Parsons to move entirely away from a view of power as a relationship between individuals and groups. Such is not, however, the case for Bachrach and Baratz. Their view of power is that of a relationship between people, whilst force and manipulation are precisely defined as lacking compliance (in Parsons's terms 'without legitimation or justification'). With actual use of violence against, to use Giddens's terms, the 'most radical conflicts' and a false consciousness developed to conceal true 'sectional interests', Bachrach and Baratz's notions of force and manipulation prove complementary to Parsons's approach.

As in his criticism of Parsons, Lukes (1974, p. 29) contends that Arendt's (1970) concept of power may also be criticized for having been designed 'to lend persuasive support to the general theoretical frameworks of their authors'. In Arendt's case, Lukes argues, her concept of power must fit with her idea of 'the *res publica*, the public thing' which is traced back to the idea of 'the power of the people' in ancient Greece. To point out that Arendt argues within the framework of political theory is hardly the same kind of argument as the suggestion that Parsons adopts a particular definition of power to ensure consistency with his social systemic theory. Arendt moves to a position close to Montesquieu, rejecting the more dominant Hobbesian view of sovereignty (Canovan, 1992, p. 208). As will be explained, Arendt's conceptual differentiation between power and violence is crucial to her earlier theory of totalitarianism but, as will also be shown, this proves its conceptual advantage.

Arendt: power, violence and the essence of government
Arendt adopts a definition of power which is conceptually distinct from violence for the very reason that, unlike Parsons, she does not wish to constrain her interests to consensual politics and, unlike Lukes, does not conceive it within a decision-making framework, even one stretched to its measurable limits by the inclusion of unperceived 'interests'. Arendt is interested not only in governments in peaceful times but also in revolution and totalitarianism. Her definition of power develops from her understanding of these phenomena.

Initially, Arendt shared the usual view of power as being over others and associated with violence (Canovan, 1992, p. 208). This is her position in her first work on totalitarianism, *The Burden of Our Time* (1951). By her second manuscript ('On the Nature of Totalitarianism', c.1952–53) Arendt had developed a quite different view (Canovan, 1992, p. 208). Power was no longer viewed, in the Hobbesian way, as something that an individual could possess independently, nor even something that was simply all the separate individuals' power added together. Rather, power was seen as something that 'springs up in between men' when they act 'in concert' (Arendt, 2nd manuscript quoted by Canovan, 1992, p. 208). In 'On Violence', first published in 1969, this appears as 'Power springs up whenever people get together and act in concert' (Arendt 1986, p. 68).

Arendt (1986, p. 59) takes direct issue with Weber's definition of the state, translating him correctly as 'the rule of men over men based on the means of legitimate, that is allegedly, legitimate violence', with Mills's 'All politics is a struggle for power; the ultimate kind of power is violence' and with de Jouvenel's 'war presents itself as an activity of States which *pertains to their essence*' (ibid.). Arendt's position against violence and war as the essence of the state also runs contrary to the subsequent works of Tilly, Skocpol, Giddens and Mann, the last of whom it will be recalled developed the term 'despotic power'. The importance of war also reflects the double edge to Trotsky's comment, taken up by Weber, 'that every state is founded on force', first uttered at the time of the signing of the Brest–Litovsk treaty in March 1918, the peace treaty which extricated Russia from World War I. In response to de Jouvenel she poses the question of 'whether the end of warfare, then, would mean the end of state. Would the disappearance of violence in relationships between states spell the end of power?' (Arendt, 1986, p. 59).

Berating the way in which terms such as violence and power are misused because of political theory's and political science's obsession with domination Arendt (1986, p. 64) argues

> Power, strength, force, authority, violence – these are but words to indicate the means by which man rules over man; they are held to be synonyms because they have the same function. It is only after one ceases to reduce public affairs to the business of domination that the original data in the realm of human affairs will appear, or, rather, reappear, in their authentic diversity.

Arendt defines power in the following way:

> Power corresponds to the human ability not just to act but to act in concert. Power is never the property of an individual; it belongs to a group and remains in existence only so long as the group keeps together. When we say of someone he is 'in power' we actually refer to his being empowered by a certain number of people to act in their name. The moment the group, from which the power originated to begin with (potestas in populo, without a people or group there is no power), disappears, 'his power' also vanishes. (Arendt, 1986, p. 64)

It follows for Arendt that the 'representative government' operates with citizens' support under laws to which they have given their consent. 'It is the people's support that lends power to the institutions of a country, and this support is but the continuation of the consent that brought the laws into existence to begin with...All political institutions are manifestations and materializations of power; they petrify and decay as soon as the living power of the people ceases to uphold them' (Arendt, 1986, p. 62). Violence, as a basis of rule, for Arendt, therefore, is the complete opposite of power. It operates exactly where there is no consent, where 'unquestioning obedience' is achieved through the use of implements (Arendt, 1986, p. 62). This stands in sharp contrast to power where 'support is never unquestioning' (ibid.). Violence is used *against* people, is distinguished exactly by this 'instrumental character' (ibid., p. 65). The least powerful forms of government are also, therefore, the most violent for the very reason that they lack (questioning) consent. Montesquieu's views on tyranny are drawn in for support and Arendt goes on to argue: 'Indeed one of the most obvious distinctions between power and violence is that power always stands in need of numbers, whereas violence up to a point can manage without them because it relies on implements' (ibid., p. 63).

Arendt (1986, p. 63) appears unaware of Bachrach and Baratz's distinction between power and force for she complains about political science's failure to distinguish between such terms and makes no reference to them in her work 'On Violence'.[4] Her example of the 'unquestioning obedience' that an act of violence can exact – 'the obedience every criminal can count on when he snatches my pocket book with the help of a knife or robs a bank with the help of a gun' (ibid., p. 62) – is very similar to Bachrach and Baratz's discussion and argument for separating force from power. Bachrach and Baratz's insistence on the crucial difference between compliance and non-compliance in distinguishing the exercise of power and force is also very close to Arendt's consent versus 'unquestioning obedience'. Linguistically, Arendt views 'force' as simply a mistaken synonym for violence, which ought to be restricted to releases of energy (ibid., pp. 64–5). Bachrach and Baratz, as explained, included the threat of sanctions as an essential part of their conceptualization of the exercise of power, leaving the actual use of sanctions as an exercise of force. Arendt rejects this individual behaviouralist approach to power but the distinction between the threat and use of implements proves helpful in understanding Arendt's argument.

More than Bachrach and Baratz, Arendt recognizes that in the practice of politics power and violence may be very difficult to distinguish and commonly they are found together, and only rarely in their pure and therefore extreme form. She notes, for example, that majority rule can lead to the suppression of minorities' rights 'and be very effective in the suffocation of dissent without any use of violence' (Arendt, 1986, p. 65). She adds, emphatically, 'but that does not mean that violence and power are the same' (ibid.). She illustrates this 'gap between theory and reality' through consideration of revolution and the disparity between the implements available to the revolutionaries as compared with those available to the government. What determines whether or not the revolutionaries will succeed in overthrowing the government, she argues, is not superiority in weapons but whether the power structure of the government holds. 'That is as long as commands are obeyed and the army and police forces are prepared to use their weapons. When this is no longer the case, the situation changes abruptly. Not only is the rebellion not put down, but the arms themselves change hands' (ibid., p. 66). Clearly, for Arendt, as for Bachrach and Baratz, the non-empty threat of violence is essential to the power structure. Arendt (ibid.) generalizes from this case:

> Where commands are no longer obeyed, the means of violence are of no use, and the question of this obedience is not decided by the command–obedience relation but by opinion, and, of course, by the number of those who share it. Everything depends on the power behind the violence. The sudden dramatic breakdown of power that ushers in revolutions reveals in a flash how civil obedience – to laws, to rulers, to institutions – is but the outward manifestation of support and consent.

The ability of government to threaten to use its 'state-owned means of violence' then rests on consent. Again, however, this difference between power and violence may be difficult to identify. In cases of governments where 'power has disintegrated' but where rebellion does not develop (for example, for the lack of those willing to test the government's strength) the absence of the visible use of violence does not constitute proof that the power structure is intact. It follows, in line with Dahl's view on power, that only the evidence of actual conflict, 'direct confrontation', can reveal this for certain.

Whilst the structure of power may rest on the capacity to threaten to use violence, power itself never rests on its actual use. If implements are used, violence, and not power, is in action. The actual use of implements is the opposite of power. 'Power and violence are opposites; where the one rules absolutely, the other is absent' (Arendt, 1986, p. 71).

Thus in Arendt's view, power can rule absolutely (the implements for the threat of violence, therefore, remaining unused); violence (implements used) can never rule absolutely. Even in the most violent regimes a power structure, where commands will be obeyed because they are consented to, that is given justification by the dominant group, is necessary. For example, in slave socie-ties, it is the 'organised solidarity of the masters' rather than the superiority of violent weapons on which their despotic rule rests (Arendt, 1986, pp. 67–8). 'Even the totalitarian ruler, whose chief instrument of rule is torture, needs a power basis – the secret police and its net of informers' (ibid., p. 67).

Violence for Arendt, being the means of coercion, is not 'of the essence of government' (Arendt, 1986, p. 68). Power is. 'Violence is by its nature instru-mental; like all means, it always stands in need of guidance and justification through the end it pursues. And what needs justification by something else cannot be the essence of anything' (ibid.). In contrast, Arendt argues, 'power needs no justification', but what it does need is 'legitimacy'. Crucially, she argues, power derives legitimacy from the initial getting together to act in concert, not from any actions that follow. Whilst legitimacy derives from past experience, justification relates to the future – the end. For this reason, Arendt contends that though violence may be justifiable it will never be legitimate, and the persuasiveness of its justification will diminish the further into the future are the ends used to justify actions (ibid., pp. 68–9).

In the reality of politics, Arendt accepts that violence and power normally appear together; she argues that, for example, even in the most peaceable of regimes, violence may sometimes be needed against violent individuals, the act given justification by the end of keeping the peace for everyone else. Because violence is measured by implements, and power by numbers giving consent, a violent regime which attacks a power government will always win. 'Violence can always destroy power; out of the barrel of a gun grows the most effective command resulting in the most instant and powerful obedience. What can never grow out of it is power' (Arendt, 1986, p. 69).

Terror and violence
The importance of this distinction between violence as the means of coercion and power as the essence of government becomes clearer as Arendt moves to a yet further distinction, that between terror and violence. Significantly, Lukes does not draw attention to this distinction in Arendt's work. Arendt distinguishes the concepts as follows:

> Terror is not the same as violence; it is, rather, the form of government that comes into being when violence, having destroyed all power, does not abdicate, but on the contrary, remains in full control. (Arendt, 1986, p. 70)

Before terror can be 'let loose', she continues, 'every kind of organized opposition must disappear', every last vestige, that is, of questioning consent. Terror, then, can substitute for power as 'the essence of government'. Violence cannot. Violence remains the means of coercion, the instruments themselves which can be used by any type of government. Violence may be used by democratically elected governments as consent slips away and against 'single individuals who, as it were, refuse to be overpowered by the consensus of the majority' (ibid.); it may be used by dictatorships and tyrannies which set themselves up through violence with their limited power basis; and it may be used in 'totalitarian domination' which destroys 'even the power of friends and supporters' (ibid., p. 71).

Criticism of Arendt
As will be explained in some detail in Chapter 3, Arendt's arguments about
terror, in order to be understood fully, need to be put within the context of her
analysis of totalitarianism. At this point, objections could be raised in respect
of her claim for the 'power basis' under the totalitarian ruler which appears to
contradict her claim that under totalitarian domination all power is destroyed.
In fact her careful use of 'totalitarian ruler' and 'totalitarian domination',
where terror is the essence of government, represents a crucial distinction
between totalitarian dictatorship, which operates through the state, and the
totalitarian regime, 'terror as government', which operates behind the state
façade. Her distinction between violence, as the instruments of coercion
which normally form part of the state but which are not of its essence, and
terror, which substitutes for power as the essence of the state, is crucial.
    Lukes's (1974, p. 31) criticism of Arendt's distinction between violence
and power because it steps out of line with the normal understanding of
power and concentrates on 'power to' rather than 'power over' misrepresents
her argument. Arendt confronts existing views but is entirely consistent with
Bachrach and Baratz's approach which separates force from power, and
which perceives the use of the coercive implements to be the important
difference. Arendt's arguments about the state are also in line with MacIver
(1926, p. 223, quoted in Walter, 1972, p. 52), who holds that 'coercive power
is a criterion of the state, but not its essence.' When Lukes (1974, p. 31)
argues that Arendt and Parsons claim that because 'power indicates a "capacity", a "facility", an "ability", not a relationship', the possibility that power is
'exercised *over* people, disappears altogether', he is misrepresenting Arendt's
position. None of these terms actually appear in Arendt's argument and, as
has now been explained, the essence of her whole thesis is that power is a
relationship, but one which is *between* people, in a questioning consenting
relationship with government. Important to her argument also is that power
relationships have histories. Lukes (ibid.), therefore, is also wrong to dismiss
Arendt's view of 'acting in concert' as influence, for to do so ignores its
historical importance for state legitimacy.
    Lukes is not only concerned that in Arendt's analysis power exercised over
people 'disappears altogether from view'; he is also concerned that what
disappears too is 'an interest in the (attempted or successful) security of
people's compliance by overcoming or averting their opposition' (Lukes,
1986, p. 31). In making this argument, however, Lukes ignores Arendt's
discussion of 'unquestioning obedience' and this relates to Bachrach and
Baratz's position on situations of 'non-compliance'. Those situations which
Lukes wants to include within his definition of power, where A exercises
power over B against B's interests even when B does not know those interests, are concerned exactly with 'unquestioning obedience'. Lukes's ideas on

power which claim to be 'a radical view' are so only to a limited extent. His views go against the Marxian tradition which separates coercion and admin-istration of things, without which distinction the logic of the communist society could not be derived. Lukes also operates within the old tradition of viewing force as the extreme form of power; the 'radical' change is that force need not necessarily involve violence where people have been duped, in a way similar to Marx's 'false consciousness'. It is Bachrach and Baratz who are more radical and it is Arendt who is most radical.

Habermas, broadly in sympathy with Arendt's view of power, nevertheless also raises important criticisms of her position.[5] Habermas (1986, p. 83) argues that Arendt's view of government is purely political, too influenced by the theory of the classical Greek *polis* and the example of the American revolution to the neglect of the reality of modern societies. In arguing that Arendt's theory is too unrelated to social reality, Habermas takes particular exception to Arendt's objections to governments playing a role in social and economic reforms, quoting her assertion in *On Revolution*, that 'the intrusion of social and economic matters into the public realm frustrates free associa-tion, the coming together in concerted political action' (Arendt, p. 256, quoted in Habermas, 1986, p. 83).[6] As will become clear, it is a theme of this book that Arendt's explanation for the origins of totalitarianism are altogether too political and it is exactly social and economic explanations which will be stressed, though by no means to the point of denying the importance of political choice. Habermas also criticizes Arendt for failing to distinguish between the 'acquisition and maintenance of political power' from its em-ployment ('rule') and 'generation' (Habermas, 1986, p. 184).

In making her claim that the use of violence cannot generate political power, Arendt employs Mao Zedung's saying, 'power grows from the barrel of a gun'. As explained, in Arendt's (1986, p. 69) reasoning, 'out of the barrel of a gun grows the most effective command resulting in the most instant and powerful obedience. What can never grow out of it is power.' Mao's saying was born in the Chinese Revolution and both revolutions in general and the Chinese case in particular prove useful in questioning Arendt's position on the acquisition and maintenance of power.

In their passage to power, revolutionaries succeed because they use vio-lence both against those loyal to the old order, and those who actively seek to defeat the revolutionaries. In this sense it is obedience which 'grows from the barrel of a gun'. However, the use of violence by the revolutionaries against these 'counter-revolutionaries' also generates support amongst others. Think-ing consent, support, grows through the development of the conviction that the revolutionaries will succeed in protecting those oppressed and attacked from the violence of the counter-revolutionaries. In China, the communist guerrilla army's defence of peasants against attack both from the Guomindang, from 1926 to 1949, and the Japanese army from 1937 to 1945, was crucial in gaining and expanding the communists' active support. Without that support the Communist Liberation Army could neither have played such a major part in defeating the Japanese nor could the communists have won the civil war of 1946–49.[7] The guerrillas came together to 'act in concert', with power, in Arendt's sense, growing up between them. Mao's portrayal of the communist guerrilla army moving as fish through water, their passage and survival made possible only by peasant support, illustrates this relationship between violence and power well.

The problem with the Chinese Revolution as a fully convincing case of the use of violence against some in the generation of support amongst others, and therefore power, is that the outcome in China was a single-party state which outlawed even non-violent opposition. The Nicaraguan Revolution where the outcome was a pluralist democracy offers a stronger case. (See Coraggio, 1986 and O'Kane, 1991, pp. 169–73.) In the passage to power the Sandinista army, itself made up of three tendencies, was borne to victory in a bloody civil war by a network of groups which covered a very wide social spectrum. This plurality of interests was first reflected in the formation of a coalition government, which was later confirmed through multi-party elections, and in a subsequent election, the Sandinista government was itself replaced by the opposition coalition.

The case of Nicaragua then nicely illustrates the argument put forward by Habermas (1986, p. 85) that 'the ability to prevent other individuals or groups from realising their interests…has always belonged to the means for acquiring and holding on to positions of legitimate power'. Habermas also points out that this struggle for power is institutionalized in the modern state. In pluralist systems disagreements are recognized through multi-party competition, multiple pressure groups, multiple sources of information and so on. Within modern states Habermas, therefore, concludes that 'power is a good *for* which political groups struggle and with which a political leadership manages things' (ibid., p. 87). Habermas here is in line with Arendt. In the first instance, in pluralist democracies, it is support not obedience 'for which political groups struggle' and, in the second case, where people have the capacity to protest and change allegiance, management is based on thinking consent.

In the running of government, which Habermas distinguishes as the 'rule' and 'generation' of power, as opposed to its acquisition and maintenance, Arendt's position that violence may be a means of power but the use of violence is not, holds. She allows, as explained, that violence against individuals justified by democratic ends may sometimes be needed even in democratic regimes. This consideration of 'violence' in social democracies raises, though, an additional worry with Arendt's terms. 'Violence' appears too strong a word to be used for countries where there is no capital punishment, and fines and probation substitute for imprisonment. This seems particularly so when comparison is being made with the use of brutal violence. Bachrach and Baratz's term 'sanctions' seems far more appropriate and the terms 'coercion' or 'force' also appear preferable. Such terms, however, do in fact suggest gradations in the amounts of violence inflicted. While a victim can be killed by a variety of means, the decision not to use capital punishment but to rehabilitate criminals relies on a whole system of implements (such as probationary services) which will not be found in brutal systems. Equally torture, on Arendt's own argument, is the 'instrument of rule' in a terror government, yet torture is not part of the means of coercion in, for example, Scandinavian countries. Implements are designed or obtained for use. The means of coercion reflect government policies and not the other way around.

State coercion and terror

In modern states, where power is the essence of government, violence, even just the threat of violence, plays a relatively small part in the day-to-day running of things. As a consequence, in pluralist democracies definitions of power designed for analysis of the decision-making process, along the lines of A gets B to do something which goes against B's interests, provide reasonable working definitions of the exercise of power. They do so, however, not only because the use of violence is rare but also because an interest in decision-making does not focus on wider aspects of politics. Where interest is focused on power 'springing up', as in Bachrach and Baratz's Baltimore race riots and Arendt's revolutions and rebellions, a definition of power designed for the narrow confines of the decision-making area is simply unworkable. A conceptual distinction must be made between power – which involves active compliance (support) and the threat of coercion (sanctions) – and violence – which involves non-compliance or unthinking obedience and the use of coercion. Where dictatorships, not democracies, are the focus of political analysis, again, this explicit interest in violence as conceptually distinct from the power found in western democracies is invaluable.

Arendt's central concern in her discussion of power, however, was not to confront the decision-making debate but to understand the nature of government itself, to take issue with the view of the state put forward by Weber, among others, in which the monopoly of the (legitimate) means of violence is of its essence and fundamental to the conflictual definition of power which Weber derived. With power and violence kept separate, power the 'essence of government' (in democracies) and violence the means of coercion, the instruments, Arendt is able to indicate how much support (as distinct from Weber's obedience) a government has. The more actual violence is used, the less support a government has. In understanding the nature of government, Arendt also wished to distinguish between governments based on power, genuine support derived from questioning consent; and governments based on terror, totally unquestioning obedience. Weber's analysis of obedience in the context of domination cannot do this.

The extreme violence in totalitarian regimes was of intense interest to Arendt and in this context the distinction between power and violence, with power idealized in terms of questioning consent characteristic of open democratic societies historically developed through people coming together in groups, though open to the criticisms made above, is highly persuasive. These criticisms levelled at Arendt's view of power do not, however, undermine her claim for power and violence to be kept conceptually separate. This view of violence as the means of coercion for use by any governments permits the crucial separation between governments based on power and totalitarian regimes where terror reigns.

Violence is the means of coercion, the instruments themselves, conceptually separate from power. So these means of coercion – the police system, military establishments, judiciary, courts, prisons, mechanisms for surveillance and the bureaucracies which serve these instruments – may be found in all states and their monopoly is a characteristic of all modern states. The existence of these instruments *per se* cannot, therefore, serve as the distinguishing feature between democratic and totalitarian governments. It is the use to which these means are put that counts.

Repressive regimes and terror systems
In democracies, state coercion is used against those who perform illegal acts. The punishment of those found guilty serves to warn of the consequences of future actions for both present and future culprits. State coercion thus serves as a means of social control. As Bachrach and Baratz suggest, past use of coercion can act as the basis upon which the threat of sanctions justifies the exercise of power within the political process. From case to case, what counts as illegal may differ and may be far more wide-reaching in some situations than in others, as for example restrictions on movement in states of emergency. Punishments may also be far more severe in some cases: sentences may be longer, prison conditions worse, the death penalty used more widely. Essentially, however, the monopoly of the means of coercion is common to these cases and the purpose of coercion, the punishment of illegal acts, is the same.

Terror is not concerned, primarily, with punishment for illegal acts. I have argued elsewhere (O'Kane, 1991, pp. 16–35) that revolutionary reigns of terror are distinguished by summary justice, where the innocence or guilt of the victim is immaterial to the process. Gregor (1982) has pointed out that Sergio Panunzio, one of the principal Italian fascist thinkers (his most important work was published in 1922), was the first to distinguish terror in terms of violence directed against innocents. This served as a justification for fascism's philosophy which argued for violence directed at the guilty, but against violence directed at the innocent – that arbitrary, indiscriminatory use of violence which is terror. On Panunzio's analysis, in the situation of 'internal war' which characterized the fascists' rise to power, the communists and socialists were not 'innocents' because they had chosen to belong to the Communist or Socialist parties. So long as they were members of these parties they were 'guilty' but they had the choice to withdraw their membership. As Gregor (1982, p. 158) explains,

> Their compliance with Fascist demands could make them reasonably confident that their immediate security was assured. Their 'guilt' was a function of their voluntary behaviour. They had chosen to behave in a proscribed manner. Their rehabilitation would turn on a specific schedule of compliance behaviours. Similarly, their 'innocence' would have been the consequence of a voluntary avoidance of prohibited conduct. In effect, Fascists were prepared to operationalise 'guilt' and 'innocence' by providing a guide to prescribed conduct. Both 'guilt' and 'innocence' involved some determinate voluntary acts on the part of the individual or individuals.

As in democratic states, the threat of violence could be used to affect people's behaviour. But in fascist states the threat of violence would be used to 'intimidate' people to change their behaviour. Again it is stressed that such intimidation is not the same as terror:

> Terrorism, on the other hand, does not intimidate its victims because it offers them no escape from deadly coercion or loss. There is no schedule of behaviours to which the prospective victim might conform. The victim is an 'innocent' – he has neither done anything proscribed nor can he undertake compliance behaviours to avoid threat. (Gregor, 1982, p. 159)[8]

Gregor differentiates 'repressive regimes' (such as Fascist Italy) from 'terror systems'. As Gregor (1982, p. 160) explains, 'In a repressive regime, individuals or groups of individuals can successfully avoid severe sanction by compliance behaviour', whereas in terror systems, 'the victims of terror can do nothing to reduce the probability of their involvement in arbitrary and indiscriminate violence.' Gregor contrasts the Special Tribunal which operated in Italy between 1926 and 1943 with the terror systems found in Stalinist Russia and Nazi Germany. In Italy, the Special Tribunal meted out 47 death sentences, not all of which were carried out, and in the remaining cases, of the 5619 defendants, 4596 were found guilty and given a range of sentences and 998 were found innocent (ibid.). Whilst, with the outbreak of war, 'charges and sentences became increasingly capricious and onerous' (ibid., pp. 160–

61), Gregor argues that the sentences were given in order to intimidate others into changing their behaviour. He also argues that while allowing that the Tribunal 'clearly violated the procedural rules of justice prevalent in liberal democracies...However repressive such a system might have been, it did not qualify as a system of terror' (ibid., p. 161).

Gregor (1982, p. 161) contrasts the case in Italy with the Soviet Union: 'thousands, hundreds of thousands of persons passed through the Special Boards in the Soviet Union. Before such boards defendants had no right whatsoever to defense and cases were brought in absentia and against entire groups of persons.' Gregor also notes in contrast with Italy that by 1937 around 10 per cent of those charged were given death sentences and he adds, 'In Gorki alone it is estimated that 50 to 70 persons were executed each day without the semblance of a trial and for the most obscure reasons' (ibid.). Gregor's central point in making these contrasts is not the level of death sentences but the fact that people were victims irrespective of guilt or innocence: 'There was nothing potential victims might do in order to increase their security against arrest' (ibid., p. 162). He specifically notes that people were often arrested immediately after being found not guilty in a court of law.

The reliability of the figures offered by Gregor may be questioned (the general problem of extracting evidence for terror regimes will become clear in Part II) but the validity of his argument remains. Importantly, Gregor illustrates the difference between a repressive system, where violence is used to intimidate people into changing behaviour, and a terror system, where violence is used against innocent victims, never in a position to choose to change their behaviour – through the case of racial discrimination. 'Since racial traits are ascriptive, there is nothing in principal that an individual can actively do to avoid social and political sanction once such traits are used to identify those subject to differential treatment' (Gregor, 1982, p. 162). He notes the discriminatory anti-Jewish legislation introduced in Italy in 1938 and also the anti-Japanese legislation introduced in the USA after the attack on Pearl Harbour, but argues that the nature of the treatment itself is important and contrasts both cases with the treatment of Jews in Nazi Germany. He notes that no Jews were executed by Italian fascists. This is confirmed in detail by Steinberg (1991). Gregor concludes, 'for all its stupidities, bestialities and injustices, Fascist anti-Semitism only approximated a policy of terror...The system remained by and large repressive and oppressive, rather than terroristic' (ibid., p. 164).

Walter (1972), concerned with regimes of terror in primitive African societies, also makes the innocence of victims central to his conception of a system of terror:

Everyone in the system may be a target, but the process needs a regular selection of victims, who are dispatched according to variable rates of destruction. In a chiefdom where terror is continual but of low intensity, the available stock of evildoers, deviants, scapegoats, and candidates for legal punishment may be sufficient. A terroristic despotism needs a larger supply. They may be selected at random or else chosen by spies and informers. The informers may be specialists or indiscriminate people who are potential victims themselves. (Walter, 1972, pp. 9–10)

In line with Arendt, Walter views violence as 'an instrument' (ibid., p. 13). He describes it as 'an instrument of power', which is consistent with Arendt in that it is not power itself. For Arendt, however, violence drives out power and in that sense cannot be an instrument *of* power, but Walter does make clear that violence can be employed with or without terror (ibid., p. 14).[9]

As does Gregor, Walter distinguishes between violence as punishment, where intimidation is used to control behaviour, and as a system of terror, where violence is used to break resistance. As will be expanded in Chapter 3 this is in line with Arendt's view of the destruction of spontaneity in totalitarianism. The example which Walter gives is that of slavery in the USA. Where the slave is whipped for a proscribed act then violence is used for punishment and is therefore repressive, not terroristic. The 'violence of punishment...shifted over to the violence of terrorism' when whippings were used to break resistance. Using Stampp (1956) as his source, Walter (1972, p. 19) explains his point: 'the lash was often used to "break in" young slaves and to "break the spirit" of insubordinate older ones.'

Walter (1972, p. 19) reflects further on the system of terror in slavery. The slave is a tool of production. If a tool offers resistance 'it must either be discarded or hammered into shape' (ibid.). In a system of terror, organized resistance (tolerance) must be eliminated. Contrasting violence meted out as punishment, based on existing laws and rules or social norms, with terror, Walter's argument exactly fits Gregor's position:

> In contrast to terrorism, deterrence implies the anticipation of a probable evil and the ability to avoid it. The fear of punishment is different from the fear generated in the terror process. There is a great deal of difference between the emotional state of a man who can calculate, 'I fear that if I take this course of action, it will lead to violent punishment', and the turbulent, irrational fear, scarcely permitting thought, stirred up in the wake of unpredictable violence.
>
> The conditions of legality imply that there must be a way of being innocent. If there is no path left open to avoid transgression, or if people are bound to be charged falsely with offences they did not commit, then it is not possible to be innocent. In the terror process, no one can be secure, for the category of transgression is, in reality, abolished. Anyone may be a victim, no matter what action he chooses. Innocence is irrelevant. (Walter, 1972, pp. 25–6)

Concerned with primitive African societies, the Zulu state under Shaka between 1816 and 1828 is detailed as the prime example of a system of terror.

'On a mere sign by Shaka, viz: the pointing of his finger, the victim would be seized by his nearest neighbours; his neck would be twisted, and his head and body beaten (to death) with sticks' (Walter, 1972, p. 134). No system, however, Walter argues, has managed to eliminate resistance completely. Shaka was assassinated in 1828. In Walter's view, of all the systems of terror throughout history Nazi Germany came closest to the complete elimination of resistance. 'In the concentration camps, the Nazis came closest to perfecting the system of terror' (ibid., p. 27).

In Arendt's argument, as totalitarianism approaches perfection, violence pushes out all power, all resistance based on questioning and concerted action is eliminated, all spontaneity destroyed. In the totalitarian regime, terror is the essence of government. While Walter does not share Arendt's view of terror as government, retaining power as domination as the general case for all governments in line with the predominant view, his general position on systems of terror, directed at innocents to destroy resistance, is absolutely in line with Arendt. Had Walter been concerned with modern as well as primitive societies his consideration of the form taken by 'resistance' in modern societies (pressure groups, competing parties and the like) might have led him towards Arendt's view.

Summary

Here it has been argued that there is virtue in keeping power, violence and terror conceptually distinct and thus perceiving governments based on systems of terror as different in kind from other governments, whether representative or repressive, even though the monopoly of the means of coercion is taken to be a feature of all states. Terror, it has been argued, is distinguished by the deliberate attack on innocents. With totalitarian regimes held to be the nearest to a perfected system of terror, and concern being with modern, not primitive, states, it is time to move the debate to modern theories and the classic cases of Nazi Germany and Stalinist USSR.

Notes

1. See Dahl (1989, pp. 244–5). Almond and Powell (1967) and Easton (1985) are just two examples of this dominant view in political science.
2. Concerned with the period of transition between capitalist to communist systems (Marx's 'dictatorship of the proletariat'), in *The State and Revolution* Lenin grapples with Marx's 'withering away of the state' theorized in the *Critique of the Gotha Programme* and argues for a 'people's militia' to replace the coercive organizations of the old order whose 'special machinery for suppression will gradually cease to exist'. (See McLellan, 1986, p. 256.)
3. Morriss (1987), adopting a philosophical approach, has also argued against the view of power as 'power over'.
4. Arendt's 'On Violence' was first published in 1969, and the two theoretical chapters in Bachrach and Baratz (1970) first appeared in the *American Political Science Review* in 1962 and 1963 as 'Two Faces of Power', 1962, **56**, pp. 947–52 and 'Decisions and Nondecisions: An Analytical Framework', 1963, **57**, pp. 641–51.

5. Canovan (1983) has shown that Habermas's interpretation of Arendt's 'communications concept of power' underplays the importance of the action of coming together in her argument which is not concerned simply with people talking to each other.
6. Habermas's point is nicely illustrated by the case of Sweden. Historically, the Swedish political system was set up exactly in line with Arendt's views on concerted action and the formation of power as government. In Sweden, groups formed spontaneously and over time secured state-run organizations. In contrast to the American example which she extols, in Sweden these state-run organizations were not only for the running of government but also for the provision of the welfare goods which these spontaneous groups originally came together to provide. Milner (1990) terms the collective bargaining system in Sweden 'concertation' and describes the case, except for this stress on welfare provision, in a way remarkably close to Arendt's ideal:

> The development of common interests naturally leads to the forming of associations to promote them. In accordance with Swedish values, promoting common interests means assuming responsibility for providing the requisite service, rather than waiting for the state bureaucracy to set up an agency or for the private market to take up the service as sufficiently profitable. It is in this synthesis of private interest and public service that the network of intermediate organizations constitutes a buffer zone at the centre of the Swedish social system. They are not, as in the pluralist conception, 'special interests' as opposed to common interests. *Their activities are incorporated into the very institutional structure of society in a complementary relationship.* (Milner, 1990, p. 78, italics added)

This stress on concerted action as both a historical basis of power as government and its continual reaffirmation is supported by the evidence that Sweden has the highest rate of adult membership of organizations in the world, with 90 per cent of Swedes members of one or more of the 150 000 local associations (Milner, 1990, p. 75). Importantly, in Sweden empowerment is aided by welfare provision: 'The young, the old, the handicapped, and the sick – are not only well cared for but integrated into – rather than excluded from – community life' (ibid., p. 187). This is achieved through social democracy, the perception being that there is a collective social responsibility to ensure that, for example, the handicapped are not disadvantaged in acting out their citizenship. All sorts of aids are available to equalize capabilities as far as possible, and this is a social responsibility, 'a responsibility above and beyond that of the designated public agencies' (ibid., p. 193).

Welfare states can 'empower' people in this sense of compensating disadvantages to enable active citizenship. Such empowerment, however, can also be achieved with or without citizens' instigation. Trade union and labour movements have been historically very important in this, but individual politicians and individual opinion leaders have also played a significant role. Ralph Nader in the USA is a good, well known, modern example of the latter. The legislation so produced does not indicate a form of domination. Such provisions are neither against citizens' interests nor do they, oligarchically, represent the sectional interests of leaders. This view is compatible with Parsons's (1963) arguments about power where leaders may sometimes act as 'brokers' who mobilize their constituents in order to enhance the collective good. (See Habermas, 1986, p. 92, fn. 23.)

The changes which have taken place recently in Sweden, and Scandinavia generally, in respect of welfare provision in particular, have led to claims for the development of more individualist rather than collectivist values. (For discussion, see Lane, 1993.) These new developments do not, however, detract from the important historical lessons which Milner draws.

7. For further discussion of these events see O'Kane (1991, pp. 192–6), where the importance of support for the communists generated through political, economic and social reforms within the 'liberated areas' is also stressed. The conclusions of that study of revolutionary reigns of terror (ibid., pp. 256–9) are consistent with Arendt's distinction between violence and power in arguing that the establishment of the post-revolutionary state rests on two bases: central control over the new revolutionary forces of coercion, and support generated through the demonstration of practical policies. I have also made the case for keeping

   power and force conceptually separate in the analysis of military regimes. (See O'Kane, 1989.)

8. Following through the logic of Bachrach and Baratz's distinction between power and force, this results in the following: whilst power is always relational and involves compliance (through the threat of sanctions), force is sometimes non-relational and always involves non-compliance (through the use of force); terror is never relational, always involves the use of force but does not involve non-compliance because the victim is given no choice whether to comply or not.

9. Failing to make a clear conceptual distinction between power and violence Walter mentions 'despotism without terror'. Under this heading he discusses oriental despotism in China and the rule of the despots in Buganda (now part of Uganda) and Jimma Abba Jifar (now part of Ethiopia). Whereas violence is used (as in systems of terror) in 'despotism without terror', violence is directed towards the guilty, judged on the basis of breaching known customs, through accepted processes. Of Mutesa ('Peacemaker') who changed his name from Mukabya ('One who makes people wail') when Kabaka of Buganda, he notes: 'the rule of Mutesa had been a despotism based broadly on consent' (Walter, 1972, pp. 272–4). Clearly a conceptual distinction between power, violence and terror would have been to Walter's advantage.

2   Modernity and the Holocaust

The study of totalitarianism has fallen out of favour. If constrained to the two classic cases, Nazi Germany and Stalin's USSR, and the possible third case, Mussolini's Italy, then the passage of time has long removed the term's immediacy. If stretched throughout Eastern Europe to more recent times, then the events in 1989 have now consigned it fully to the terminology of yester-year. If preserved, as is sometimes the custom, to be applied to any Marxist regime, wherever found, current focus on transitions to democracy have provided the term with a natural built-in obsolescence. The lessons of history so reveal that though studies of hideous episodes in countries' pasts may be valuable, they are not central to the understanding of politics today.

Yet Zygmunt Bauman in *Modernity and the Holocaust*, coincidentally published in 1989, has argued that far from belonging to the outer edge of social theory the Nazi political order stands right at its centre: 'The Holocaust was an outcome of a unique encounter between factors by themselves quite ordinary and common' (Bauman, 1989, p. xiii). 'Ordinary and common', that is, in every modern society.

Bauman's argument is not intended to convey the view that modernity caused the Holocaust – though, certainly, without modern society it could not have happened – but to extend our understanding of the nature of the modern world and the dangers which lie within its natural development. As such, though 'unique', a similar episode of genocide could occur again and Bauman makes it clear that direct comparisons can be made with Stalin's USSR, itself a product of modernity. If Bauman is right, then it is clear that, far from being consigned to the archives, modern genocide remains with us today as a permanent, underlying threat to modern 'civilization'.[1]

The structure of Bauman's argument is first to identify the necessary underlying factors and then the immediate conditions which are together offered as sufficient explanation for the Holocaust. Modernity is relevant to all aspects of his argument but is of particular importance in respect of the underlying conditions because it is here, in their ordinariness and common-ness for all modern societies, that the general lessons of the Holocaust are to be found. These conditions are: the existence of a state rational bureaucracy; the availability of modern science and technology; the rational, logical approach to problem-solving which, accompanying both these phenomena, permeates modern society, and lastly the state's centralization of coercion. The importance of these conditions for his argument is that they combine to remove the modern person from individual moral responsibility. The first three conditions serve to distance the perpetrator from the victim, so creating, in reality, the laboratory conditions of Milgram's psychological experiment. The third condition, rational action, gains the cooperation of the victims. The fourth condition, the state's centralization of coercion, in Bauman's view the very basis of 'modern civilization', reinforces this obedience in people and renders them defenceless

These conditions, common to all modern societies, make each capable of modern genocide. 'Truly modern genocide' differs from 'normal genocide' in two important ways. First, modern genocide has a purpose, which is to create a 'perfect society' (Bauman, 1989, p. 91). Second, the victims themselves are made to cooperate in the genocide. This, Bauman argues, has never happened before and could not happen outside of modernity (ibid., p. 22).

Though the potential for modern genocide exists in all modern societies, the Holocaust is unique. Here the immediate condition for the Holocaust is crucial: Nazis in power. What was special about the Nazis was that they engaged in social engineering. Social engineering, Bauman argues, is itself a modern idea. 'Racism is a policy first, ideology second' (Bauman, 1989, p. 74). Social engineering, he argues, is 'like all politics, it needs organization, managers and experts' (ibid.), the very things, that is, that he identifies as exclusive to modern society. In any modern society with a government set on a goal of a 'radically different society', modern genocide could then occur in the very midst of modern civilization. Recognizing the actual rarity of the Nazi phenomenon, Bauman offers 'countervailing and mitigating circumstances' which have counteracted this general potential for genocide. These circumstances, he argues, are to be found in political democracy, that is, in the existence of both political and social pluralism, the availability of social networks and political groups. After due consideration of political democracy he concludes:

> The conditions propitious to the perpetuation of genocide are thus special, yet not at all exceptional. Rare, but not unique. Not being an imminent attribute of modern society, they are not alien phenomenon either. As far as modernity goes, genocide is neither abnormal nor a case of malfunction. It demonstrates what the rationalizing engineering tendency of modernity is capable of if not checked and mitigated, if the pluralism of social powers is indeed eroded – as the modern ideal of purposefully designed, fully controlled, conflict flee, orderly and harmonious society would have it. (Bauman, 1989, p. 114)

Bauman's theory of the Holocaust

Necessary underlying conditions

Modern bureaucratic culture   Bauman's explanation for the Holocaust hinges on Weber's theory of the growth of rationalization: the development of modern, functionally efficient, rule-following, career-structured, meritocratic, hierarchical, task-divided, objective bureaucracy. Bauman (1989, p. 14) offers a long quotation from Gerth and Mills's (1970, p. 214 and p. 215) translation of Weber's work:

> Precision, speed, unambiguity, knowledge of the files, continuity, discretion, unity, strict subordination, reduction of friction and of material and personal costs – these are raised to the optimum point in the strictly bureaucratic administration... Bureaucratization offers above all the optimum possibility for carrying through the principle of specializing administrative functions according to purely objective considerations...The 'objective' discharge of business primarily means a discharge of business according to calculable rules and without regard for persons. (Weber)

The Holocaust, in Bauman's view, was 'a product of routine bureaucratic procedures: means–ends calculus, budget balancing, universal rule application' (Bauman, 1989, p. 17). With the goal set by Hitler to make the Reich *Judenfrei*, free of Jews, the means to achieve this – the final solution, extermination – took the natural bureaucratic path. A number of possible, logical solutions involving forced emigration were considered: to Poland (rejected as too difficult to police); to Madagascar (thought too distant and too costly in ships under threat from the British Navy); to Russia beyond the Archangel–Astrakan line (until it became clear in the summer of 1941 that the USSR was not about to be defeated). Faced with this latter new element in the calculation, on 1 October 1941 Jewish emigration was stopped and the 'final solution' begun:

> The task of getting rid of the Jews had been found another, more effective means of implementation: physical extermination was chosen as the most feasible and effective means to the original, and newly expanded, end. The rest was a matter of co-operation between various departments of state bureaucracy, of careful planning, designing proper technology and technical equipment, budgeting, calculating and mobilizing proper resources: indeed the matter of dull bureaucratic routine. (Bauman, 1989, pp. 16–17)

The whole operation of the Holocaust, Bauman argues, was managed by the Economic Administration Section of the Reichssicherheithauptampt, the Central Security Office – RSHA (ibid., p. 103). What had taken place was goal-displacement, 'the tendency of all bureaucracies to lose sight of the original goal and to concentrate on the means instead – the means which turn into the ends' (ibid., p. 106). At the same time this goal-displacement could not have been put into operation had people not been willing to carry it through. Here again it is rational bureaucracy which Bauman offers in explanation. There is nothing, he argues, in 'the typically modern, technological–bureaucratic patterns of action and the mentality they institutionalize, generate, sustain and reproduce' (ibid., p. 95) which rules out the Holocaust. Indeed he states, 'the rules of instrumental rationality are singularly incapable of preventing such phenomena,…there is nothing in those rules which disqualifies the Holocaust-style methods of "social-engineering" as improper or, indeed, the actions they served as irrational' (ibid., p. 18).

Central to Bauman's argument is the claim that this 'bureaucratic culture' characteristic of modern society provided the very conditions whereby 'moral inhibitions against violent atrocities' (ibid., p. 21) were eroded. This effect was achieved by the very separation of tasks, the pursuit of rational calculation, the dispassionate conduct of business and the objective application of rules laid down from above, the violence officially authorized, the actions routinized. Crucially, each task done was only a small part towards the total outcome, the destruction of human life.

Bauman (1989, p. 24) quotes Hilberg (1983): 'it must be kept in mind that most of the participants (of genocide) did not fire rifles at Jewish children or pour gas into gas chambers…Most bureaucrats composed memoranda, drew up blueprints, talked on the telephone, and participated in conferences. They could destroy a whole people by sitting at their desk.' Killing for most of them was done 'at a distance' with each bureaucrat able to ignore overall moral responsibility through concentration on the small task, the small problem to be solved.

In support of his arguments about the importance of distance between perpetrator and victim and the role of modern bureaucracy in achieving this, Bauman (1989, pp. 151–68) considers the famous Milgram (1974) electric-shock experiments. The results of these experiments showed that as the distance between victim and perpetrator grew, so the willingness to use cruelty increased. Putting a wall between the two so that the torturer could not see the victim had the most noticeable effect of all. Milgram's conclusion was that, psychologically, responsibility is most easily ignored when one is an intermediary in a chain of action leading to a cruel outcome and as distant from the consequences of that final action as possible.

Bureaucratic organization, for structuring this 'distance', Bauman argues, is the very vehicle for destroying individual responsibility:

Indeed mediating the action, splitting the action between stages delineated and set apart by the hierarchy of authority, and cutting the action across through func-

tional specialization is one of the most salient and proudly advertised achievements of our rational society…The more rational is the organisation of action, the
easier it is to cause suffering – and remain at peace with oneself. (Bauman, 1989,
p. 155)

Science and technology   Modern society, Bauman stresses, is characterized
not only by the growth of rational bureaucracy but also by the progress of
science and industrial technology. These features of modernity, he argues,
combine to serve further that all-important distance between actors and victim which creates the conditions for shedding moral responsibility. 'Task-
splitting', that 'specifically modern form of authority – expertise' and the
'language of technology' are each seen as crucial in this (Bauman, 1989,
p. 196).

Even at the point closest to the victim, the killing point, Bauman makes
much of the nature of the gas chambers themselves which 'reduced the role
of the killer to that of the "sanitation officer" asked to employ a sackful of
"disinfecting chemicals" through an aperture in the roof of a building the
interior of which he was not prompted to visit' (ibid., p. 26). Killing could
itself be distanced by the language of technology. In support, Bauman offers
a memorandum concerning modifications to gas trucks with the aim of achieving greater efficiency, written by a technical expert, Willy Just, and sent to the
company which assembled these vans. Bauman (1989, p. 197) quotes the
memo with all of Browning's inverted commas:

> A shorter, fully loaded truck could operate much more quickly. A shortening of
> the rear compartment would not disadvantageously affect the weight balance,
> overloading the front axle, because 'actually a correction in the weight distribu-
> tion takes place automatically through the fact that the cargo in the struggle
> toward the back door during the operation always is preponderantly located there'.
> Because the connecting pipe was quickly rusted through the 'fluids', the gas
> should be introduced from above, not below. To facilitate cleaning, an eight-to-
> twelve-inch hole should be made in the floor and provided with a cover opened
> from outside. The floor should be slightly inclined, and the cover equipped with a
> small sieve. Thus all 'fluids' would flow to the middle, the 'thin fluids' would exit
> even during operation, and 'thicker fluids' could be hosed out afterwards (Brown-
> ing, 1985, pp. 64–5).

The capabilities of modern science and technology and the expertise which
this knowledge generates, in combination with rational bureaucracy, each
essential characteristics of modernity, together lead, Bauman contends, to 'a
substitution of technical for moral responsibility'. This substitution, he argues, would be 'inconceivable without the meticulous functional dissection
and separation of tasks' whereby the bureaucrat's narrow area of concern
becomes the 'end' (ibid., p. 107). 'To put it bluntly', he concludes, 'the result

is the irrelevance of moral standards for the technical success of the bureaucratic operation' (ibid., p. 101).

Rational action and the cooperation of the victim   In a modern society this
rational, logical approach to problem-solving which pervades the whole society, Bauman also views as the means through which the cooperation of the
victims can be achieved. In demonstration of this he concentrates on the
evidence provided by the Judenräte. These Jewish councils created the conditions for the outcomes of the rational decision-making of the Jews to be
towards the goal which the Nazis desired: 'The Jews could therefore play into
the hands of their oppressors, facilitate their task, bring closer their own
perdition, while guided in their action by the rationally interpreted purpose of
survival'. This, Bauman argues, could be done because of the workings of
rational bureaucracy, 'bureaucratically administered oppression'. (For the
above see Bauman, 1989, pp. 121, 122.)

First the Jews were separated from the outside world, with the outside, at
the same time, being subjected to anti-Semitic propaganda, in order to widen
the gulf between Jews and non-Jews. This distinction, furthermore, he argues,
was subjected to precise definition and enhanced by the Nuremberg Laws
(ibid., pp. 124, 125). Within their lonely world, rationality was then exploited
as piecemeal bureaucratic rules and regulations were received and reacted to
by the Jewish councils, rationally calculating at each point how survival
could best be achieved in the face of the latest instruction. So life was
structured in the rational–bureaucratic form of the final goal, concealed by
rule-following, hierarchy and task-splitting with only a small aspect of the
final goal being revealed. As a consequence, Bauman argues, 'At each state of
the destruction – except the final one – there were individuals and groups
eager to save what could be saved, to defend what could be defended, to
exempt what could be exempted; and thus – although only obliquely – to
cooperate' (ibid., p. 34).

One of the examples which Bauman gives of cooperation is the 'rescue-
through-work campaign' where the Jewish councils in the large East European ghettos sought to demonstrate the indispensability of the Jewish workers to the regime (ibid., p. 137). In so doing, they contributed to the war effort
but also helped those who were fighting for their elimination. He also supports his argument with the rational way in which decisions were made by
the members of the Jewish councils (to achieve their own survival) when
ordered to draw up the lists for deportation, the method by which Jews were
exterminated by instalments. As the choices were more and more restricted
and the conditions worsened within the ghettos, reaching a situation of desperate starvation, the one thing that stayed firm, Bauman contends, was the
modern rational way of problem-solving.

The centralization of coercion   In addition to the existence of a rational
bureaucracy, science and technology and the bureaucratic technical culture
thereby developed, affecting even the victims, Bauman (1989, p. 96) argues
that one other common aspect of modernity was needed to be available for
the Nazis to harness: the state's centralization of coercion.

   Modern civilization, in Bauman's argument, is built upon state centralization of coercion where violence is hidden behind the façade of an 'apparently
peaceful and humane, legalistic and orderly society' (ibid., p. 87): 'The popular image of civilized society is, more than anything else, that of the absence
of violence; of a gentle, polite, soft society' (ibid., p. 96). This centralization
of coercion, he argues, leads to the 'obedience to authority' (ibid., p. 90)
which accompanies the bureaucratic scientific culture and which allows the
state to take control over people's lives: 'Pacification of daily life means at
the same time its defencelessness' (ibid., p. 107).

   In Nazi Germany, Bauman argues, 'violence had been turned into a technique. Like all techniques, it is free from emotions and purely rational' (ibid.,
p. 98). Both Stalin and Hitler wished to embrace the 'modernist dream' and
genocide was used as 'a means to an end' (ibid., p. 90). The end was, in
Stalin's case 'a communist world', in Hitler's case 'a racially pure, Aryan
world' and 'in both cases, a harmonious world, conflict free, docile in the
hands of the rulers, orderly, controlled' (ibid., p. 92). Bauman concludes,
therefore, 'The two most notorious and extreme cases of modern genocide
did not betray the spirit of modernity. They did not deviously depart from the
main track of the civilizing process. They were the most consistent, uninhib-
ited expressions of that spirit' (ibid., p. 93).

The immediate condition: Nazis in power
Modern technology, in combination with modern bureaucracy and the existence of state centralization of coercion, was necessary before the Holocaust
could take place. Bureaucratic organization, scientific and technological know-
how and centralized violence were all of necessary practical importance, but
the mentality which they combined to produce was critical. The bureaucratic–technological culture which replaced moral responsibility, the rational
action of victims, the defencelessness of the individual when the state had
centralized violence in the name of 'civilization', all produced obedience.
Without obedience, the very product of modernity, the Nazis could not have
carried through the Holocaust. With the Nazis in power the sufficient conditions for the Holocaust were achieved. Nazi ideas too were the product of
modernity. Bauman argues as follows:

   Bureaucracy is intrinsically capable of genocidal action. To engage in such an
   action, it needs an encounter with another invention of modernity: a bold design

of a better, more reasonable and rational social order – say a racially uniform, or a classless society – and above all the capacity of drawing such designs and determination to make them efficacious. Genocide follows when two common and abundant inventions of modern times meet. It is only their meeting which has been, thus far, uncommon and rare. (Bauman, 1989, p. 106)

Bauman's view of the 'Nazi revolution' is that of 'an exercise in social engineering' where 'racial stock' was 'the key link in the chain of engineering measures' (ibid., p. 66). Modern science and technology were the key to solving the problem of 'the Jewish question' and racism the basis upon which Jews were 'estranged', to be weeded out in order that the grand plan, the perfect Aryan society, could be achieved 'Racism is a policy first, ideology second. Like all politics, it needs organization, managers and experts' (ibid., p. 74). Without modern bureaucracy and the rational culture of technical and scientific problem-solving which accompanies it, the Holocaust would not have been possible. Without the centralized state coercion found only in 'modern civilization', the Holocaust could not have been implemented.

Countervailing and mitigating circumstances
Given Bauman's claim that the potential for a Holocaust is present in all modern societies, he naturally seeks to delineate the 'countervailing and mitigating circumstances' which prevent modernity from normally moving towards genocide in its 'modern drive to a fully designed, fully controlled world' (Bauman, 1989, p. 93). The answer he offers is 'the pluralism of the human world' (ibid.) which precludes the state from attaining 'absolute power'. What prevented this pluralism from developing in Nazi Germany, according to Bauman, was 'the collapse (or non-emergence) of democracy' (ibid., p. 111) in the weak Weimar Republic: 'In the absence of traditional authority, the only checks and balances capable of keeping the body politic away from extremities can be supplied by political democracy' (ibid.).

In contrast to the upheavals in traditional societies, where loyal, local, social networks are in general left intact, in modern times, Bauman argues, great upheavals, such as revolutions, break down social networks and it is exactly under these conditions that the state takes control over society (ibid., p. 112). Such was the case, he argues, after the Russian Revolution and after the weak Weimar Republic; in both cases old political, economic and social forces were replaced with new, centralized state-controlled organizations (ibid., pp. 112–13). In particular, Bauman draws attention to the dismantling of local government and trade unions and the enclosure of state secrecy. Under such conditions ordinary people were 'malleable and helpless', unable to resist the encroachments of the state. So he concludes, 'the voice of individual moral conscience is best heard in the tumult of political and social discord' (Bauman, 1989, p. 166).

Problems with Bauman

Persuasive though Bauman's theory appears, there are important problems with his arguments. The first set of problems is common to much of social science involving the relationship between attitudes and behaviour and the evidence which is required to support the relationship between the two.[2] Bauman's theory relies heavily on the development of a new, modern, rational–technical mentality. Yet Bauman pays scant attention to evidence for the existence of such a mentality governing behaviour, outside of the evidence of the behaviour itself. This will not do, for the thing to be explained, behaviour, is then used to prove the existence of a mentality which is offered to explain it. The argument is circular. The difficulty, of course, is that the objective evidence for a mentality separate from behaviour is very difficult to imagine and, in so far as mentality could be seen as a set of attitudes, in Nazi Germany the evidence is not available, for it was not a regime in which people were free to express their opinions.

In a society like Nazi Germany, rational action would be either to keep one's head down and hope not to get noticed or, perhaps, actively to adopt supportive behaviour. In both cases, and in the former case most clearly the consequent behaviour would not constitute proof of a felt absence of moral responsibility – only that behaviour was constrained by conditions. In the *Judenräte*, for example, evidence is offered of actions taken within the constraints of fear produced by violence, terror and starvation. There is nothing new and modern about human beings having a basic instinct for self-preservation. Neither is there anything new and modern about humans rationalizing actions in order to 'put on a brave face'.

It is the bureaucratic structure of modern society which is fundamental to Bauman's argument, both in respect of the piecemeal orders in the *Judenräte* and, more generally, in the distance which modern bureaucracy creates between perpetrator and victim, with technical responsibility replacing moral responsibility. Here again, however, similar arguments apply. Moral responsibility might remain part of the bureaucrats' 'mentality' but, constrained by terror and secrecy, their behaviour would be unable to reflect this. The rapid changes possible in Germany after Hitler's defeat supports this view of individuals with complex sets of attitudes, where activation of any particular combination of them is dependent upon the actual conditions faced.

Consideration of this problem of evidence in Bauman and the relationship between attitudes and behaviour highlights two further problems. The first is a straightforward one about the exact definition of a bureaucrat. On Bauman's definition, the secret police, concentration camp guards, torturers and experimenters alike are bureaucrats, as is any bureaucratic pen-pusher. This will not do. The secret police, though they may be employees of the state, are no more bureaucrats than are teachers. This is not to rule out the likelihood of their bureaucratic mentalities; soldiers have a bureaucratic mentality in the sense that they follow rules and orders in a hierarchical organization, but it suggests that this is not their only important attribute. As we shall see in the chapter to follow, Arendt argues that it is the secret police who have real power and not the state, which is merely a façade. What sets the secret police apart is their capacity to terrorize.

This characteristic raises the second type of problem with Bauman. An integral part of his argument is that the modern state has central control over the means of coercion which, over time, renders the population at large defenceless. This may be so, but if the monopoly of violence facilitated Nazi control this does not constitute proof that it was either the implements of coercion of ordinary modern states which they employed, albeit on a horrific scale, or that the use to which the coercion was put was the same as in either representative or repressive governments. These points have been central to the discussion of the differences between terror, power and coercion in Chapter 1. For example, in the first instance, coercion in the modern state would normally involve the army and the police rather than rely on the terror of a secret police and concentration camps, and, in the second instance, in such states coercion is directed at the guilty rather than acting as a deliberate policy against innocents. The detail of the differences between these cases must await expansion below, but here it raises the possibility that, in respect of terror at least, Nazi Germany constituted something other than a unique combination of what is 'common and ordinary' in modern society.[3]

Whilst state monopoly of the means of coercion is common to civilization, the use of terror is not. Indeed as explained in Chapter 1, Walter (1972) has found a system of terror as a means of control both in primitive African and slave societies. Under Arendt's (1958) formulation, as will become clear in the following chapter, terror in the totalitarian regime is operated in a way completely contrary to that of the rule-following, legalistic rationality portrayed in Bauman's conception of modernity. It follows that once in power Nazis destroyed rather than utilized the attributes of modernity. As will be explained, this is in line with Friedrich and Brzezinski's (1965) view that the modern scientific approach is destroyed under totalitarianism.

Political democracy   Bauman's claims about the importance of political democracy as a countervailing factor in the relationship between modernity and genocide presents logical problems for his argument in two ways. First, the existence of political pluralism turns out, on Bauman's own admission, not to be wholly independent of the Nazis (or Communists) being in power. He argues as follows:

The Nazis must first have destroyed the vestiges of political pluralism to set off on projects like the Holocaust, in which the expected readiness of ordinary people for immoral and inhuman actions had to be calculated among the necessary – and available – resources. In the USSR the systematic destruction of the real and putative adversaries of the system took off in earnest only after the residues of social autonomy, and hence of the political pluralism which reflected it, had been extirpated. (Bauman, 1969, pp. 165–6)

Now, the problem is that if having the Nazis or Stalinists in power proved sufficient to wipe out political pluralism then the argument about political democracy's countervailing powers is made redundant. If Nazis and their ilk can destroy political pluralism, then political pluralism cannot counteract Nazi-type social engineering. Bauman shows awareness of this problem and stresses that where political democracy has not been in place long enough to be properly established it can be pushed aside: 'political democracy…is not…quick to arrive, and it is slower still to take root once the hold of the old authority and system of control has been broken – particularly if the breaking was done in a hurry' (ibid., p. 111). Whilst established political democracy, deep-rooted in strong social networks, represents obstacles to modern geno-cide, severely damaged social networks and shallow-rooted democratic insti-tutions offer no such resistance. The latter situation, Bauman argues, was characteristic of the social and political systems, both in Russia after the revolution, and after the weak Weimar Republic.

This line of argument, however, does not extricate Bauman. In raising the important point that Weimar Germany and Stalin's Russia lacked sound po-litical and social pluralism for special historical reasons he opens the way for the possibility that these historically specific conditions offer a more satisfac-tory explanation for the Holocaust and the excesses of Stalinism than do the claims made about modernity. On the logic of the comparative method meas-ures for similarity and difference against controls, it is the absence of sound, deep-rooted political democracy and the presence of a recent history of far-reaching political and social upheaval that is significantly different about these two cases and not the conditions of modernity (rational bureaucracy, science and technology and centralized state coercion) for they are similar for all cases.[4]

The attraction of historical accounts is that they offer an explanation, or at least a partial explanation, of why the Nazi Party gained support. If the arrival of the Nazis in power has a history which is itself linked to underlying conditions, however, then it ceases to be simply an immediate condition in the chain of causal explanation. In essence, at the very least some explanation for the rise of Nazism and support for the Nazi Party is required. Similarly some parallel understanding of the development of Stalinism is needed. Mo-dernity may, indeed, be necessary but against the weight of other factors the central plank of Bauman's whole argument could prove of relatively little importance. Decision about such matters must await the empirical analyses of the chapters to follow, but even if it is Bauman who is proved right and the historically specific factors are simply intervening rather than causal, Bauman still faces another problem.

The second problem relating to Bauman's argument about political democracy is that his account of modernity may itself be biased, and biased in such a way as to project political pluralism into the role of intervening factor. In essence political democracy of the social and political pluralist kind is itself an aspect of modernity. That is, pluralist democracy is only to be found in modern society, and part of the reason for this, as Weber made clear, is that modern democracy (even in its purely liberal democratic form) cannot exist without a rational–legal bureaucracy. If modernity and, perhaps more strikingly, civilization today is bound up with pluralist democracy, then the Nazi Holocaust and Stalin's USSR, rather than being modernity's logical extension, are aberrations of modernity, even taking the problem of goal-displacement into account. As will be shown, Weber's own arguments support this rather than Bauman's view and do so not only through stressing the counteracting effects of plebiscitary democracy on the dangers which the growth of rational bureaucracy threatens for individual freedom, but also through stressing the importance of capitalistic enterprise.

The link made by Bauman between the Holocaust and modernity hangs on the importance of rational bureaucracy and its tendency for goal-displacement, and it is Weber's conception of modern bureaucracy which holds the key to Bauman's argument. What is lacking in Bauman's account, however, is a full consideration of Weber's preoccupation with the growth of bureaucratic power and the dangers to individual freedom which this entails.

Weber's fears for bureaucracy and his countervailing factors

Political: plebiscitary democracy
Rational–legal bureaucracy for Weber was a 'technical instrument', 'technically the most perfectly adapted for achieving the highest level of performance'. As Beetham (1985, p. 65) comments, bureaucracy for Weber, 'though a supremely effective technical instrument, was nevertheless *only* an instrument', in Weber's terms, 'precise, soulless and machine-like'.[5]

The dangers of bureaucracy which Weber foresaw stemmed from his belief in its inevitable growth, for the very reason that it was so technically superior, so perfectly designed for the complexities of modern society. Rational–legal bureaucracies, he believed, had an 'inherent tendency' (Beetham, 1985, p. 67) to become more than simply administrative and to form a power group pursuing its own goals. The function of goal-setting, Weber was adamant, belonged to politicians and was not the role of bureaucracy, a role, in any case, for which bureaucrats lacked training (ibid., p. 65). Weber was also aware of the limited social background from which bureaucrats were drawn (ibid., p. 66). The essential source of the bureaucracy's power, for Weber, stemmed from bureaucrats' knowledge, both specialist and official, backed up by secrecy. Without separate sources of knowledge, politicians were vulnerable to bureaucrats presenting a case for policies which suited the bureaucrats. Whereas the role of politicians was to take personal responsibility, and assess policies on the basis of the support they would be likely to have, bureaucrats did not have to face individual responsibility in this way. Their job was to follow the rules set down.[6]

This taking of personal responsibility by politicians was, for Weber, a crucial counter to the dangers of bureaucracy. Personal responsibility or personal initiative, Weber argued, was also characteristic of entrepreneurs. If the inherent tendency of bureaucracy to exceed its administrative functions was to be countered then politicians, responsible to the electorate (for future election), and capitalistic enterprises, independent of the state, were necessary.

Socialism, which lacked both privately run firms and politicians obliged to seek support for policies was, for Weber, just the sort of system under which the bureaucracy would grow unchecked. Individual freedom and initiative would be squashed under the weight of the bureaucratic machine and inefficiency would characterize the system as rule-following displaced accountable policy-making. It was in any case, Weber believed, impossible for total economic planning to be achieved. (For the above see Beetham, 1987, pp. 62–7.)

Within capitalist systems, the problem of keeping bureaucracy under political control remained for Weber. The solution which he offered – leadership democracy – centred on the importance of the gifted politician, personally responsible for policies, and answerable to the electorate. He believed that the nature of the political system would have an important bearing on the production and training of such politicians. His preference was for a strong form of parliamentary democracy, though he later favoured a presidential system where the president was elected by the people rather than within the parliament. Universal suffrage, competing mass parties and charismatic leaders appealing directly to the electorate for support for policies initiated by the political parties and their leaders (not by the masses themselves) were the crucial elements of his political counterbalance to the routine nature of bureaucracy. Universal suffrage was important for Weber because it encouraged mass participation in an orderly and regular way, unlike the disorderly, intermittent, irrational mass interventions characteristic of undemocratic political systems. Elections were important because if leaders lost support for their policies then they would be voted out of office. (For the above see Beetham, 1985, pp. 95–107.[7])

Weber's proposed political counter to bureaucracy has been criticized and in particular for its élitism.[8] As Beetham (1987, p. 11) points out, it offers no solution to ministers colluding in secrecy. The flow of democracy is also always top–down, never bottom–up. The people do not formulate policy demands to be adopted by parties and politicians and there is no room in Weber's analysis for the pluralist democracy, which is based on the free formation of interest groups to play a significant part in the policy process. This is an important element in Bauman's idea of strong political democracy, rooted in social networks. The portrayal of liberal democracy which Weber offers, based on regular elections, is one which appears vulnerable to the demagogic leader. With bureaucracy stripped of individual initiative and responsibility, and a plebiscitary system in which leaders mobilize support for their policies at election, there is a danger that one such elected leader might stop further elections and destroy the parliamentary system. The leader in mind, of course, is Hitler.

Weber was quite clear in his view that the Wilhelmine political system was a poor example of the kind of democratic system that he had in mind as a counter to mechanical bureaucracy. The Reichstag offered a poor training ground for politicians of ability. Government ministers were mostly appointed from the bureaucracy with responsibility to the Kaiser, not parliament. This domination of civil servants meant that government was rule-following and lacked the personal initiative characteristic of a system where ministers were dependent on the electorate for re-election and had to defend policies against opposition. This all-important personal responsibility for policy was lacking in the German system. Crucially the system encouraged the kind of politician who 'lived off politics', rather than the kind who 'lived for politics'. Politicians with a vocation gained office through winning popular support and learnt skills necessary for political office, such as oratory, through public debates and speeches.[9]

On Weber's argument, then, the Wilhelmine state had not offered the conditions for nurturing strong leaders and so such leaders were not available to serve in the Weimar Republic. This is clearly a different argument to Bauman's explanation for the weakness of the Weimar Republic which stressed the absence of political democracy.

While Weber's recommended form of democracy, leadership democracy, can be criticized for opening the way for a demagogue, such as Hitler, Weber was clear that his ideal leaders would be liberals. As Beetham (1985, p. 243) explains, 'Weber's plebiscitary leader was never a pure demagogue; he had also to possess the essential quality of "Sachlichkeit", a recognition of the limits of the possible.'[10] This was why he was explicitly critical of socialist leaders within the Reichstag, and doubly so as he believed that the 'limits of the possible' had to include an expectation of the continuation of the capitalist system (ibid., p. 244).

Economic: formal rationality in the capitalist system

For Weber, the capitalist system afforded an important counter to the inherent anti-democratic tendency of bureaucracy for three reasons, and the first of these hinged on the importance of money. First, private economic organizations each had their own bureaucracies which could compete, in both technical competence and expertise, with the state bureaucracy. Second, entrepreneurs, like strong politicians, exercised individual responsibility and the success of the enterprise depended on the entrepreneurs; the profit motive encouraged the initiative and flair so lacking in rule-following bureaucrats. Third, Weber believed that the market was more formally rational than bureaucratic central planning. The unpredictable could never be taken into account in a completely planned system and only free exchange and competition would determine prices accurately. Without these prices planning could not be calculated rationally. Money accounting was central to Weber's thinking about the advantages of modern capitalistic economies. Money provided the means by which formal rational calculation could be made. Clear prices, whether for goods or labour, costs or profits, were essential if the highest levels of formal rationality were to be achieved.

The distinction made by Weber between 'formal' and 'substantive' rationality in the economy was central to his thinking. 'Formal rationality of economic action' exists where calculations and accounting are entirely quantitative and actions are based on these accurately calculated numbers (Weber, 1964, pp. 184–5). In modern society, money is crucial, calculations in traditional societies are in kind. 'Substantive rationality' (ibid., p. 185), in contrast, is not based solely on numerical calculations at each stage but in terms of the outcome of economic actions. As Weber explains,

> it is necessary to take account of the fact that economic activity is oriented to ultimate ends of some kind, whether they be ethical, political, utilitarian, hedonistic, the attainment of social distinction, of social equality, of anything else. Substantive rationality cannot be measured in terms of formal calculations alone, but also involves a relation to the absolute values or to the content of the particular given ends to which it is oriented. (Ibid.)

As examples of such ends he mentions 'scholastic and communistic standards' and 'in furtherance of the power of a political unit' (ibid., pp. 185–6). Under circumstances such as these, Weber contends, 'the mere formal calculation in money terms may seem either of quite secondary importance or even as fundamentally evil in itself, quite apart from the consequences of the modern methods of calculation' (ibid.).

Weber then contrasts the modern capitalist system, not only with socialism (and, in Weber's view, its historically antecedent centrally planned states such as Ancient Egypt) but also with war economies. On the war economy, Weber argues as follows:

> In war time the whole economy is oriented to what is in principle a single clear goal, and the authorities are in a position to make use of powers which would generally not be tolerated in peace except in cases where the subjects are 'slaves' of an authoritarian state. Furthermore it is a type of economy which inherently tends towards bankruptcy. The overwhelming urgency of the immediate end over-shadows almost any concern for welfare in the coming era of peace. Precision of calculation exists only on a technical level. Economically, however, except for materials of which a grave shortage threatens, and above all, for labour services, calculations are very rough. (Weber, 1964, p. 209)

On the planned economy Weber argues the following:

> A planned economy oriented to want satisfaction must, in proportion as it is radically carried through, weaken the incentive to labour....Where a planned economy is radically carried out, it must further accept the inevitable reduction in formal rationality of calculation which would result from the elimination of money and capital accounting. This is merely an example of the fact that substantive and formal rationality are inevitably largely opposed. This fundamental and, in the last analysis, unavoidable element of irrationality in economic systems is one of the important sources of all the problems of social policy, above all, the problems of socialism. (Ibid., pp. 214–15)

Weber's description of a war economy surely fits Bauman's image of 'modernity' in Nazi Germany: the 'single clear goal', 'the authorities...in a position to make use of powers which would generally not be tolerated in peace except in cases where the subjects are "slaves" of an authoritarian state'. Careful monetary calculation is absent; calculations are rough, 'budgetary' ones of a 'relatively primitive level'. War economies, unlike rational–legal societies, pursue only one goal, and the market is not permitted to determine prices, either of goods or labour. As a consequence, genuinely rational calculations cannot take place, decisions are all immediate. The war economy lacks the 'genuine economic character – that is, so far as it takes account of alternative ends and not only of means for a given end' (ibid.).

This pursuit of a single goal, present both in a war economy and in a planned economy, is absent in a modern capitalist economy. Weber further emphasizes the importance of a wage system in a modern rational economy. He argues that there are 'three primary conditions affecting the maximization of calculable performance by labour in carrying out specifications: (a) the optimum of aptitude for the function; (b) the optimum of skill acquired through practice; (c) the optimum of incentive for work' (Weber, 1964, pp. 261–

2). The third, (c), he argues is determined either by the individual's 'strong interest in the outcome on his own part' or by 'direct or indirect compulsion' (ibid., p. 262). This compulsion may either take the form of the threat of physical punishment or reduction in earnings for 'unsatisfactory perform- ance'. The earnings-related incentive, he argues, is 'essential to a market economy' (ibid., p. 262). With 'freedom of selection according to perform- ance' in the labour market the economy achieves 'a high degree of formal rationality' far higher than any system of compulsion can achieve.

An open, wage-system labour market also encourages what is, for Weber, the all-important individual responsibility on the part of the worker. By contrast, a system of unfree labour is nowhere near as rational as the piece- rate system. (For the above see ibid., pp. 262–3.) Leaving aside objections that can be levelled at the harshness of the free market for the unemployed and those disadvantaged by lack of skills, the important point here, again, is that for Weber a modern rational system must include incentives for hard work. Work for set wages, irrespective of quality of work or aptitude for the work, or fully compulsory work without wages (such as slave labour or labour camps) would not be formally rational, that is rational in the modern sense.

Weber's economic analysis, then, leads directly to a rejection of Bauman's thesis which views modernity as the underlying cause of the Holocaust. Whereas, as explained, Weber also offers an alternative explanation to Bauman's arguments about 'political democracy', it is Beetham's criticisms of Weber on bureaucracy which lead to a political refutation of Bauman's theory, through political analysis.

Bureaucracy and secrecy
Beetham shares Weber's view of bureaucracy as essential for democracy but takes issue with his position in two ways. First, he rejects the easy distinction between the means – the realm of the technical–rational expert bureaucrat – and the ends (policies) – the realm of the politician. Policies, he argues, are part means and part ends. Consideration of, for example, feasibility and ways of implementation are important features of policies. Technical help can be sought outside the bureaucracy and bureaucrats too may seek such independ- ent help. There is no inherent need for bureaucracies to be secretive. Indeed, Beetham argues, in an open society where interest groups are free to form, where expert opinions can be sought and policies are formulated on the basis of negotiation in conditions of freedom to form and express opinion with ready access to information, bureaucracy can offer a truly democratic, non- secretive service. (For the above see Beetham, 1987, pp. 106–8.)

Second, Beetham (1987, pp. 112–15) rejects Weber's view of bureaucracy as an autonomous system functioning independently of government, with inherent anti-democratic tendencies. Rather, Beetham argues, it is secrecy which creates the conditions for bureaucracy's independence, and the need for secrecy is itself dependent on the policies which it is called upon to administer. The need for secrecy reflects, to a greater or lesser degree, the anti-democratic nature of the government and its 'great power' role in either aspiration or practice. Beetham offers three tasks which push bureaucracy towards 'independence and self-enclosure' (ibid., p. 112). The first, 'the management of unresolved conflict', follows from the Marxist theory of bureaucracy for, as Beetham argues, 'the control of labour requires a secretive, self-enclosed administration – in both industry and state' (ibid., p. 113). Beetham extends this point beyond class to race, gender and any subordinate groups where there are significant cleavages. The second point, 'the dynamics of the overextended centre', derives from the liberal objection to command economies and the problems of the overcentralized state which is obliged to intervene increasingly to impose corrections to its own mistakes, overriding and destroying local initiative.

Beetham's third cause of bureaucracy's closing in on itself is 'the protection of the state's security interests', where secrecy is required at home to protect against potential foreign enemies and is extended to the weapons industries. Beetham elaborates as follows:

> Of course the degree of bureaucratic self-enclosure is partly dependent upon the extent of any external threat, and how far it is replicated internally. But it is also a matter of the state's own political posture and mode of defence. A great power role, or pretensions to it, is the posture most conducive to the expansion of the military related bureaucracy within the state, and to its infecting other areas of the apparatus; reliance on nuclear weapons systems leads to the most intense and ramified secrecy. (Ibid., p. 114)

In contrast, he argues, the neutral, non-nuclear state with a 'citizen militia' would encourage openness.

Bureaucracy closes in on itself most, then, exactly where government policies require it. As Beetham (1987, p. 115) stresses,

> Common to all three processes – the deregulation of social subordination and conflict, the dynamic of the overextended centre, the protection of state security – is the need to control a population, or significant sections of it: to treat them as the objects of management, with all the sophisticated techniques that now implies, rather than as the autonomous subjects of social and political activity. To this end secrecy is required and the informational and organizational capacities necessary to modern administration have to be transformed into an instrument of control and surveillance, and protected by a process of bureaucratic self-enclosure and independence.

The question naturally arises as to whether these conditions requiring secrecy and so conducive to bureaucratic self-enclosure are an inherent part of modern society. Beetham's disclaimer for neutral, non-nuclear states with a citizens' militia suggest that they are not. Again, in order to regulate social disorder and law-breaking all modern societies must have a police force. Clearly, however, the extent to which secrecy is necessitated by this regulation must depend upon the openness of the procedures themselves. Police forces 'governed' within the local community under citizen control may be less conducive to bureaucratic secrecy than those entirely under central orders. (See Dahl, 1989, p. 245.) Such regulation will be the least conducive to secrecy where the role of police is to uphold laws, openly laid down, and to follow proper procedures with their actions subject to scrutiny and the laws themselves open both to public debate and to pressures for reform from the relevant interest groups within society.[11]

Beetham is clearly right in stressing the openness of society itself and the democratic nature of policies as the main counters to bureaucratic self-enclosure. In respect of the second factor, the 'overextended centre', again his arguments are persuasive: a central organization which is under scrutiny at every point from the relevant freely-formed interest groups and is capable of reacting to the unexpected problems which arise will not depend on secrecy. The very openness of society and the nature of the policies implemented, namely, that they are in harmony with the views of the relevant sections of the population affected by them, will be crucial in preventing the growth of central control.

Beetham (1987, p. 116) notes that in the USSR in the 1920s and 1930s all three policy factors pushing for bureaucratic self-enclosure, and therefore autonomous power, were present: 'the assertion of state security interests against external and internal challenge; the overextension of the centre in the service of the command economy; the compulsory extraction of a surplus from both peasantry and proletariat in the interests of rapid industrial development.' In German, under Hitler, though the balance might have differed, the system was equally heavily weighted towards secrecy and bureaucratic self-enclosure. Hitler pursued a militaristic policy of armament and sought world-power status. He also extracted surplus through the forced labour of Jews, Slavs, and other *Untermenschen*. (The case will be covered in detail in Chapters 7 and 8.) The overextension of the centre also occurred as the command system took increasing control. But by more than any of these things secrecy was encouraged by the extraordinary policies of concentration camps and eventually the concealed extermination of millions of people.

The difficulty arises that the policies found in Stalin's USSR and Hitler's Germany are so strikingly different from those found in more open societies that it seems insufficient simply to recognize all three conditions for bureau-

cratic self-enclosure to have been present to reach an understanding of secrecy in these cases. The nature of the policies, the absence of interest
groups, competing parties and a free press and so forth certainly help. Following Arendt (1958), however, not only the bureaucracy became secretive
but the whole society became 'a secret society'. Furthermore, the state bureaucracy was not so much straightforwardly self-enclosed as closed off
within itself with deliberate duplication of offices in a system of terror (Arendt's
argument will be covered fully in Chapters 3 and 4). Following Beetham,
however, policies are almost always a combination of means and ends. The
use of terror may in part be a policy decision and in part be the natural
development of bureaucratic self-enclosure under special social and political
conditions. But this is to jump ahead of the analysis of cases.

At this juncture, the important point is that if Beetham's argument is
accepted that bureaucracy does not have an inherent anti-democratic tendency towards anti-democracy, then modernity cannot be given the general
blame for the Holocaust in the sense of providing its necessary conditions,
as Bauman argues. Modern legal–rational bureaucracy does not possess an
inherent anti-democratic tendency towards technical rule and displacement
of ends by means as a goal. The self-enclosure of bureaucracy is itself a
reflection of policies and policies are themselves a combination of means
and ends.

Against modernity
The lessons for Bauman's thesis are clear. To characterize modern society in
terms of Weber's rational–legal bureaucracy and the expertise of science and
technology is to disengage bureaucracy from society. For Weber this society
was to possess a free-market capitalist system, with its concomitant competitive wage-labour system. It was also to be a liberal democracy where leaders
competed for votes in a system of universal suffrage. Under these circumstances, in Weber's view, the anti-democratic tendencies of bureaucracy could
be countered. Furthermore, only in a modern capitalistic system could bureaucracy achieve its highest level of formal rationality. Only via a money
economy with a free market in goods, employment and ownership of capital
could proper numerical calculations of prices, incomes, profits, costs, labour,
budgets and so on be made. That is, only in such a society could high levels
of formal rationality be attained.

At the furthest extreme from such a society is one where the economy is
based on substantive rationality – the pursuit of a single goal, where there is
compulsory labour, lack of entrepreneurs and little, if any, proper accounting,
based on money – and the political system lacks competition between political parties so that politicians are neither required to compete for electoral
support nor held accountable for their actions in government.

A policy of forced labour stands in direct opposition to that of free-market capitalism in which wage labour forms an integral part. Not only political and social pluralism stand in the way of another Holocaust in rational modern society but also 'free' labour within a plural economic system, where private firms exist in competition with any state-run enterprises, each with their own independent bureaucracies. Each organization may be run on modern rational calculations based on rule-following and problem-solving, each epitomizing 'modernity' in Bauman's sense, but by ignoring competition and the capacity for people to move between organizations, Bauman overlooks a crucial attribute of truly modern societies, one which makes them very different from both Nazi Germany and Stalin's USSR.

Which goal?

Bauman's argument, then, rests on a view of bureaucracy which does not approximate modern legal–rational bureaucracy, for it is the substantive rationality of the system which is his concern, the pursuit of a single goal – Germany free of Jews – which in the end becomes displaced by 'the final solution'. As such, Bauman's (1989, p. 106) claim that 'bureaucracy is intrinsically *capable* of genocidal action' cannot be supported, for its actions depend on the nature of the policies it is directed to pursue and the secrecy which those policies encourage or require. The claimed natural link between modernity and the Holocaust which is said to follow from rational bureaucracy is not then sustained.

Substantive, not formal, rationality was characteristic of the Nazi regime. However, while it may be true that the Nazis pursued a goal, it is neither necessarily the case that Bauman has identified the correct goal, nor that only one goal (whether displaced or otherwise) was involved. That Hitler wanted to make Germany 'free of Jews' is undoubtedly true, but this could have been as much means as end and, as an end, one among several. Arendt (1958), for example, stresses the expulsion of Jews as a means to develop and intensify anti-Semitism abroad, through the deliberate creation of stateless people, with the Nazis' ultimate goal to take over the world, under which sole condition total domination could be fully achieved. Arendt also contends that the Nazis had the added goal of racial purification which involved the extermination of Jews. Following Arendt's position, the 'final solution' was not, then, a case of goal-displacement, for forced migration of Jews was both a policy in the earlier years and a means to a longer-term extermination policy intended for later years once conditions had been created to make its implementation possible. These arguments will be expanded fully in Chapter 4.

Taking over the world, the creation of the 2000-year Reich is, clearly, also an important contender for Bauman's goal of 'getting rid of Jews'. Bauman (1989, p. 94) himself recognizes the importance of war to Germany. He quotes Gordon (1984, pp. 48–9): 'systematic extermination, as opposed to sporadic pogroms, could be carried out only by extremely powerful government, and probably could have succeeded only under the cover of wartime conditions'. For Bauman, then, war was a means to the end of getting rid of Jews. Geyer (1984, p. 198) has gone so far as to argue that it was Hitler's 'main and ultimate goal'. In line with Beetham's position, however, it is doubtful that the separation between means and end is helpful.

Expulsion of Jews could only work so long as there were places beyond German territories to which Jews could be sent. On this logic, win or lose the war, Jews would in the end have to be exterminated. If the war was won and world domination achieved then the Aryan race would people the world and there would be no place to which Jews could migrate. In this case, no goal-displacement would have taken place; only the means would have changed. Losing the war, however, would equally have meant that Jews would have to be exterminated: as the Reich ceased to expand further and began to contract, the eventual Aryan purpose remained, so that Jews would have to be got rid of inside old, rather than outside new, German borders. In this sense, killing Jews was both a means and an end and the policy changes which occurred in reality were not the result of goal-displacement through the natural laws of bureaucratic growth, but changes in policy as a reaction to changing circumstances.

It is, in general, true that the major criticisms of theories are derived from the availability of alternative explanations. These are amply provided, as comments have already indicated, by the existing theories of totalitarianism, which predate Bauman by more than three decades. As will be shown in the chapter which follows, these alternative explanations offer some support for Bauman but also challenge his position at various critical points They raise not simply the possibility that alternative goals were important, but in Arendt's case, contrary to Bauman, deny the existence of a rational state, under totalitarian government. The theories also challenge Bauman's conception of the importance of the centralization of coercion, by directing attention to terror. In focusing attention on the secret police they also point to the problem which Bauman faces in respect of the bureaucrat as pen-pusher and bureaucrat as killer. The theories also offer a different explanation to that of 'distance' for the absence of 'moral responsibility'.[12] Each theory also approaches the significance of science and technology in a challenging way. Most importantly, though, in drawing direct comparison between Stalin's Russia and the Holocaust they offer generalizations which, though less sweeping in their claimed potential relevance, in practice offer broader application.

Notes

1. A similar stress on the relationship between modernity and totalitarianism, though within the wider context of modern nation-states and the use of violence, is also to be found in Giddens (1985, pp. 294–310). In Giddens's view 'Totalitarianism is a tendential property of the modern state' (p. 295). Giddens (ibid., p. 301) accepts Friedrich's (1969) and Friedrich and Brzezinski's (1965) concept of totalitarianism 'to be accurate and useful'. The classic theories of totalitarianism will be covered in Chapters 3 and 4.

2. For a particularly interesting and persuasive demonstration of the problem for Weber's *Thesis on the Protestant Ethic and the Spirit of Capitalism* see Marshall (1982).

3. These criticisms in respect of Bauman's arguments about modern states and their monopoly of violence also apply to Giddens (1985) where surveillance is given particular prominence and in totalitarian regimes is seen as essentially an intensification of what takes place in other nation-states. Torture is viewed as just an extreme means of extracting confessions from those holding 'deviant political views' (ibid., p. 304). How being a Jew in Nazi Germany classifies as a 'deviant political view' is not faced. 'Tanks, mortars, machine-guns deployed in the reference to a civilian population' (ibid.) are stressed as the modern means of coercion available to the modern nation-state and concentration camps are interpreted as the intense 'concentrated application of force against minority groupings' (ibid.), these minorities being those classified as deviant.

4. On the logic of the comparative method see Sartori (1970, 1991).

5. The quotations from Weber are taken from Beetham (1985, p. 64). The expression 'technical instrument' is Albert Weber's, the brother of Max Weber. The other quotations are respectively from Max Weber, *Wirtschaft und Gesellschaft* (Tübingen, 1972) and *Schriften des Vereins für Sozialpolitik*. These quotations are translated from the German by Beetham.

6. For the above see Beetham (1985, p. 74) Beetham's sources are *Gesammelte Politische Schriften* (Tübingen, 1958), *Gesammelte Aufsatze zur Sociologie und Sozialpolitik* (Tübingen, 1924) and *Wirtschaft und Gesellschaft* (Tübingen, 1972).

7. Beetham draws mainly on *Gesammelte Politische Schriften* (Tübingen, 1958).

8. For discussion of these criticisms with some defence, see Beetham (1987, pp. 113–16).

9. For the above see Beetham (1985, p. 99 and 1987, p. 67) and, in particular, M. Weber, 'Politics as a Vocation' in Gerth and Mills (1970) and M. Weber, 'The Introduction of Parliamentary Government and Democratization' in Lassmann and Speirs (1994, pp. 209–33).

10. Here Beetham's sources are *Gesammelte Politische Schriften* (Tübingen, 1958) and 'Politics as a Vocation' in Gerth and Mills (1970).

11. These considerations also have a bearing on Giddens's (1985) arguments about modern techniques of surveillance and the nation-state. Surveillance, in the sense of information collection, can be an aid not to secrecy but to openness through greater access to more information. Furthermore, where modern surveillance equipment is widely available surveillance may equally be seen as a counter to totalitarianism. This serves to reinforce Arendt's view that violence (here surveillance) should not be seen as the 'essence of the state'; it is the uses to which it is put which is critical to the nature of states.

12. Within the social psychology literature it should also be noted that Milgram's experimental procedures and the analytical deductions made from them have provoked considerable debate. For an account of this debate see Mixon (1989). Mixon's own position is that the behaviour of the experimenter would have affected the subject's belief in the reality of pain inflicted. If the experimenter remained calm at all levels of pain inflicted then the subject would feel more assured that it would be all right to continue. In this line of argument, then, it is not the 'distance' between subject and object that would be crucial but the behaviour of the experimenter and the reaction of the subject to that behaviour. The less emotional, then, the superior bureaucrat about issuing orders, the less affected would be the inferior bureaucrat (ibid., pp. 12–40). Deception effected through secrecy would have the desired result of getting inferiors to carry out orders. In Mixon's view issues of moral responsibility belong essentially at the top of the command hierarchy, not lower down.

In limitation of Mixon's arguments, however, it must be accepted that at the point of actual killing and torture, there is no equivalent to the 'experimenter' present. The subject can see when screams derive from real pain and when death is a fact. Moral responsibility must remain a central concern here. As argued, however, the torturer, and the executioner, are not 'bureaucrats'. It follows from the analysis offered here that the advantage of concentration camps and killing fields in underpopulated areas is that of secrecy. Not letting people know what is going on, preventing them knowing that moral responsibility is an issue, is an essential part of terror as government in the midst of 'modern civilization'.

3 Totalitarian dictatorship and totalitarian regime

The view of Nazi Germany as a phenomenon of modernity is not new. Both the classic works on totalitarianism, Hannah Arendt, *The Origins of Totalitarianism* (1958, first published 1951) and Carl Friedrich and Zbigniew Brzezinski, *Totalitarian Dictatorship and Autocracy* (1965, first published 1956) see totalitarianism as a purely twentieth century phenomenon. Though there are similarities between these works there are also important differences. The debate generated from these positions strengthens the case against Bauman's claims for the direct and central importance of modernity in explanation for the Holocaust and also focuses attention on government.

Bauman's work does not engage directly with the debate on totalitarianism. Its aim, as explained, is to comment on modern societies in general through the case of the Holocaust, rather than to develop a general conceptual construction for application to limited cases. Arendt's conception of the totalitarian regime is highly restrictive, applying to only two cases, Nazi Germany and Stalin's USSR. In contrast, Friedrich and Brzezinski's syndrome of totalitarian dictatorship is designed for far wider application, but contrary to Bauman's position, the syndrome is constructed so as to be distanced as far as possible from the 'modern civilization' of western capitalist liberal democratic societies. These are the very societies which Bauman views as inherently possessing the potential for modern genocide.

There is a tendency to assume that where concepts vary, synthesis can be achieved to produce progress in understanding. This can sometimes be so, but often positions are actually oppositions and disagreements so fundamental that if one view is accepted, even in part, then the other must be rejected. Such is the case in the debate about the concept of totalitarianism. Even though they share important areas of emphasis, Arendt and Friedrich and Brzezinski are in fundamental disagreement. In essence, Friedrich and Brzezinski develop a concept of totalitarian dictatorship whereas central to Arendt's view is the emphasis that totalitarian government is not a dictatorship, even of a new and modern kind.[1]

The purposes for which Arendt's as opposed to Friedrich and Brzezinski's concepts were conceived differ in significant ways. Friedrich and Brzezinski propose a six-point syndrome in order to further political science. It is offered as a comparative device to separate out a proposed new form of political system to be applied to future cases. As such, Friedrich and Brzezinski do not seek a causal explanation of this new phenomenon but offer understanding of how the separate parts work together to create an entirely new whole. In contrast, it is exactly the origins of the phenomenon in which Arendt is interested. While Friedrich and Brzezinski must extract their syndrome from context in order to achieve their scientific ambitions, Arendt must investigate the past and develop an intricate picture, not an abstract. Though strictly Arendt's theory was formed before Friedrich and Brzezinski's view, for the very clarity of its abstraction, it is best to begin with Friedrich and Brzezinski's conception of totalitarian dictatorship.[2]

Friedrich and Brzezinski's six-point syndrome of totalitarian dictatorship

The attraction of Friedrich and Brzezinski's conception of totalitarianism is their clear and concise list of characteristics. Though not always appreciated as such, the list is a syndrome, which implies an interdependence of parts to form in their terms an 'organic' whole.[3] A totalitarian dictatorship exists only where all six characteristics are present. Each can exist separately, for example points five (monopoly of arms) and six (central control and direction of the economy) are specifically mentioned as present in some constitutional democracies.

The six points are summarized by Friedrich and Brzezinski (1965, p. 22) as follows:

1. An 'elaborate ideology' which is official doctrine covering all 'vital aspects' of people's lives, rejecting the existing society and aiming for a perfect future society through world conquest.
2. A 'single mass party typically led by one man, the dictator', consisting of fanatical supporters of the ideology; the party is 'hierarchically, oligarchically organized and typically either superior to, or completely intertwined with the government bureaucracy'.
3. A 'system of terror', physical or psychological, carried out through 'secret police or party directed social pressure' with the secret police both 'supporting' and 'supervising the party for its leaders' and directed against 'demonstrable "enemies" of the regime' and also 'more or less arbitrarily selected classes of the population'. Here it is expressly commented that modern science and particularly 'scientific psychology' are exploited by the terror system.
4. A 'technologically conditioned near-complete monopoly of control' of mass communications by the party and government, including the 'press, radio and film'.
5. 'A similarly technologically conditioned, near-complete monopoly of the effective use of all weapons of armed combat'.

6.   A centrally controlled and directed economy through the coordination by the bureaucracy of once independent businesses and other economic associations.

Friedrich and Brzezinski recognize that there may be variations between totalitarian dictatorships. For example, the ideology of the 'Marxist–Leninist bible' (p. 23) is contrasted with fascism in Germany and Italy where the party leader formulated ideology. Following from the corporatism of fascism and the doctrines of communism they also argue that differences of public and private property existed in the respective economies. These variations are recognized and other relevant variables are also accepted as of possible importance, but what is new is the coming together of the six traits and it is the syndrome they create which constitutes totalitarian dictatorship. Examples offered by Friedrich and Brzezinski are the USSR, pre-World War II Germany under Hitler, Italy under Mussolini, and the post-World War II communist countries in Europe, China, Cuba and Ghana. These latter cases, naturally, appear only in the later edition of their book.

As the six-point list makes clear, there are important areas of sympathy with Bauman's position. Not only are science, technology and bureaucracy stressed but the monopoly of coercion is central as, too, in the stress on the single party, is the absence of what Bauman terms 'political democracy'. On closer examination, however, it becomes clear that Friedrich and Brzezinski's earlier work offers an important challenge to Bauman's link between modernity and modern genocide.

Modern science and technology
In common with Bauman's theory, modern science and technology is central to Friedrich and Brzezinski's analysis. As they point out, 'In short four out of the six traits are technologically conditioned' (Friedrich and Brzezinski, 1965, p. 24). Advanced science and technology are crucial to the monopoly of weapons. The monopoly of communications would be impossible without modern technology, and propaganda is central to totalitarian dictatorship with the link between terror and propaganda singled out as the combination that distinguishes totalitarian dictatorship from 'other terror regimes and autocracies' (ibid., p. 171). Modern science and scientific psychology are 'exploited' in the 'system of terror'. The authors also point out that the centrally directed economy presupposes the reporting, cataloguing and calculating devices provided by modern technology' (ibid., p. 24). Twentieth century technology is also essential for the party to indoctrinate youth (ibid., pp. 60–69). Furthermore, Friedrich and Brzezinski (1965, p. 317) conclude that

totalitarian dictatorship is itself the 'logical' outcome of some of these technological trends. This is not true in the sense of modern technology's having 'caused'
totalitarianism, but in the sense of having made it possible. Without it, several of
its distinctive traits, more especially propaganda, the terror, and central planning,
would be quite impossible.

At the same time, however, it is also clear that Friedrich and Brzezinski
have a very functional view of the role of science and technology which
contrasts with Bauman's. They view science as an agreed method of investigation within a particular discipline, and not the knowledge itself. This is
important, because the scientific method must involve disagreement and critical analysis which generates new ideas and discoveries. They draw particular
attention to this in respect of universities, institutes of technology and the like
which they perceive as 'islands of separateness' threatening the totalitarian
need for unanimity, imposed ideological consensus (ibid., pp. 316–28).[4]

Wishing to employ the products of science, but threatened by the critical
and open interests found within these institutions of higher learning and
research, the totalitarian system develops in defence, Friedrich and Brzezinski
claim, 'a crude utilitarian view of science as merely a means to an end' (ibid.,
p. 316). Such regimes, they argue, become in effect 'parasitic', using scientific
discoveries but at the same time thwarting the open scientific experimental
method, imposing bureaucratic controls and insisting on 'narrow specialization' (ibid., p. 323). Whereas Bauman views such specialization as the natural
development of modernity, Friedrich and Brzezinski view it as a political
imposition and one, furthermore, which because it stunts inquiry threatens to
destroy the regime. In Friedrich and Brzezinski's view, totalitarian dictatorship could not have occurred without modern science and technology, but at
the same time totalitarian dictatorship could only be achieved through the
stunting of scientific inquiry and the imposition of tasks to be performed
through bureaucratic control.

Bureaucracy
The importance of bureaucracy is also obvious in Friedrich and Brzezinski's
analysis. They state clearly: 'modern totalitarianism, unlike more traditional
dictatorships, is a highly bureaucratized system of power' (Friedrich and
Brzezinski, 1965, p. 35). As noted, party organization is 'hierarchically,
oligarchically, organized' and either above 'or completely intertwined with,
the governmental bureaucracy' (ibid., p. 22). Bureaucracy is needed for the
centralization of arms, for the control over technology, for the operation of
technology and for the process of terror. The judicial system also becomes
part of the bureaucracy (ibid., p. 34). Most strikingly characteristic, however,
is the role of the state bureaucracy in the control of the economy. Bureaucracy is the means through which the once independent businesses, trade

unions and cooperatives are coordinated. Bureaucracy is essential for planning, and central planning in Friedrich and Brzezinski's view is a major characteristic of totalitarian dictatorships (ibid., p. 214).

Though the bureaucratic nature of totalitarian regimes is stressed as a factor which differentiates the totalitarian from other dictatorships, Friedrich and Brzezinski conflict with Bauman's view of the importance of modern bureaucracy. Under totalitarian dictatorship, they argue, bureaucracy is retrogressive, turning from the legal–rational form back to more traditional forms. In the highly hierarchical party, those just below the leader are viewed as of the 'feudal type' with the leader having 'absolute power' (ibid., p. 140). Stressing this point Friedrich and Brzezinski (1965, p. 206) argue as follows:

> What we find under totalitarian dictatorships is, however, a marked deviation and retrogression where previously a higher degree of bureaucratization existed. Centralization of control and supervision yields to a conflict between the bureaucracies of party and government; centralization is superseded by local autocrats like the Gauleiters, and party loyalty replaces professional qualifications for office, though from the totalitarian regime's standpoint such ideological commitment constitutes a kind of qualification for office.

For Friedrich and Brzezinski, the development of bureaucracy in its totalitarian form is not, as Bauman contends, the product of modernity but, in line with Beetham, the consequence of political decision: 'The very shapelessness of the vast bureaucratic machinery is part of the technique of manipulating the absolute power that the dictator and his lieutenants have at their disposal' (ibid., p. 34). It is central to Friedrich and Brzezinski's claim that in totalitarian dictatorships those in power choose to implement an ideology which has devastating consequences.

Elaborate ideology
Totalitarian ideology is defined by Friedrich and Brzezinski (1965, pp. 88–9) as: 'a reasonable coherent body of ideas concerning practical means of how totally to change and reconstruct a society by force or violence based upon an all-inclusive or total criticism of what is wrong with the existing or antecedent society'. It is 'an official body of doctrine' which is Utopian, in pursuit of world rule and which covers all aspects of the lives of everyone in the pursuit of the totally reshaped society which is to be 'revolutionised economically, socially and culturally' (ibid., p. 162). Representing truth, disagreements are allowed neither within the party nor society (ibid., p. 105).

Violence, the means to achieve the ends of a totally reshaped society and world rule, is justified within the ideology itself. Both communism and fascism are claimed to fit these requirements, though it is stressed that while both these ideologies have their roots in the 'complex and variegated tapestry' of western intellectual ideas, this justification for violence does not (ibid., p. 106). In this respect, the strands of western ideas are exploited. In Friedrich and Brzezinski's words, 'the specific totalitarian ingredient – the employment, even glorification, of violence for the realization of the goals that the ideology posits is largely absent from the thought of those whose ideas these ideologies have utilized and, in utilizing them, distorted' (ibid., p. 106). It is, in their view, the 'insistence' of both communism and fascism on 'the revolutionary fulfilment of the "truths" of their doctrine' that leads to the need for a disciplined party (ibid., p. 105). Narrowly, the ideology of Nazism is described as racial purity (anti-Semitism) and communism is class war.

These views are close in some respects to Bauman's account of Nazis in power, the 'Nazi revolution, an exercise in social engineering' a 'bold design of a better, more reasonable and rational social order'. Ideology is not, however, given a significant part in Bauman's argument. Racism, it will be recalled, was 'a policy first and an ideology second'. Bauman's arguments about goal-displacement also conflict with Friedrich and Brzezinski who debate the possibility that leaders manipulate ideology but conclude that they do not, though they accept that ideology may evolve (ibid., pp. 107–15).

Propaganda, terror and the 'vacuum'
The reason why ideology is perceived as so fundamentally important to totalitarian dictatorship stems from the role given to propaganda 'directed ultimately to the maintenance in power of the party controlling it' (Friedrich and Brzezinski, 1965, p. 131). The party requires unanimity. Propaganda and educational training are viewed as the means for achieving the 'total ideological integration' of the people. Any group which disagrees must be removed. One of the most important roles of propaganda is to create stereotypes of the 'enemy'. This use of propaganda, however, they argue, leads to the use of terror, because propaganda creates what they term 'the vacuum' (ibid., p. 135). The 'vacuum' comes to surround the leadership, rendering it out of touch with ordinary people's views and also creating problems of effective communication inside the party hierarchy. Propaganda, they contend, leads in the end to disbelief and rumours. The absence of alternative sources of information, such as a free press, is crucial in this, because without genuine information people as a whole tend to become indifferent, whereas within the hierarchy officials become more concerned to say what they think wants to be heard rather than what may be the truth (ibid., pp. 135–6).

The spread of this 'vacuum', Friedrich and Brzezinski (1965, p. 136) argue, has highly damaging consequences:

A slow disintegration affecting all human relations causes mutual distrust so that ordinary people are alienated from one another; all the bonds of confidence in social relationships are corroded by the terror and propaganda, the spying, and the denouncing and betraying until the social fabric threatens to fall apart...Isolation and anxiety are the universal result. And the only answer the totalitarian dictatorship has for coping with this disintegration of human relationships is more organized coercion, more propaganda, more terror.

Moreover, the inhibition of 'truthful reporting', not only within the population, but also within the party and the secret police, they argue, interferes with industrial planning: 'The vacuum works like a cancer in the totalitarian systems' (ibid., p. 143).

This move to terror exists within the ideology itself. The stress on violence has already been mentioned, but it also follows, Friedrich and Brzezinski (1965, p. 162) argue, from the goal of total change. The 'organization of total terror' is used to prevent opposition developing and in the end everyone is engulfed. At first, violence is used against open enemies, in order to effect unanimity, but the 'overlapping groups' of acquaintances and associates of these 'enemies of the people' are drawn in and totalitarian terror gradually extends through society such that unpredictability becomes a part of its process (ibid., p. 163). In short, terror is defined as 'a process in which activities of deliberate violence are undertaken by the power wielders to strike general and undefined fear into anyone who dissents' (ibid., p. 170). As explained in Chapter 1, however, this clearly fits within Gregor's definition of a repressive rather than a terror regime.

The system of terror

Whilst the monopoly of the effective use of all weapons of armed combat strikes a chord with Bauman's attention to the centralization of coercion (if without the theoretical connection to distance), Friedrich and Brzezinski's separate stress on terror does not. The military, for Friedrich and Brzezinski (and in direct contrast with ordinary dictatorships), is totally under the control of the totalitarian party (ibid., pp. 201–14).

This 'system of terror' is effected neither through the army nor the police. Terror is perpetrated through the secret police and party control, with the secret police, as explained, 'supporting but also supervising the party'. The terror, which can be physical or psychological, is used by governments in 'the deliberate effort to intimidate'. 'Governmental terror seeks to frighten those under its sway into conformity and obedience. It therefore may create a measure of consensus and willing cooperation' (ibid., p. 129). The effect of the terror is to generate 'a pervasive atmosphere of anxiety and a general sense of insecurity' (ibid.). The link between terror and propaganda, with propaganda spreading terror and terror strengthening the monopoly of communication, is argued to be crucial and, as explained, it is this link which is viewed as the aspect of totalitarian dictatorships which distinguishes them from other terror regimes and autocracies (ibid., pp. 129–30). In sympathy with Bauman's claims about political pluralism as the counter to modern genocide, Friedrich and Brzezinski (1965, p. 171) argue that the clearest indication of the non-existence of terror is the presence of organized groups that criticize those in power both publicly and continually.

The essential role played by the secret police, Friedrich and Brzezinski argue, is not the total destruction of 'enemies' but 're-education', though they add that 'the National Socialists seemed less hopeful on this score' (ibid., p. 174). Though indoctrination is the combined role of terror and propaganda, liquidation of people – 'vast masses' of people – they argue to be 'much more typical'. For all this a 'machinery of terror' is required. In the USSR, this machinery, they contend, began with the Cheka, under Lenin, though they admit that after 1953 and the removal of Beria after Stalin's death, there was no secret police member in the Praesidium. In Italy, they argue, the blackshirts (*squadristi*) were the machine of terror. In Germany they were at first the SA (Stormtroopers), which were then replaced by the SS (which also took over the police) and then, with Himmler as head of the SS, the SS took over the Gestapo in 1936. (For the above see Friedrich and Brzezinski 1965, pp. 175–9.)

Friedrich and Brzezinski also argue that purges and concentration camps are unique to the totalitarian system. The main functions of purges, they claim, are to undermine stabilization, especially in the provinces, and to ensure élite circulation (ibid., p 189). Purges, labour camps and confessions together, they argue, make their contribution to the terror by which the totalitarian regime reinforces the propaganda that in time produces the consensus any government requires in the long run, whether it be 'democratic, autocratic, constitutional or totalitarian' (ibid., p. 201).

Party and dictator
Along with the failure to make a distinction between centralized state coercion and a system of terror, Bauman also pays scant attention to the party and the leader. The party and dictator play a very important role in Friedrich and Brzezinski's analysis. The whole idea of a totalitarian 'dictatorship' rests on the claim that '...the power of decision is completely concentrated in a single leader' (Friedrich and Brzezinski, 1965, p. 34). They continue, 'any constitution is merely a disguise by which a "democratic" framework is being suggested, a kind of window dressing or façade for the totalitarian reality'. Legislative bodies are there to 'acclaim' decisions made by the leader. Crucially too, the role of the party is 'to provide a following for the dictator with which he can identify' (ibid., p. 47).

The party, as already explained, is bureaucratic and intertwined with, or 'superior to' the state bureaucracy, with party loyalty being the main criterion for promotion, position and authority within the bureaucratic hierarchy. The totalitarian party is élitist, undemocratic, more like a 'club' or 'exclusive brotherhood' (ibid., p. 45). There is no open recruitment and membership would not be allowed to exceed 10 per cent of the population. The discipline required within the party Friedrich and Brzezinski relate to both the ideology ('the revolutionary fulfilment of the "truths" of their doctrines') and the 'infallible leadership', which leads 'through science or intuition towards the 'utopian apocalypse' (ibid., p. 105). Power is entirely centralized and the party is the hub of a wider movement aimed particularly at the recruitment of future members. Youth movements, such as the Hitler Youth and Komsomol, are set up for the purposes of indoctrinating the next generation of party members (ibid., pp. 60–69).

Economic planning: production and labour

Totalitarian dictatorships, according to Friedrich and Brzezinski, also share in common a centrally directed and controlled economy. Economic success is seen as vital to political success (Friedrich and Brzezinski, 1965, p. 244). The authors make it quite clear, however, that their arguments are not about the outward structures of the economy but about the role of economic planning and its effects. They 'readily concede that the differences between the fascist type of industrial arrangement and the communist one are many and obvious' (ibid., p. 243). They accept that in fascist economies private enterprises are mostly formally left in place with big businessmen presiding over board meetings, whereas in the communist economies the state owns and runs industry. They contend, however, that these differences are not fundamental, arguing as follows: 'One needs to go below the surface and ask: who controls the industrial development, who sets its quotas and allocates resources, who determines the ultimate objectives of industrial production, who regulates awards, who controls the personnel, who establishes political standards of loyalty for all those involved?' (ibid., p. 243).

It is, then economic planning which Friedrich and Brzezinski argue to he crucial to totalitarian dictatorships, and it is the leader who makes the basic decisions about the organization of the plan. In the Soviet Union, they argue, the plan was 'originally' that of industrialization. In Nazi Germany it was 'that of eliminating unemployment and preparing for war', in China industrialization combined with 'land reform' and in East Germany initially that of providing 'the large-scale reparations the Soviet Union demanded'. 'These goals of planning', they argue, 'are the most decisive issues to be settled in a totalitarian society' (Friedrich and Brzezinski, 1965, p. 219). They specifically mention the five-year plans in the USSR (and in China) and the importance of this plan and the four-year plan in Nazi Germany, begun in 1936 and taken over by Speer in 1942 (see ibid., pp. 221–9).

They argue, however, that plans do not have to succeed when the dictator and party have control over information. As they explain, 'Planning in Germany never became effective due to Goering's incompetence and Hitler's lack of understanding of economic problems' (ibid., p. 227). It is not simply control of production of goods which Friedrich and Brzezinski have in mind. In addition to five-year and four-year plans, they also stress central control over trade unions and the destruction of workers' independent representation and control over their conditions of work and eventually conditions of life. Crucially, labour is not free either to form associations or to choose jobs. Trade unions become the agents of governments, not the agencies of representation of workers' needs. (See ibid., pp. 243–59.) They stress, in particular, a 'system of labour conscription' whereby a 'special government body' assigns workers to jobs where needed, draws up long-term contracts or sends workers long distances away to labour camps (ibid., p. 251). They also point out that 'beyond this general subjugation of labour in the Soviet totalitarian system, there existed for many years the outright slavery of the labour camp' containing 'millions of people' (ibid., p. 252).

In Russia, they contend, the system of labour camps was in full swing by 1928, following peasant resistance to collectivization and the first Five-Year Plan produced millions of similar so-called 'criminals'. They draw attention both to the contribution of slave labour to Soviet output (ibid., p. 253) and to the fact that in Nazi Germany a system of slave labour developed during the war (ibid., p. 254).[5] They also stress the importance to the National Socialist Party of the Charter of Labour (20 January 1934) and the National Labour Front formed by the party to include workers and managers, around 25 million in all, which took over the whole trade union structure (including its property). Compulsory assignment to jobs began in 1939 under the Four-Year Plan in 1938, becoming more burdensome as the country entered war and eventually faced defeat. In addition they note that at the start of the war, the government also took on the right to determine both maximum and minimum wages. The labour market ceased to be either free or competitive and was no longer, therefore, capitalist in this sense (for the above see ibid., pp. 254–6). In Italy, they argue, the workers were one of the 'pillars' of the corporate organization. There the Charter of Labour was introduced on 21 April 1927. Under it workers and managers lost their autonomy and despite the measures of social welfare, it became a means for disciplining workers. Thus the workers become 'a cog in the totalitarian centrally directed economy' (ibid., pp. 257–9). Friedrich and Brzezinski's image of the totalitarian economy clearly fits within Weber's substantive rationality.

As with industrial workers, Friedrich and Brzezinski also argue that totalitarian regimes try to extend control over peasants and farmers. They note the collectivization policies and disastrous consequences for agriculture and peasant lives in the Soviet Union. Arguing that agricultural production is, by its nature, 'unsuited to large-scale organization and control' and viewing it as the 'Achilles heel' of fascist regimes, they link Hitler's policy of 'living space' (*Lebensraum*) to the drive for additional land as 'a way out of the difficulties involved in making the available land more productive' (ibid., p. 274). This 'ideology', they argue, 'reinforces the totalitarians' propensity to foreign conquest' (ibid.).

Problems with Friedrich and Brzezinski
Friedrich and Brzezinski's syndrome of totalitarian dictatorship has been criticized a good deal. Criticisms have concentrated, in particular, on the cases: the differences between Russia and Germany; the issue of whether or not all or any of the Eastern European cases other than the USSR should be included; whether Russia under Khruschev should be under the same classification as Russia under Stalin; whether Italy under Mussolini was actually totalitarian; whether China, since 1949, and Cuba, since 1959, should at all times or at any time, particularly in the latter case, be classified as a totalitarian dictatorship.[6] Generalizations invariably play down specific differences and run the risk of squeezing evidence to fit expectations, and Friedrich and Brzezinski have, not surprisingly, been accused of doing both. As discussion above of their sixth point, control over the economy, has shown, however, they are aware of differences and their aim is to identify the similarities which lie below surface dissimilarities.

In a sense Friedrich and Brzezinski are caught between two stools. On the one hand they wish to develop a scientifically precise description of totalitarianism which can be applied to many cases, future as well as past and present. On the other hand their conception is actually of a syndrome. Given that the syndrome's characteristics are interdependent, scientific identification of each point, which requires independent variables, is, to say the least, difficult. For example, the role of the party is important to each of the six points. The possibility of objectively rejecting a single-party case from classification on the grounds of the absence of one of the characteristics is, therefore, problematic. This is especially the case when all political parties aiming at change (which all do, if to differing degrees) can thereby be classified as having an ideology. Yet to include every single-party system is clearly excessive, for it begs the need for a special category of totalitarian dictatorships when 'one-party state' will do.

The notion of a syndrome also conveys the idea not only that these characteristics occur together but that, as in a disease, they develop over time, first getting worse and eventually ending either in cure or death. This is clear in Friedrich and Brzezinski's (1965, pp. 367–78) discussion of the 'stages of development' of totalitarian dictatorship. The 'typical' sequence they suggest

to be ideology, movement, party and government, with totalitarian dictatorship then emerging 'sometime after the seizure of power by the leaders of the
movement that has developed in support of the ideology' (ibid., p. 369). The
dictatorship has 'emerged', they suggest, when 'unadorned violence' is used.
Expanding on how this development takes place, they suggest (ibid., pp. 373–
4) that first the ideology produces violence, then the movement develops into
the party, and the party then becomes increasingly bureaucratized. The 'totalitarian breakthrough' comes with party purges and the secret police needed
for total terror. At this stage the total planning of the economy imposes itself,
for by this point disorganization has developed.

There is something inherently unsatisfactory in the idea of stages of development which attempts only to describe how something grows rather than to
examine the conditions which led to its original existence, and nurtured it in
the early stages of growth before it emerged complete. The issue of the party
again serves to illustrate the problem. Ideology, movement, party and government is suggested as a typical development yet it is also clear that, on their
argument, the party is itself reshaped through purges and becomes, in effect,
a retrogressive bureaucracy substituted for the state bureaucracy – retrogressive because it is run on traditional (patrimonial) rather than rational–legal
lines and its main role is to keep the leader in power. In essence, then, the
movement becomes the replacement – retrogressive bureaucracy. Conceiv-
ably, the same outcome could occur without a party. For example in Ethiopia
a mass movement developed through the dergs (local military movements)
and in Iran mosque-based movements formed around the Komitehs. In both
cases, terror regimes developed and whereas in Iran the Islamic Revolutionary Party was instituted but eventually disbanded, in Ethiopia a variety of
single political parties failed to take power from the military. (See O'Kane,
1991, chs 10 and 11.)

It also follows from Friedrich and Brzezinski's position that whilst a totalitarian dictatorship may be identified by the concurrence of the six characteristics, there will be different stages of the 'disease'. This is bound to make
comparison problematic and though death might be readily identified (as in
Hitler's and Mussolini's defeat in war), miracles aside, cure will be rather
more difficult to judge as recovery too takes time and occurs in stages. The
clearest example of this problem tor Friedrich and Brzezinski can be found in
their assessment of China. Following a discussion of brainwashing, they
conclude, 'In both Stalinist Russia and Hitler Germany, the totalitarian terror
increased in scope and violence as the totalitarian system became more stable
and firm. But it would appear now that this was due to special factors, more
especially the character of the leader, rather than any inherent trait of totalitarian dictatorship' (ibid., p. 168). This is only one of a number of possible
conclusions that Friedrich and Brzezinski could have drawn. They could have

preserved the stress on physical terror and declared China, at some point, no longer a totalitarian system, or perhaps even admitting that they had been wrong to include it in the first place.[7]

Friedrich and Brzezinski's whole argument about the 'vacuum' produced by propaganda and the consequent move to violence, then terror, and finally 'total terror', is lost in their desire to keep China in. Given their emphasis on the 'slavery of labour camps' and the 'liquidation of people', their stress on purges in the 'developed totalitarian regime', indeed their whole conception would have been strengthened had they chosen to remove cases, rather than to adapt and loosen the concept.[8] This is especially clear in the light of their discussion of the stages of development where they stress again that developed totalitarian dictatorship has emerged when 'unadorned violence' is used and the 'totalitarian breakthrough' to 'total terror' is said to occur through the purges and the secret police (ibid., p. 369). Every emphasis that Friedrich and Brzezinski make pushes them towards the importance of terror in its most physical form and on a large scale.

Because they choose to adapt their conception in order to keep communist countries in, it is no wonder that Friedrich and Brzezinski have been accused of being unscientific in the sense of not being 'value-free'. They fail to discriminate between communist systems and overlook concurrent excesses outside of communist countries. They gloss over the contrast between Russia under Stalin compared with Russia under Khrushchev; ignore the differences between Czechoslovakia, Poland and Hungary compared with Romania and Albania; and include Cuba under Castro, while failing to consider the human rights abuses taking place within neighbouring Latin American dictatorships, such as Haiti under the Duvaliers and the Dominican Republic under Trujillo. These are not arguments to suggest that all or any of these are totalitarian systems, but considered together these cases do support an objection to Friedrich and Brzezinski's syndrome on the grounds that if a scientific definition is to be achieved it must include not only the characteristics of what it is, but also of what it is not. (See Sartori, 1984.) The use of propaganda to change the way people think is simply not the same as the use of torture leading to death, and it seems far-fetched to expect that the consequences of the process would produce the same kind of system. In any case, following the logic of 'the vacuum', propaganda cannot survive without eventually leading to terror.

Friedrich and Brzezinski's argument about this vacuum are, however, unconvincing apart from a consideration of the actual effects and intentions of government policies. Propaganda in combination with tangible benefits, like good harvests, full employment or improved wages, would be less likely to produce distrust than propaganda without such tangible rewards. This may be why central control over both communications and the economy go together.

It may be that terror develops not simply to remove those not duped by propaganda but also those who are not benefiting tangibly under the system. On the other hand it might be the case that the system is specifically designed to benefit some at the expense of others, and propaganda may be employed to make this more palatable to the beneficiaries. This, indeed, seems to have been the case both in Stalin's Russia and Nazi Germany: those who did not own private property in the former case, those who were not Jews in the latter. On this line of argument propaganda would not turn into terror: they would be part-and-parcel of the same package, but designed for different groups within each society.

Friedrich and Brzezinski view violence as being used first against open oppositions, and gradually expanding into terror as 'overlapping groups' are drawn in, but if propaganda and terror form part of the same package then the persecution of innocents is entailed in the policy in the first place. It is particularly hard simply to view Jews as 'opposition' in Germany when Nazi policies were so evidently directed at them. The definition of terror as 'a process in which activities of deliberate violence are undertaken by the power wielders to strike a general and undefined fear into anyone who dissents' (ibid., p. 170) clearly cannot fit the Nazi case. Jews did not 'dissent' by being Jewish. The same is true where present labour and possessions are ignored in favour of noticing only the social position of a parent before the revolution, as under collectivization in the USSR. It is clear that in spite of stressing the importance of violence in fascist ideology Friedrich and Brzezinski fail to draw the lessons derived by Gregor (1982) from the work of the fascist philosopher, Panunzio, as elaborated in Chapter 1. Coercion directed at the guilty is justified in fascist ideology; terror, defined as violence directed deliberately against innocents, is not. Although Friedrich and Brzezinski allow that 'unpredictability' (ibid., p. 163) plays a part in terror, their essential emphasis on real enemies, as actual dissenters, stands in direct contradiction to Arendt's view of totalitarianism.

Arendt and totalitarianism
Arendt's conception of totalitarianism is highly restrictive. It is reserved for Stalin's USSR and Hitler's Germany. Arendt's aim is exactly to explain the origins of totalitarianism which Friedrich and Brzezinski avoid. Not aiming to develop a scientific tool for comparison, her analysis naturally lacks the precision which is Friedrich and Brzezinski's attraction. At the same time, however, and in spite of the restriction to Germany and Russia, and skewed at that greatly towards Germany, it is Arendt's work which offers the superior comparative method. This is so because rather than gathering like cases together for similarities in support, as do Friedrich and Brzezinski, Arendt also examines cases which are dissimilar.[9] For example, Arendt compares

both France and Britain with Germany in order to discover why, in spite of some similarities in respect of bureaucracy, imperialism, party system and anti-Semitism (in France), the outcomes were different. Rather than claiming, as do Friedrich and Brzezinski, that Russia and Germany and others were essentially similar, Arendt compares Russia and Germany for similarity of outcome but recognizes differences in development. For example, in Russia Arendt claims that Stalin created a mass society whereas in Germany one already existed and, whilst Russia experienced civil war, in Germany civil war conditions were 'artificially created'. Italy under Mussolini too is brought in for comparison of how the nature of the regime differed from those in Germany and Russia. From Arendt's work, therefore, it is possible to know not only what, in her view, totalitarianism is, but also what it is not. It is also possible to know not only what she believed led to the development of totalitarianism, but also what hindered or prevented its development.

Arendt's view of totalitarianism contrasts with and challenges Friedrich and Brzezinski's in six ways:

1. She rejects that it is a dictatorship, even of an entirely new and modern kind.
2. She has a quite different view of the nature and role of terror in the final stage of totalitarianism: its primary purpose is not aimed at dissidents in order to create fear.
3. Propaganda is not part of the developed totalitarian system.
4. Arendt rejects the idea of totalitarianism as an ideological movement which unites the party and ties it to the leader.
5. Arendt rejects any functional relationship between totalitarianism and the economy.
6. Arendt contradicts the whole image of a bureaucratic society, even one, as portrayed by Friedrich and Brzezinski, where the state bureaucracy, distorted by party bureaucracy, has regressed to patrimonialism, and even one, as drawn by Bauman, suffering goal-displacement.

The totalitarian regime
Although Arendt does not lay out her image of a totalitarian regime in a systematic way there are, nevertheless, four clear strands to her conceptualization. As with Friedrich and Brzezinski's syndrome, these four strands are interrelated to form a whole. The four aspects must go together for what they, crucially, produce through total terror is a secret society under total domination. These four parts are the following: terror aimed as a deliberate policy towards the innocent; the real power of the secret police and the ostensible power of the state; the leader principle operating in a mass society; and concentration camps. Unlike Friedrich and Brzezinski's view of six characteristics

which have existed elsewhere coming together, enabled by twentieth century technology, Arendt's four characteristics are not only novel in combination, they are each newly arrived at. As twentieth century phenomena their origins are the product of modernity in the sense that they can be traced back to events following the French Revolution (and not before), but for Arendt history reveals modernity as political and social and not merely rational and scientific.

Terror aimed as a deliberate policy towards the innocent   For Arendt, terror is absolutely central to her concept of totalitarianism and she makes this clear in the very opening pages of her book when rejecting totalitarianism as either dictatorship or autocracy:

> A fundamental difference between modern dictatorships and all other tyrannies of the past is that terror is no longer used as a means to exterminate and frighten opponents, but as an instrument to rule masses of people who are perfectly obedient. Terror as we know it today strikes without any preliminary provocation, its victims are innocent even from the point of view of the persecutor. This was the case in Nazi Germany when full terror was directed against Jews, i.e. against people with certain common characteristics which were independent of their specific behaviour. (Arendt, 1958, p. 6)

Arendt expands on the relevance of this in Russia too, where 'arbitrariness of terror is not even limited by racial differentiation, while the old class categories have long since been discarded, so that anybody in Russia may suddenly become a victim of the police terror' (ibid.). Arendt's theory is not static and she, like Friedrich and Brzezinski, is aware that such terror does not occur overnight; it develops, and also has origins. 'Terror, however', Arendt argues, 'is only in the last instance of its development a mere form of government' (ibid.).

In contrast to Friedrich and Brzezinski's view, where terror directed at 'real enemies' and then at innocents by accident as 'overlapping groups' become affected, Arendt's view of terror is that of a deliberate policy of arbitrariness. The purpose of this policy is not to generate fear in order to stop dissents, as Friedrich and Brzezinski hold. Arendt recognizes, of course, that fear is bound to develop, 'the ultimate consequence of rule by terror – namely, that nobody, not even the executors, can ever be free of fear' (Arendt, 1958, p. 6). The purpose of this policy of terror against innocents is to permeate society with 'mutual suspicion' (ibid., p. 430) so as to isolate people, destroy spontaneity and make them perfectly obedient, perfect for a government of total domination:

> The aim of an arbitrary system is to destroy the civil rights of the whole population, who ultimately become just as outlawed in their own country as the stateless

and homeless. The destruction of a man's rights, the killing of the juridical person in him is a prerequisite for dominating him entirely. And this applies...to every inhabitant of a totalitarian state. Free consent is as much an obstacle to total domination as free opposition. The arbitrary arrest which chooses among innocent people destroys the validity of free consent, just as torture – as distinguished from death – destroys the possibility of opposition. (Arendt, 1958, p. 451)

The real power of the secret police and the ostensible power of the state   Such terror cannot be operated without a secret police system and, Arendt argues, a system of concentration camps. This secret police system, however, again contrasts with Friedrich and Brzezinski's portrayal. The secret police system is not run by party or state bureaucracy as part of a wider totalitarian state involved in planning and economic control of communications and weaponry. Totalitarian domination does not derive from the party system (Arendt, 1958, p. 419). For Arendt the state has 'ostensible' but not 'real' power. It is a façade and behind it lies the real 'power nucleus', the secret police (ibid., p. 420).

The 'so-called totalitarian state' (ibid., p. 392) is nothing like Weber's modern legal–rational system. The system is characterized by lawlessness. Arendt observes how the 1936 Constitution in Russia was totally ignored, and how the Nuremburg Laws in Germany and the Weimar Constitution, which remained intact throughout Nazi rule, were completely disregarded (ibid., pp. 394–5). Furthermore, the state system itself is characterized by its 'shapelessness' (ibid., p. 398) through its 'multiplication of offices' and 'duplication of functions' (ibid., p. 399). As illustration of this 'shapelessness' at all levels of administration in the Third Reich, Arendt offers the two National Socialist student organizations, the two Nazi women's organizations, the two organizations for university professors, lawyers, doctors and so on and also the way in which the SA, then the SS and then the Gestapo duplicated functions over time. In Russia, Arendt also draws attention to the multiplication of offices and overlapping functions between the soviets, state and party. (For the above see ibid., pp. 396–7.) Arendt also points out that 'fake departments' were set up in Nazi Germany to look like a regular state administration (ibid., p. 371).

The totalitarian 'movement', a term Arendt prefers to 'party', as a party would have structure whereas a movement has only direction (ibid., p. 398), she characterizes as having a 'peculiar onion-like structure' where 'every layer was the front of the next more militant formation' (ibid., p. 413). Each layer, as if separated by a skin, was in place to preserve secrecy. Regular purges are viewed by Arendt as a deliberate means to turn over the machinery of administration, to perpetuate movement rather than stability, to prevent loyalty developing and to turn into 'accomplices' those who take the jobs thereby vacated (ibid.).

The leader principle in a mass society   In addition to this lawlessness, duplication of functions and multiplication of offices, orders are also 'deliberately vague'. This is part of the 'leader principle' (Arendt, 1958, p. 404). The leader principle is not 'authority', it is not a form of dictatorship, and in conflict with Friedrich and Brzezinski's position there is neither 'ruling clique' nor hierarchical party domination (ibid., pp. 404–7). The leader principle is based not on a total ideology, as in Friedrich and Brzezinski's conception of totalitarian dictatorship, but on 'systematic lying' (ibid., p. 413). Existing ideologies, whether anti-Semitism, pan-Germanism, or communism, are used by the leader. The leader in his 'dual capacity as chief of state and leader of the movement...combines militant ruthlessness and confidence-inspiring normality' (ibid., p. 413). In a society where everything else is chaotic and arbitrary, and relationships disintegrate into 'mutual suspicion', the leader is the one (safe) common factor to which people can attach themselves.

The key to the attraction of the leader is his prophetic infallibility: 'The chief qualification of a mass leader has become unending infallibility; he can never admit an error' (Arendt, 1958, pp. 348–9). What the leader engages in is 'prophetic scientificality', infallible prediction (ibid., p. 350). So Stalin talked of 'the dying classes' which, prophetically, died and Hitler talked of 'the incurably sick and those not fit to live' who also, just as he prophesied, lost their lives (ibid., pp. 349–50). 'As soon as the execution of the victims had been carried out, the "prophecy" becomes a retrospective alibi: nothing happened but what had already been predicted' (ibid., p. 349). While the leader principle is important to the mass movement it is only under totalitarian rule, in a mass society of isolated individuals, that this systematic lying can be carried through to full effect.

Arendt's view of the leader clearly contrasts sharply with Friedrich and Brzezinski's dictator and this follows through to their differing positions on propaganda. On Friedrich and Brzezinski's argument a 'vacuum' develops around the dictator through the use of propaganda which leads to terror. On the surface, the argument seems similar: Friedrich and Brzezinski's discussion of 'mutual distrust', Arendt's of 'mutual suspicion'. Arendt's argument, however, develops in a quite different way. Rather than social disintegration through mutual distrust being the 'cancer' of totalitarianism, it is the very life-blood of the leadership principle, no accidental consequence of propaganda, but the goal of arbitrary terror.

The aim of arbitrary terror, terror deliberately aimed at the innocent, is to stop people thinking, to eliminate spontaneity, to destroy judgement, to 'murder the moral person', so that in the end people become just like Pavlov's dog (ibid., p. 438). Then the 'leader principle' will have achieved its utmost aim – total domination: the leader will have everyone under his spell, behaving exactly in accordance with his every command.

The contrast between the 'mass person' that Friedrich and Brzezinski have in mind and the one portrayed by Arendt is again striking. For Friedrich and Brzezinski, the masses are indoctrinated by the total ideology whose aim is expressly to reshape everyone into a completely new type of thinking and behaviour suited to the redesigned Utopian society. For Arendt, the perfect mass person is apathetic, emptied of thought, capable only of reflex actions, and demoralized. The contrast with Bauman is also striking in this latter respect. For Bauman it is the scientific approach to problem-solving and the separation of tasks which, in creating distance between victim and perpetrator, destroys moral responsibility. For Arendt, moral responsibility is destroyed through a deliberate policy of terror against the innocent in a state which is irrational in the Weberian sense. It is not simply that people are able to ignore the consequences of their actions, or disclaim responsibility, their courage and endurance are destroyed.

Concentration camps   A society in which people dare not mention disappearances, even of close members of their family, even to close members of their family, is a 'secret society' (Arendt, 1958, p. 435) The secret about which no one dares speak involves the operations of the secret police and the concentration camps. Concentration camps, Arendt argues, are 'the true central institution of totalitarian organizational power' (ibid., p. 438). They are 'the most essential to the presentation of the regime's power than any of its other institutions'. Within concentration camps, at one and the same time the microcosm of the perfect totalitarian society and also the 'central institution of totalitarian organizational power', spontaneity is totally eliminated. With spontaneity completely destroyed the leader principle, which requires total domination, is fully achieved. In the concentration camp the perfect mass person is created, for there total terror destroys 'the space between people' (ibid., p. 466).

Again the contrast between Bauman and Arendt is equally clear. It was not individual moral responsibility destroyed by 'distance' which was the true characteristic of Nazi Germany, but existence as an individual destroyed in a mass.

Comparison with Bauman

Arendt's conception of the totalitarian regime offers a broad challenge to Bauman's view of the Holocaust. For Bauman, goal-displacement occurred in a rational bureaucratic system and took the form of extermination camps. The rational–scientific method of problem-solving and the separation of tasks and rule-following, the epitome of rational bureaucracy characteristic of modern society, were the means through which individual moral responsibility was destroyed. This outcome was essential for the Holocaust to take place. Arendt's contention, however, is consistent neither with Bauman's nor Weber's, but with Beetham's arguments about bureaucracy. Deliberate policies shrouded in secrecy and requiring secrecy in their operation are crucial in stimulating bureaucracy's growth and destroying its capacity to serve democracy. Furthermore, rational bureaucracy and goal-displacement were not, in Arendt's view, the means for destroying moral responsibility; neither was the concept of 'distance', created by modern rational ways and means of problem-solving. It is not Milgram's experiments that Arendt has in mind but Pavlov's. In totalitarian regimes people do not deny responsibility as a consequence of being just one link in a long chain of actions, they are stopped from thinking, and spontaneity is turned into reflex actions.

Arendt also makes a very clear distinction between bureaucrats and the secret police, which Bauman fails to consider. For Arendt, it is the secret police who have real power, and not the state. Her idea of 'planned shapelessness' is to ensure that the real power of the secret police operates behind the façade of the state and not through it. 'Through it' would imply an ordinary dictatorship. Crucially, too, Arendt's construct is built upon the importance of absolute terror, terror against the innocent, not Bauman's modern state monopoly of force where governments base their power on the threat of force against lawbreakers.

The development of totalitarianism

For Arendt, as we have seen, 'terror is only in the last instance of its development a mere form of government' (Arendt, 1958, p. 6). This fits, as explained in Chapter 1, with her contrast between power as government and terror as government. The establishment of a totalitarian regime involves a process. Here Arendt argues for the importance of propaganda linked to ideology. These are points of compatibility with Friedrich and Brzezinski's theory.

'In order to establish a totalitarian regime', Arendt (1958, p. 6) argues, 'terror must be presented as an instrument for carrying out a specific ideology; and that ideology must have won the adherents of many and even a majority before terror can be stabilized'. Crucial to Arendt's position, and in direct contrast with Friedrich and Brzezinski's view, neither the Soviet Union under communism nor Germany under Hitler were totalitarian regimes, in this sense of terror as government, until part-way through their duration. Germany, she argues, established itself as a totalitarian regime only in 1938, more than five years after Hitler came to power. In the USSR this last stage of totalitarian domination was not entered until 1930, excluding, therefore, not only Lenin's rule but the entire period of the New Economic Policy (NEP). Stalin's Russia after 1930 and Hitler's Germany after 1939, Arendt holds to be the 'only two authentic forms of totalitarian domination' (ibid., p. 419). This leaves open the possibility, however, that other regimes may have shared important similarities with this earlier stage.

Propaganda and organization in the development of totalitarianism
Before the totalitarian regime can be established, Arendt argues that it is first
necessary to gain mass support. This is done through organized propaganda
which exploits existing ideologies: 'an ideology which has to persuade and
mobilize people cannot choose its victims arbitrarily' (Arendt, 1958, pp. 6–
7). In this process, 'organization and propaganda (rather than terror and
propaganda) are two sides of the same coin' (ibid., p. 364). Propaganda,
though preserved for outside consumption in the totalitarian regime, ceases to
be a constituent part of the 'last instance' of totalitarianism: 'Where the rule
of terror is brought to perfection, as in concentration camps, propaganda
disappears entirely' (ibid., p. 344). She adds for emphasis, 'it was even expressly prohibited in Nazi Germany'. The role of propaganda before this
point is to build up the image of the infallibility of the leader and to win over
the support of the masses, in order to develop the totalitarian movement
(ibid., pp. 348–50).

Winning the support of the masses is achieved through the exploitation of
existing ideologies, ideas and prejudices: 'Totalitarian propaganda perfects
the techniques of mass propaganda, but it neither invents them nor originates
their themes' (Arendt, 1958, p. 351). These themes, she argues, 'were prepared for them by fifty years of the rise of imperialism and disintegration of
the nation-state when the mob entered the scene of European politics' (ibid.,
p. 351). Anti-Semitism, which was not original to the Nazis (it had been
around in Europe since the Middle Ages) was exploited in propaganda to get
the masses to believe lies. Both the Protocols of Zion and the Dreyfus Affair
in France were lies. Similarly, she argues that communism was exploited by
Stalin: 'Totalitarian movements *use* socialism and racism by emptying them
of their utilitarian content, the interests of a class or nation' (ibid., p. 348).

Propaganda alone, even that based on existing themes, however, is not
enough; organization is equally crucial. Organization is the means through
which the state institutions are undermined, to be turned into a façade, while
the secret police become the real centre of power (ibid., p. 368). She explains
how, in Germany, the 'fluctuating hierarchy' was developed: first the SA, the
Stormtroopers, founded in 1922, and then the SS, founded in 1926 out of the
élite of the SA. This was then continued with the Shock Troops being formed
out of the SS, and then the Death's Head Units (the concentration camp guard
units) which then merged, later, to form the Waffen SS and finally the Security Service and Office for Questions of Race and Resettlement (ibid.). In
Russia, the successive purges in the party had the same effect, undermining
existing organizations and promoting the 'real power' of the secret police
(ibid., p. 371).

Through this process of propaganda and organization – the 'planned shapelessness' of the state – the development of the terror organization for isolating

individuals and the crystallization of the leader principle took place. Thus conditions were prepared for the final stage of totalitarian domination.

Problems with Arendt
There are, nevertheless, practical problems with Arendt's concept of the totalitarian regime. The first is essentially similar to that found with Bauman's 'bureaucratic mentality', namely the difficulty of obtaining the necessary evidence. It is essential to Arendt that terror towards the innocent be a policy to create mutual suspicion throughout society, and that the multiplication of offices and duplication of functions be deliberately done in order to turn the state into a mere façade behind which the real power of the secret police operates. It may be possible to discover evidence of widespread suspicion, and records and accounts may help to reveal the scale of the non-accidental deaths of innocents. In a secret society where truth is suppressed and in any case so frequently taken to the grave, evidence such as is available cannot be taken as either fully reliable or completely valid. The evidence that large numbers of innocents did die could not, of itself, prove the intention of the policy to have been the creation of mutual suspicion. For example Nazis may straightforwardly have wanted Jews dead. Similarly, the fact that organizational multiplication and duplication occurred within the state could not, without other evidence, prove deliberate manipulation. Both the deaths of innocents, even on a large scale, and the lack of coordination within the state could be compatible with chaos produced by policies which do not work – policies, that is, which have unintended outcomes.

The evidence ideally available would be statements of intent by the leader and secret police – evidence of attitudes and 'mentality', that is, separate from behaviour. Not only is such evidence inherently difficult to obtain in a secret society, with its onion-like structure of organizations, but the most supportive evidence would ironically be the absence of evidence. The problem is similar to Bachrach and Baratz's (1970) 'other face of power', where groups operating behind the scenes have the greatest power. Exactly when it is the most difficult to observe and where 'the mobilization of bias' is strongest, real power may actually be impossible to measure. In a society subjected to propaganda the possibility of people expressing their true attitudes (about for example who is innocent, or the point of the task they perform) is clearly curtailed and where terror is rife, even if true attitudes remain, it is obviously to be expected that behaviour (including statements of opinion) will accord with the authority's position and not people's own beliefs.

In short, the problem is that if Arendt is right, then the evidence she requires about intention of policy and deliberateness of action will be inherently impossible to obtain. Relevant partial and circumstantial evidence may be brought to bear, but such evidence will be open to alternative interpretation.

There is a further problem with Arendt's definition of the totalitarian regime. The last stage of totalitarianism, terror as government, is not separate from the explanation which she offers for its development. For Arendt, the purpose of terror as government is to destroy spontaneity in order to achieve total domination, but the leader principle and mass society are offered both as explanation for the totalitarian regime and feature as part of its defining characteristics. There are two possible ways around this. One is to remove these as characteristics of the totalitarian regime, the other is to offer an explanation for the phenomenon which is more distant from the thing being explained. An alternative explanation for terror as government will be developed in the next chapter, but Arendt's distinction between totalitarian dictatorship and totalitarian regime remains crucial.

Totalitarian dictatorship
Arendt's distinction between the totalitarian regime – 'terror as a form of government' – and the 'pre-power stage' is a critical one (ibid., p. 364). This earlier stage, unlike the last, shares features in common with dictatorship. The so-called 'leader principle' is in itself non-totalitarian: it has borrowed certain features from authoritarianism and military dictatorship. This development stage, where propaganda is important and the real power of the secret police is being constructed, but the state institutions are not yet undermined, has parallels beyond Germany and Russia. Arendt stresses how fascist party dictatorships, such as those in Italy, Spain and Portugal, ruled 'through the state machine without drastically changing the power structure of the country, being content to fill all government positions with party members' (Arendt, 1958, p. 257). Spain and Portugal remained 'ordinary nationalist dictatorships' and Mussolini's Italy only became a totalitarian dictatorship from 1938, when Mussolini developed a fascist movement (ibid., pp. 257–8). Continuing to rule Italy through the state, however, Mussolini never took the country to the last stage. Italy never became a totalitarian regime and remained a totalitarian dictatorship. Indeed, 'Mussolini who was so fond of the term "totalitarian state" did not attempt to establish a fully-fledged totalitarian regime and contented himself with dictatorship and one-party rule' (ibid., p. 308).

Italy
Emphasizing this distinction between dictatorship through the state and the totalitarian regime which operates behind a state façade, Arendt (1958, pp. 258–9) develops her argument about Italy as follows:

> The Fascist movement, a 'party above parties', because it claimed to represent the interest of the nation as a whole, seized the state machine, identified itself with the

highest national authority, and tried to make the whole people 'part of the state'. It did not, however, think itself 'above the state', and its leaders did not conceive of themselves as 'above the nation'. As regards the Fascists, their movement had come to an end with the seizure of power, at least with respect to domestic policies; the movement could now maintain its motion only in matters of foreign policy, in the sense of imperialist expansion and typically imperialist adventures.

In support of her view Arendt (1958, p. 258, fn. 95) offers quotations from *The Fascist Era* (published by the Fascist Confederation of Industrialists, Rome, 1939, ch. iii): 'No group outside the State, no group against the State, all groups within the State…which…is the nation itself rendered articulate.'

Arendt (1958, pp. 308–9, fn. 11) also offers 'proof of the nontotalitarian nature of the Fascist dictatorship', the absence of 'terror as government' in 'the surprisingly small number and the comparatively mild sentences meted out to political offenders'. Between 1926 and 1932 ('particularly active years') the special tribunals pronounced only seven death sentences and though many were imprisoned (albeit only 257 to sentences of ten or more years) or exiled, 12 000 political offenders were arrested and found innocent. This is in complete contrast with the totalitarian regime where terror is deliberately directed at the innocent (ibid.).

This view is supported by Gregor (1982). In Italy, though violence was part of the fascist philosophy, the difference between guilt and innocence turned on actual voluntary conduct. It was possible to avoid punishment by not performing proscribed acts. People could be intimidated through violence because they knew what they had to do in order to avoid it.

In Italy, Gregor argues, the function of the Special Tribunal for the Defence of the State, instituted on 25 November 1926, was to intimidate, not to terrorize. From 1926 to 1943, when the fascist regime collapsed, only 47 death sentences were passed. Of the 5619 people prosecuted, 998 were found innocent, and although after the war sentencing was sometimes 'capricious and onerous…For all that the Tribunal, which clearly violated the procedural rules of justice prevalent in liberal democracies, was qualitatively different from institutionalised terrorism' (Gregor, 1982, p. 161). Gregor contrasts the repressive Tribunal with the system of terror in the Soviet Union where 'severe punishment', including 'corrective labour', which to all intents and purposes meant death in a labour camp, could be meted out by the administrative organs of the state, in effect, the People's Commissariat for Internal Affairs, the NKVD. The Special Boards gave defendants no right to defence; nor was defence possible for cases brought in absentia and against groups of people at a time without specific charges (ibid., p. 161). Drawing on Conquest's (1971, p. 638) evidence, Gregor demonstrates the stark differences between the Italian and Soviet cases:

> By 1937 about ten per cent of all those charged by the extra juridical administra-
> tive bodies were receiving death sentences...In Gorki alone it is estimated that
> from 50 to 70 persons were executed each day without the semblance of a trial
> and for the most obscure reasons. By 1938, five per cent of the total population
> was involved, and arrests and punishments were applied indiscriminately. By
> 1938 there was a call for a systematic attack on the 'silent', those who had not
> taken any actions during the events of the preceding years. (Gregor, 1982, p. 161)

More recent evidence may reduce these estimates (this evidence will be
considered in Chapters 5 and 6) but the point of Gregor's argument remains
unaffected: summary justice is an inherent part of a system of terror, and the
killing of innocents a deliberate part of terror. The point is not to create fear
in order to intimidate and prevent other people behaving in proscribed ways,
but to destroy spontaneity. As noted in Chapter 1, Gregor (1982, p. 162)
argues that racial discrimination 'harbours some of the principal species traits
of terrorism' because once racial traits are used to identify victims there is no
behaviour which the accused can adopt to avoid sanction. Jewish parentage
was not something that intimidation could remove. There was no 'defence',
no means to avoid victimization. To the extent that Italy introduced anti-
Semitic legislation in 1938, potential for terrorism entered the fascist system,
though 'mitigations' were allowed and many Jews were 'Aryanized'. Gregor
points out that although 7495 Jews were deported, of whom 6885 were killed
by the Germans, 'none were executed by the Fascists, and the question of
Fascist complicity in the deportations has not itself been resolved' (ibid.,
p. 163). Ironically, Mussolini's move to anti-Semitism served as proof that
his was not a totalitarian regime but a totalitarian dictatorship, organized
through rather than from behind a state façade.

In early 1942 mass deportations of Jews from German-occupied European
countries began. Though the true nature of the 'solution' could not be broached
directly with the Germans, the Italians as their allies were in a position to
develop a pretty good idea of what was going on (Steinberg, 1991, p. 50). As
Jews fled from Germany into the Italian territories of Southern Europe, the
issue was raised of setting up an Italian-run concentration camp offering a
'guarantee of their safety and a minimum of humane treatment' in Croatia
(ibid., p. 53). General Roatta, the commanding general of Slovenia and Dal-
matia, refused, arguing as follows:

> We have guaranteed them a certain protection and have resisted Croatia's pressure
> to deport them to a concentration camp. It is my opinion that if Jews who have
> fled to annexed Dalmatia were to be consigned to the Croatians they would be
> interned at Jasenovac, with the well-known consequences. (Roatta's reply sent on
> 16 June 1942, quoted in Steinberg, 1991, p. 53)

Jasenovac was a death camp. In August the Italian government was asked 'to instruct its military authorities in Croatia to adhere to the measures agreed between the Croatian and German governments and to arrange for a "transfer in mass" of the Jews from the Italian zone as well' (Steinberg, 1991, p. 56, quoting from the telegram signed by Ribbentrop). On 21 August Mussolini sanctioned the memorandum for compliance – 'nulla osta...M' – Mussolini had 'no objection' to the 'dispersion and elimination' (the words employed in the memo) of Jews from the Italian zone (ibid., p. 57). By the end of August the Jews in the German zone of Croatia had been deported. 'What happened next stands out in the entire history of the Second World War...Italian soldiers, diplomats and civil servants simply refused to obey those orders' (Steinberg, 1991, p. 58).

This 'resistance' involved the very highest generals and members of the state, beginning with Count Luca Pietromarchi, the senior diplomat responsible for Italian-occupied territories, and Colonel Cigliani, the colonel in charge of the Office of Civilian Affairs at the Headquarters of the VIth Army Corps:

> Our entire activity has been designed to let the Jews live in a human way...[It was impossible to surrender the Jews] because we would not be true to the obligations we assumed...they have given us no trouble of any sort. (Colonel Cigliani, documents, 27 August 1942, quoted in Steinberg, 1991, p. 59)

Their tactic was 'one deeply rooted in the Italian bureaucracy to do nothing in the most officious possible way' (Steinberg, 1991, p. 59). Such delaying tactics could not have worked had the dictatorship operated other than through the state. The bureaucracy had never been replaced by the party (ibid., p. 139). There was no system of terror, no troops separate from the army, no organization operating in secrecy, no equivalent to the SS. The decision to ignore the Duce's order was helped by his poor health, but again this confirmed his dictatorship. Mussolini was not spun about by infallibility, his humiliations in battle were known. As Steinberg remarks, purposefully contrasting the case with Arendt's portrayal of the Nazi case, 'at the end, the Duce regained his grip on the limits of the possible' (ibid., p. 192); people like Bastiani dared to tell him the truth. In November Mussolini revoked his 'nulla osta'. On 27 November 1942 General Roatta visited the largest of the Jewish concentration camps at Kraljevice (Porto Re) and formally told them that they were under Italian protection (see ibid., p. 84). As the true facts of the Holocaust became clear between November 1942 and July 1943, the Italians also defended Jews in Greece and France as the fortunes of war turned (see ibid., p. 33). In July Allied troops landed in Sicily and the Supreme Command of the Italian army told Mussolini to surrender (ibid., p. 141). In the early morning of 25 July 1943, the old order was restored by a vote of the Fascist General Council.

The following day, Mussolini was arrested. Divisions of the German army entered Italy. Visas were quickly issued to return Italian Jews to Italy with full speed; the Italians continued to frustrate the final solution in their occupied zones and to refuse to comply with German orders to hand over Jews for forced labour (Steinberg, 1991, p. 158). On 8 September 1943 the Italian government surrendered to the Allies. In the same month the SS began to arrive to implement the final solution themselves (ibid., p. 163).

In the Italian Social Republic of 1944–45, controlled by the Germans with the freed Mussolini set by them as its head, totalitarianism was mirrored to a degree – in particular the police were given extraordinary powers. Sarti (1990, p. 27) argues, however, that without the war and 'German prodding' fascism would have gradually been replaced by 'Mussolinismo': 'The record shows that Mussolinismo meant, above all, a strong bureaucratic state based on law rather than a police state driven by a revolutionary vision of a future society' (ibid., pp. 27–8).

Totalitarian dictatorship and totalitarian regime
Mussolini's Italy never developed into the 'last instance' of totalitarianism, the totalitarian regime. Dictatorship was conducted through the state; a system of terror was not operated behind a state façade. Arendt allows that fascist Italy was a totalitarian dictatorship, as opposed to an ordinary dictatorship, because it developed a mass movement.

The restriction of totalitarianism as total domination to Nazi Germany from 1938 and Stalin's Russia from 1930 will be shown to be supported by the evidence.[10] To restrict the concept of totalitarian dictatorship to Russia 1917–29, Germany 1933–38 and Mussolini's Italy from 1938, however, is too narrow. There is value in differentiating the ordinary dictatorship, which operates through the army and has as its principal aim to keep the dictator in power, from those dictatorships which, through state structures and usually the single party, and with the aid of propaganda, mobilize mass movements in support and aim for substantive changes. Friedrich and Brzezinski's stress on bureaucracy, party, propaganda, repressive terror, the vacuum, the leader, planning and centralized coercion are all consistent with a view of totalitarian dictatorship operated through the state. The emphasis on modern science and technology, so important for propaganda, central planning and centralized coercive control, is also consistent with the modernness of totalitarian dictatorships in comparison with 'ordinary' dictatorships and autocracies.

In essence, however, just as Arendt argues, what separates dictatorships, including totalitarian dictatorships, from totalitarian regimes is the system of terror. Unlike in totalitarian dictatorships, where terror is used against the guilty to intimidate the rest of the population, in totalitarian regimes terror is deliberately directed at innocents. In Gregor's terms, this is the difference between repressive regimes and terror regimes. The years 1930 and 1938 are chosen by Arendt as the crucial points of differentiation between totalitarian dictatorship and terror as government in the USSR and Germany respectively because these years mark the dates when the concentration camps were overwhelmed with 'completely "innocent" inmates' (ibid., p. 450). In spite of concern with totalitarian dictatorships, however, Friedrich and Brzezinski's focus on economic factors proves highly pertinent to a new understanding of the causes of totalitarian regimes.

Notes

1. There have been many publications on totalitarianism since Arendt's and Friedrich and Brzezinski's classic works. Essentially these later works divide between those in sympathy with Friedrich and Brzezinski's view of totalitarianism as an extreme form of government through state structures and organizations, and those in sympathy with Arendt who are not. As examples of the former see Schapiro (1972) and Curtis (1979) who view totalitarianism as dictatorship of a new kind and Aron (1968) and Unger (1974) who stress the role of the single party. See also Giddens (1985) who considers 'Friedrich and Brzezinski's concept of totalitarianism to be accurate and useful' (ibid., p. 301) but like Schapiro and Curtis stresses leadership rather than the party. In sympathy with Arendt is Buchheim (1968), who argues that the state 'withers' (p. 92) under the totalitarian movement and the state is 'stripped' of its monopoly of the use of force (p. 90). There are important differences within these positions, but in comparison with the fundamental disagreement between the two views of the state the differences within each camp amount only to differences of emphasis. Only Talmon (1952) takes the view that 'totalitarian democracy' is not a twentieth century phenomenon, tracing its origins back to the French Revolution. Connecting 'totalitarian democracy' in the Soviet Union with that under the Jacobin dictatorship, Talmon fits within the state dictatorship view of totalitarianism. I have elsewhere taken issue with Talmon's account of the Jacobin dictatorship. (See O'Kane, 1991, p. 71.) As will become clear, it is also the view here that both Arendt's and Friedrich and Brzezinksi's works are far richer sources than has generally been acknowledged and that the fundamental differences between these works have wrongly been ignored in the search for synthesis.
2. The first edition of Hannah Arendt, *The Origins of Totalitarianism* was published in 1951, the first edition of C.J. Friedrich and Z.K. Brzezinski, *Totalitarian Dictatorship and Autocracy* was published in 1956 and the general conception of totalitarianism first appeared in C.J. Friedrich (ed.), *Totalitarianism* in 1953. In the second edition (1958) of her book, Arendt does not refer to Friedrich and Brzezinksi's work, though Friedrich and Brzezinski (1958) use Arendt's work in support in a few places, taking direct issue with her only in respect of her claims that Pan-Slavism was more important to developments in the USSR than was communism (p. 364).
3. See, for example, Gregor (1974, p. 222) who criticizes Friedrich and Brzezinski for not saying whether 'all or some of the traits' are necessary for classification as totalitarianism.
4. The other 'islands of separateness' which Friedrich and Brzezinski (1965) consider are the family, churches, writers and artists. Their imagery is that of islands within a 'totalitarian sea' (ibid., p. 279).
5. For 1941, Friedrich and Brzezinski (1965, p. 253) offer the following figures on slave labour production in the Soviet Union: 5 325 000 metric tons of coal; 11.9 per cent of timber and firewood; 14.49 per cent of furniture; 22.58 per cent of railroad ties; 40.5 per cent of chrome ore. They estimate the number of people working in the labour camps as 8–14 million plus those working in the satellite camps.
6. For a list of eight criticisms of totalitarianism compiled from the literature on the Soviet Union see Sartori (1993). For criticism directed more specifically at Friedrich and Brzezinski

see Ebenstein (1958), Groth (1964), Burrowes (1964) and Gregor (1974, pp. 214–37). Alternative conceptions of totalitarianism also constitute criticisms. Schapiro (1972) stresses the leader as more important than the party and Curtis (1979) argues that the factors that were common for Germany, Italy and Russia were the use of terror, the role of the dictator and the mobilization of the population. The common criticism that Friedrich and Brzezinski fail to offer a theory, as explanation of totalitarianism, is defended by Gregor (1974) on the grounds that they do not claim to offer a theory. In general terms, Sartori (1993) reinforces Curtis's defence in making clear what a model is and that totalitarianism is a 'typological construct'. Sartori, however, continues to view totalitarianism as a species of dictatorship. As will become clear this is acceptable for totalitarian dictatorships but not the highly unusual totalitarian regime.

7. See, in particular, Curtis (1969) for a sustained attack on Friedrich and Brzezinski's position on this point, arguing 'the process of indoctrination (in China), stifling though it is, is of a quite different order from the terror and concentration camps of the Stalin and Hitler regimes' (ibid., p. 82). In the same volume, however, Friedrich (1969) reaffirms his position.

8. On the logic of concept formation see Sartori (1984) and on the effects of 'conceptual stretching' see Sartori (1970). See Burrowes (1964, p. 286) where Friedrich and Brzezinski are specifically criticized for broadening their denotative definition rather than narrowing their connotative definition.

9. The essential purpose of comparative analysis is the investigation of variance against controls (see Sartori, 1970, p. 1035).

10. For Nazi Germany there is also to be found theoretical support in Chapman (1970) where 1933–39 is viewed as a qualitatively different type of police state from that of 1939–44. Chapman chooses early 1939 as the date marked by the setting up of the Reichssicherheitshauptampt (RSHA). In line with Arendt, modern works on Nazi Germany choose the end of 1938, marked by 'Crystal Night'.

4   From origins towards causes of terror regimes

Arendt is not content, as are Friedrich and Brzezinski, simply to consider the development of totalitarianism, for her real concern is its origins. As has become clear, Arendt views the development of totalitarianism as deliberate policy, executed once the totalitarian leader has come to power. Its perfected form, 'terror as government', with concentration camps and total domination over the secret society, takes time to set up. As explained, in preparation for the totalitarian regime, which dated from 1938 in Germany and from 1930 in Russia, propaganda is employed while the state is undermined and the totalitarian terror organization is put in place. As totalitarianism rests on mass obedience, this process involves not just the systematic telling of lies and enforcement of their belief, but also the development of a binding allegiance to the 'infallible' leader. In this the existence of a mass society, a society made up of atomized and isolated individuals, is crucial.

The mass society: precondition and policy
For Arendt, the existence of a mass society is necessary for the development of the totalitarian mass movement but the isolation and atomization of individuals has to be matured for the establishment of the totalitarian regime. A society of isolated and atomized individuals is then a goal of dictatorial terror (the stage before totalitarian terror) and also a precondition of totalitarian power. As the fully perfected 'secret society', the society of mass individuals under the total domination of the infallible leader, the mass society is also a characteristic of the totalitarian regime. This complicates Arendt's argument and it has been criticized above for failing to separate definition and explanation, but it fits with and is a necessary part of her emphasis on movement. The mass society is not a static thing. It has origins, changes naturally over time and is also capable of being deliberately manipulated. As a consequence, Arendt's arguments for Russia and Germany are not the same. In the case of Germany, Arendt (1958, p. 315) argues that the military defeat, inflation and unemployment brought by involvement in World War I produced a mass society ready to be manipulated into a mass movement: 'The masses grew out of the fragments of a highly atomized society whose competitive structure and concomitant loneliness of the individual had been held in check only through membership in a class' (ibid., p. 317).

Arendt argues that Russia before the revolution of 1917 (also bludgeoned by war) similarly displayed the characteristics of mass society. Arendt (1958, p. 318) describes Russia before the revolution as 'a country where a despotic and centralized bureaucracy governed a structureless mass population'. In her view, however, the revolution changed all that and under Lenin's policies (the New Economic Policy – NEP – in particular) classes with common interests and organizations had emerged. Stalin, therefore, had to destroy these classes. As Arendt explains, 'Stalin had first to create artificially the atomized society which had been prepared for the Nazis in Germany by historical circumstances' (ibid., p. 318). She argues that Stalin prepared the conditions for totalitarian government by first destroying what remained of power in the soviets, then liquidating classes: first the peasantry through collectivization, then the workers through the Stakhanov system, promoting individualism and destroying teamwork, and finally the bureaucracy (ibid., p. 319). Through 'skilful use of repeated purges' (ibid., p. 322), Arendt argues, mass atomization was gradually achieved.

It is obviously the case that Stalin's and Hitler's passages to power differed and it is a strength, not a weakness, in Arendt's argument that it takes this into account. Stalin manipulated himself into position from within the enfolding post-revolutionary state, whereas Hitler was elected to power in 1933 through the liberal democratic rules set out under the Weimar Republic, in place since November 1918. As Arendt explains, Hitler achieved power as the head of 'a typically nationalistic little party', but once in power, just as Stalin exploited Marxism to his advantage, so Hitler changed his party programme completely (Arendt, 1958, p. 324). As it is not programmes but lies and manipulation that are characteristic of totalitarian leaders in power, it follows for Arendt that examination of Stalin's and Hitler's support before coming to power will provide little understanding of the origins of totalitarianism, which is developed as a political force only once a leader is in power.

The origins of totalitarianism
There is great significance in Arendt's choice of the term 'origins', for she offers no straightforward causal explanation of totalitarianism. The factors which she identifies as significant begin as a series of threads, each one a phenomenon of modernity in the sense that they first appeared after the French Revolution. These threads become woven together over time but in the process change both within themselves and in respect of their interrelationships with each other. In this way preconditions are created for politicians to come to power and to go on to develop totalitarianism. Her arguments are complex. They involve both the growth of the nation-state in Europe during the nineteenth century and its breakdown between the wars. They also involve ideas of foreign imperialism and their adaptation to colonialist ideas

within Europe. The arguments also take account of both developments within political systems and the effects of social and geographical mobility, the latter leading to the crucial 'stateless' people wandering around Europe.

Imperialism: race-thinking

Arendt begins her explanation from her position that existing ideologies are used in totalitarianism and that totalitarianism itself is based on 'systematic lying', not original ideology. Her 'origins', therefore, start from an analysis of the existence of the right kinds of themes to be exploited in the generation of the totalitarian movement: 'an ideology which has to persuade and mobilize people cannot choose its victims arbitrarily' (Arendt, 1958, p. 7). The 'victims' chosen and the ideology or ideologies exploited need not be the same for each case, but ideologies must be of the kind which are victim-directed.

Arendt starts with the specific direction of attack against Jews in Germany. She identifies the existence of anti-Semitic movements in France, Austria and Germany from 1871. Anti-Semitism had a very long history but these were forms of 'modern anti-Semitism', which, she argues, is a form of 'race-thinking' – not only a modern phenomenon, but an attitude of mind with consequences for behaviour which go far wider than the narrow category of Jews. 'Race-thinking', in Arendt's view, stems from imperialism. Race 'as a principle of the body politic', as a 'substitute for nation', she argues, was one of the two devices which imperialism used to rule over foreign peoples. (For the above see Arendt, 1958, p. 185.)

The difference between race and nation in this thinking was politically significant because it undermined the ideas of citizenship within the nation-state which developed in Europe throughout the nineteenth century. In the 'continental' (rather than 'foreign') form which it took in Europe, imperialism developed both the ideas to justify the denial of rights to people within a country and identified the peoples to whom such rights could be denied. Lacking colonies abroad, continental imperialist movements developed, in Russia and Germany most strikingly, which looked for 'colonies on the continent' (ibid., p. 223). Arendt opens her chapter on continental imperialism with the declaration that 'Nazism and Bolshevism owe more to Pan-Germanism and Pan-Slavism (respectively) than to any other ideology or political movement' (ibid., p. 222). In Europe, 'tribal nationalism' developed and with the Pan-movements inclusion of some people, though outside the state's borders, and the exclusion of others, though inside the state's boundaries, race-thinking became a powerful political force.

The nation-state and rights of citizenship
The historical conditions which made these Pan-German and Pan-Slavic ideas so potent in Arendt's analysis were, together, the growth of the nation-state and the expansion of citizenship rights within each country in combination with the increase of movement around Europe. The result was the growth of 'stateless' people, whose numbers escalated as a consequence of World War I (ibid., pp. 267–9). The post-World War I treaties, furthermore, artificially drew boundaries such that all sorts of people found themselves in new states (ibid., p. 261). These newcomers were resented. Stateless people, lacking rights, became a characteristic of post-World War I Europe: refugees, beggars, Jews, Trotskyists, and so on, all denied citizenship, all viewed as 'undesirables' (ibid., p. 269). With the special problems brought by defeat in the war and followed by unemployment, this potent combination of race-thinking, Pan-movements and a mass society set the conditions for a totalitarian movement.

Imperialism: bureaucracy
Given the generality of these conditions in Europe (defeat in war aside), the obvious question is why a totalitarian leader was not brought to power outside Russia and Germany. Here Arendt's answer is essentially political and she draws together her two themes of imperialism and citizenship. Her second device of imperialism is bureaucracy, used 'as a principle of domination' (Arendt, 1958, p. 185). Observing that both Stalin and Hitler admitted their debt to Pan-Slavism and Pan-Germanism, with race 'as a principle of the body politic', Arendt argues that neither one admitted their indebtedness to the second device of imperialism – 'bureaucracy as a method of rule' (ibid., p. 222). She writes: 'Legally, government by bureaucracy is government by decree, and this means that power, which in constitutional government only enforces the law, becomes the direct source of all legislation' (Arendt, 1958, p. 243). A political system historically structured around a strong bureaucratic state, government by decree, will then be the one best suited to the totalitarian leader. As parties must be undermined and replaced by movements, a party system conducive to this will also be needed.

Party system differences
The one form of party system that Arendt argues could not be undermined and turned into a movement was the two-party system, as found in Great Britain, a system based on a strong parliament, strong government, but not a strong state (ibid., p. 250). The important difference between the Anglo-Saxon two-party and 'continental multiparty' systems relates to the role of the 'opposition as the future party of government' (ibid., p. 252). Because the administration is organized for 'alteration' the state does not stand above government, and citizens

(organized in parties and so 'acting in concert') have control, therefore, over both the government and the state. In the continental party system, however, the state is above parties, for 'each party defines itself consciously as a part of the whole, which in turn is represented by state above parties. A one-party rule therefore can only signify the dictatorial domination of one part over all others' (ibid., p. 253). Arendt also contends that coalition governments are in a similar position of inferiority to the state, as are single-party governments. She also adds that in coalition systems ministers cannot be chosen on the basis of their competence, whereas in the British system there is a choice of competent ministers from the 'large ranks of one party'.

Arendt also points out that in a coalition system no one person or party ever takes full responsibility. Furthermore, in such systems, if one person or party dominates with an absolute majority, this will end either in dictatorship or 'bad conscience', as in post-World War I Germany and Austria. She also draws attention to the differing roles played by party ideology in the two systems: the one restricted; the other, in the multiparty system, always needing to appeal to the wider whole, above the party. Arendt considers the effect of this on citizens whose patriotism, therefore, requires abandonment of party and draws people towards nationalism and away from class interests (ibid., p. 255). Where the state is above parties, nationalism is encouraged and class loyalties are discouraged so that the rise of totalitarian movements is made possible and the conditions for the 'mass' to turn against parliament are developed. In practice, with the influx of stateless people, the continental parties proved incapable of defending anything other than the *status quo* and so the party system broke down.

In important respects the similarities between Bauman and Arendt on the underlying conditions of the Holocaust are striking: 'race-thinking' for Bauman as 'a policy not an ideology'; bureaucracy as a device for domination (though, for Arendt, used only in the stage before the totalitarian regime in order to undermine the state); and the weak state of 'Anglo-Saxon' democracy as the countervailing and mitigating circumstance of Bauman's 'political democracy'. Arendt's argument, however, is more intricate than Bauman's 'modernity', which makes no differentiation between either types of bureaucracy or types of political democracy, and fails even to provide any kind of explanation for 'race-thinking'. This is the one part of his argument where Bauman fails to make a connection with modernity.[1] More striking than similarities between Arendt's and Bauman's later arguments, however, are the similarities between Arendt's and Weber's views on politics: government by bureaucracy being government by decree; the importance of a strong parliament to counter the state and the role envisaged for responsible politicians in mass parties; and specifically arguments in favour of the British parliamentary system over the German.

Through critique to new explanations

In offering so intricately woven an explanation, it is not surprising that Arendt has been subject to criticism and that critics, wanting bold clear threads, have complained that her arguments are hard, sometimes impossible, to follow. (See, for example, Burrowes, 1964.) What Arendt tries to do is to explain how Nazi and Stalinist Terror could have happened. She is not intent on the discovery of scientific laws to demonstrate these outcomes to be inevitable. Arendt's position is that back in the nineteenth century the possibility for totalitarianism was set and the probability grew gradually, but that there was no inevitability in Hitler coming to power in Germany, nor of Stalin taking over in Russia. Once in power they set about creating the conditions for totalitarian terror.

Arendt's explanation, though very broad in conception, is very narrow in application. Her origins are highly specific to a certain period of modern history and while some of her conditions continue to have relevance, not least since 1989 and the break-up of Eastern Europe with its displaced peoples and refugees, her particular explanation is rooted in a specific time. It is the narrowness of the application of Arendt's theory which has been of greatest concern to political scientists. Not only that: political scientists and historians alike have objected to her account of the two cases which she does include, arguing that conditions in Germany and Russia differed in fundamental ways. Historical assessment wail be covered in the chapters to follow. Here it is the logic of her argument which is of interest.

The main problem with Arendt's theory is not so much what she puts into her analysis, but what she leaves out. Arendt is a political theorist and it is not surprising, therefore, that the focus of her enquiry and the emphasis of her analysis should turn on ideas, actors and politics. This is not, of course, to say that her analysis must therefore be wrong, but simply to draw attention to what she may, as a consequence, overlook or underplay. For example, the idea of a society turned from a class society to a mass society entails a prior explanation for the society being a class society. Without industrialization, the class structure in Europe would not have developed as it did during the nineteenth century and parties would not have developed based on class affiliations. The growth of the nation-state was also connected with economic change. Market protection could only be achieved through the development of clear national borders and national governments. Not only markets for goods but also markets for labour developed and became restricted through national legislation. In playing up the importance of political explanation, Arendt plays down economic explanation, yet in the logic of her argument there seems room for both.

War, civil war and scapegoats

Applying Ockham's razor, an explanation for the combination of the large numbers of stateless people in Europe after World War I, the specific political conditions in both Germany and Russia, and the economic devastation experienced in each case could all be put down to the effects of war. As such, war, with particularly devastating consequences, could suffice as explanation for the origins of totalitarianism. On such an account, the tracing back of these conditions to imperialism would be redundant, and such a position might be strengthened by the observation that 'race-thinking' was not important in Russia. But this would, perhaps, be to do an injustice to Arendt, for preconditions themselves have histories. World War I did not materialize from thin air and imperialism clearly lay behind its outbreak. Indeed Arendt's arguments could have been strengthened further by historical analysis of the causes of the war.

At the same time, discovery of the particular conditions which led to World War I remains tied to a specific period of history. The claim for the direct importance of wars has the attraction of general applicability. Furthermore, such a claim can be linked not only to the movement which Arendt stresses, that is the movement of people having been displaced by war, but also, potentially, to the more general atomized conditions which she highlights. Where both death rates and rates of geographical movement are high, traditional ways of life and social networks are easily destroyed. Where economic devastation accompanies and follows war, rapid social mobility is also likely to occur: upwards for those replacing people killed in war; downwards for those hit by the economic downturn.

There is also another advantage in concentrating directly on the importance of war. It is central to Arendt's argument that imperialism provided the basis upon which both 'race-thinking' developed and the political condition of statelessness grew. Yet again this seems an unnecessarily complicated argument, determined to put the concerns of political theory (citizenship, freedom and democracy) at the centre. On a lower level, what is at stake is the need to find an explanation for scapegoating; why Jews, in particular, were picked on in Germany and why they were able to be exploited by totalitarian leaders bent on the development of a totalitarian regime; why, in other words, a Germany 'free of Jews' (*Lebensraum*) could have such appeal; and why, in Russia, similarly, 'Trotskyists' could be exploited by Stalin.

At one level, it is possible to find potential scapegoats in any society. Anyone who does not 'fit in' easily with common practices, whether religious, economic, social or political, is a potential target to be exploited by governments when faced with problems which they are failing to resolve, those relating to the economy, perhaps. As a device finding scapegoats works well in deflecting attention or apportioning blame. So long as governments wish to employ the device of scapegoating then the chances are that scape-goats will be available; history will dictate whom to choose. This does not, of course, mean that 'scapegoating' will work for the government, but if there are conditions under which the chances of it doing so are especially high, then these surely are those following civil war. After civil wars neighbours have recently been enemies and trust is therefore low. Following foreign war, too, the idea of foreigners as 'enemies' remains strong within a country. Civil war and foreign war conditions, particularly where combined with economic crisis (which civil wars and foreign wars ending in defeat generally are) produce circumstances ripe for exploitation by governments in two crucial ways. They produce potential scapegoats and they create a disrupted and mobile society, dislocated in all ways – socially, geographically, economi-cally and politically.

Following Arendt, as totalitarian politicians, once in power, ignore all promises made, it is not necessary to make the difficult causal connection between these dislocated societies and a desire for ruthless government. This is especially so given the very different routes to power taken by Stalin and Hitler. Stalin had no need for popular appeal in his passage to central control in the Soviet Union. Ruthlessness and singlemindedness were what he needed. Hitler's election to power demands an explanation only for the proportion of the electorate who supported the National Socialist Party. In a country suffer-ing severe economic problems, with high levels of unemployment and infla-tion, such as was the case in Germany, support for extreme parties is not unusual and an explanation for why around a third of the electorate voted for this 'typically nationalistic little party' does not seem difficult to find.

Force and government

Arendt's view of the dominance of the state over government as a common condition for totalitarianism in both the Soviet Union and Germany is, in general terms, convincing, However, in directing the weight of her argument towards the nature of party systems Arendt, again, ignores another similarity between the two cases. Not only was the state strong in respect of the bureaucracy, but also in respect of the army and police. Again this develop-ment is related to the features of civil and foreign war.

In the suppression of rebellion in both countries – the civil war in Russia, 1918–21, and the failed revolution in Germany with, in particular, the upris-ings in the Ruhr until 1921 – the importance of force as the basis of govern-ment was strengthened. This is obviously the case in Russia where, through-out the civil war, the Red Army and the Cheka (the All-Russian Extraordinary Commission for Combating Counter-revolution and Sabotage) played a cru-cial part in Bolshevik success and where, after the civil war had ended, Lenin abolished competing political parties. In Weimar Germany, with its democratic organizations, the case is less obvious, but nevertheless valid. The secret deal with the army was made on 11 November 1918 between Ebert and General Gröener just two days after the Social Democrat, Ebert, was handed the government as Germany met defeat. In the Weimar Republic not only the bureaucracy but also the army was more powerful than the government. In Russia, the case was more complex. The army and the Cheka were not 'over' the government in 1921; Lenin gained central control over the forces of coercion through measures introduced at the Tenth Party Congress of March 1921. The civil war government, Sovnarkom, soon ceased to be the centre of power, but government reliance on the coercive forces remained. The weakness of government, or otherwise, should not then be judged only in relation to bureaucratic power but also in relation to the forces of state coercion.[2]

In concentrating on political theory explanations, Arendt, then, underplays both the direct effects of recent history and the importance of economic factors. Her underplaying, indeed outright rejection of economic explanations for the behaviour of totalitarian leaders once in power, has particularly serious consequences for her theory.

Concentration camps: anti-utilitarian versus economically useful
It is important to Arendt's argument that concentration camps were anti-utilitarian, like the 'madness and unreality' of Hell with people 'sealed off' from the outside world (Arendt, 1958, p. 445). If concentration camps were economically functional then her whole explanation of totalitarian government is brought into question. For Arendt, totalitarian society is a secret society, designed to achieve total domination, total obedience to the leader through the destruction of spontaneity. It is to this end that concentration camps are required. They are essential for the disappearance of the 'objectively innocent' of whose absence no one, not even close relatives, dare speak. In the secret society, the best-kept and most central secret in the whole construction of the totalitarian regime is the concentration camp: 'the real secret, concentration camps, those laboratories in the experiment of total domination is shielded by the totalitarian regimes from the eyes of their own people as well as from others' (ibid., p. 436). These laboratories served the 'fundamental belief of totalitarianism that everything is possible' (ibid., p. 437). Their primary function was to sustain the reflex-action obedience of the population suspended under the will of the infallible leader. If the concentration camps are shown to have other, more utilitarian purposes, then this would constitute a serious challenge to Arendt's entire position.

Arendt is specifically defensive against the alternative claims for the utility of the forced (slave) labour within the camps. She argues as follows: 'The concentration camp as an institution was not established for the sake of any possible labour yield. The only permanent economic function of the camps has been the financing of their own supervisory apparatus, Thus from the economic point of view the concentration camps exist mostly for their own sake' (ibid., p. 444). Arendt does allow that 'in times of acute labour shortage, as in Russia and in Germany during the war', 'concentration camp inmates were used for work, but essentially, she argues, 'from the point of view of normal society [the inmate] is absolutely superfluous' (ibid.). The claimed utilitarian goals of the totalitarian leader, 'the building of socialism in one country' or 'realising the Volksgemeinshaft' (ibid., p. 422) are simply the systematic lies of totalitarianism, the genuine, prime goal being total domination.

Arendt's arguments are more difficult to make for Russia than for Germany. She notes (ibid., p. 444, fn. 135) that Dallin 'has built his whole book on the thesis that the purpose of Russian camps is to provide cheap labour' and recognizes that he is not alone in this, with 'current theories about the Russian camp' being similar. She offers two arguments against this utilitarian interpretation. The first is that work could have been developed more cheaply under different conditions. The second is that, given that forced labour was the condition of all Russian workers, there would be no special utilitarian purpose in concentration camps.

Here, however, Bauman's stress on goal-displacement is relevant. While by the final stage the labour in concentration camps may have lacked economic utility this does not rule out the possibility that forced labour had been an important plank of policy in earlier years, whether as ends or means, or a combination of the two which, as Beetham points out, most policies are.

Arendt views the use of forced labour in the Soviet Union in these earlier years only as means to an end, the replacement of a class society by a classless mass society. Lenin's policies, Arendt argues, had 'emancipated nationalities' (ibid., p. 319) and, through the New Economic Policy in particular, had developed social stratification: 'All these new classes and nationalities were in Stalin's way when he began to prepare the country for totalitarian government' (ibid.). 'In order to fabricate an atomized and structureless mass', she argues, 'he began first to destroy what was left of the Soviets and to Russify the nationalities through centralized party bureaucracy' (ibid.). He then began the 'liquidation of classes', and started, 'for ideological and propaganda reasons with the property-owning class, the new middle class in the cities and the peasants in the country' (ibid., p. 320). The liquidation of the peasants, Arendt argues, 'was carried through by artificial famine and deportation under the pretext of expropriation of the Kulaks [wealthy farmers] and collectivization'. Economic changes and occurrences are then purely designed to create a mass society.[3] She continues on this theme of 'massness':

> the liquidation of the middle and peasant classes was completed in the early thirties; those who were not among the many millions of dead or the millions of

deported slave labourers had learned 'who is master here', had realized that their lives and the lives of their families depended not upon their fellow-citizens but exclusively on the whims of the government which they faced in complete loneliness without any help whatsoever from the group to which they happened to belong. (Ibid., p. 320)

In support of her case, Arendt speculates that around two years before Stalin died he proposed to reform the collectives on a larger scale and that he did so because 'collective interests', or communal interests, being the greatest threat to a totalitarian regime, had formed over the passage of time. She is convinced that, had he lived, Stalin would have succeeded in this plan and that the economy would have suffered even more than in the first liquidation. She concludes: 'there is no class that cannot be wiped out if a sufficient number of its members are murdered' (ibid.).

After the peasants it was the workers' turn to be liquidated. They were a weaker class because factories were already state property, and here, Arendt argues, it was the Stakhanov system which produced isolation. From the early 1930s to 1938, the Stakhanov system

broke up all solidarity and class consciousness among the workers, first by the ferocious competition and second by the temporary solidification of a Stakhanovite aristocracy whose social distance from the ordinary worker naturally was felt more acutely than the distance between the workers and the management. (Ibid., p. 321)

In 1938, when the labour book was introduced, this process, she argues, was completed, with the entire working class turned into 'a gigantic forced-labour force' (ibid.). Following the atomization of the workers, the next to be liquidated, on Arendt's account, was the bureaucracy in the 1936–38 purges. By the end of these purges workers, from the highest to the lowest levels and in all areas of administration, including the army, and even the GPU (State Political Administration) itself, had all, Arendt contends, joined the ranks of forced labour and all sources of group power had been destroyed.

In support of her argument that this destruction of human lives was carried through with the purpose of creating an isolated and atomized society, Arendt counters the alternative position that it was done to deal with real problems faced by the Stalinist regime. This she does in two ways. In the first place she argues that the groups representing class interests which were destroyed were neither an actual nor even a foreseeable threat to the regime (ibid., p. 321). Actual, organized opposition, Arendt argues, had been ended by 1930. By this point too foreign opposition to communist rule had diminished greatly and trade and other agreements had been made with capitalist countries. (For the above see ibid., pp. 321–2.)

The second argument which Arendt makes is that the liquidation of classes and purges were economically counterproductive: 'If the liquidation of classes made no political sense, it was positively disastrous for the Soviet economy' (ibid., p. 322). She points to the dire repercussions for the economy of the 'artificial famine of 1933', the 'chaotic imbalance' in industry produced by the Stakhanov system from 1935, and the particular devastation of destroying much-needed new technical 'know-how' when factory managers and engineers were liquidated along with other bureaucrats (ibid.).

The utility of these policies is not, however, as easily countered as Arendt supposes. Rejecting official Soviet information, Arendt accepts (ibid., p. 321, fn. 29) that little was known of what actually took place in the Soviet Union at the time she was writing. It follows, therefore, that she cannot disprove the existence of real opposition to the regime, even into the late 1930s. Furthermore, even if this opposition were not organized, as she insists, it could perhaps be that unconcerted political and economic disruption took place. In either event strongly coercive action in combination with new experimental economic policies might be one of the possible rational actions taken by a regime. This consideration, however, raises the second difficulty with Arendt's arguments.

While government behaviour might, to our eyes, appear anti-utilitarian because of the economic chaos which resulted from policies, such evidence could neither constitute unequivocal proof of deliberate anti-utilitarian policy nor, more specifically, count as evidence of intention to create a mass society. The problem here is that people's actions have unintended consequences and this is most likely to be the case where actions taken are new and untried, where time is short (and so inadequate for reflection in the light of unforeseen outcomes) and where the people undertaking the actions are operating in new or unsettled circumstances. All this was surely true of the Soviet Union, which, faced with economic devastation after foreign war, revolution and civil war, embarked on entirely new and untried anti-market policies of centrally planned, rapid industrialization. Central planning had never been tried before. The fact that economic chaos resulted from Stalin's policies cannot then rule out the possibility that these policies were intended to achieve economic improvement.

This point about plans going wrong is implicit in Friedrich and Brzezinski's discussion of the role of economic planning in totalitarian dictatorship. Plans do not have to succeed, they argue, for the very reason that the dictator and party have control over information (Friedrich and Brzezinski, 1965, p. 227). In Germany, it will be recalled, they argue that planning was ineffective because Goering was incompetent and Hitler lacked understanding of the economy (ibid.). Furthermore, their particular stress on economic planning similarly concentrates on the 'system of labour conscription' (ibid., p. 251) where wage rates are determined and where 'a special government body' (ibid.) assigns workers to jobs and uses labour camps for 'slave labour' (ibid., p. 253).

Friedrich and Brzezinski's arguments, however, raise the question of why the dictators were planning the economy if propaganda had to be used to conceal errors. The idea of the 'vacuum' goes some way towards offering an answer to this. Propaganda, they argue, leads to disbelief and rumours. The absence of alternative sources of information, such as a free press, is crucial in this. Friedrich and Brzezinski use this argument to explain the development of public indifference to propaganda and the development of 'mutual distrust' which moves the dictatorship towards terror (ibid., p. 136). This terror then further inhibits 'truthful reporting' everywhere and interferes with industrial planning, 'the vacuum working like a cancer in the totalitarian systems' (ibid., p. 143).

This idea of a vacuum, however, contains a convoluted argument in respect of economic plans. Weber's arguments about the inefficiencies of systems based on substantive rationality, as outlined and discussed in Chapter 2, offer a direct explanation for the problems of economic planning. In an economic system based on substantive rationality, lacking calculations based on real prices at every stage, the system itself would directly undermine the availability of accurate information. Certainly a system of terror would add to the problem of concealment of information but a system of substantive rationality would entail inefficiencies, chaos, bankruptcy and the need to conceal errors emanating from decisions made at the top.

Evidence of economic disutility cannot prove that economic policies were undertaken in order to create a mass society. In a system of substantive rationality, planning problems would soon arise, naturally, for lack of accurate figures upon which to base plans. The extent to which a mass society was created as at least part of a deliberate policy must await analysis of the cases in the chapters to come. Within Arendt's writings, in any case, is to be found a position on war which leads logically to a claim for intended economic utility in totalitarian policies.

War as policy
Though it is given somewhat uneven treatment for Germany and Russia, world conquest, total domination across the globe, is an essential element of totalitarianism for Arendt. For Germany, war is viewed as particularly important because, without an increase in territory, the country was not large enough to have moved to 'terror as government'. Explaining why, outside Russia and Germany, the existence of totalitarian movements failed to lead to the 'last instance' totalitarian government, stopping at totalitarian dictatorship, she argues that the size of a country's population acts as a critical

constraint. Arendt (1958) stresses that in smaller European countries 'the would-be totalitarian ruler of masses was forced into the more familiar patterns of class and party dictatorship. The truth is that these countries simply did not control enough human material to allow for total domination and its inherent great losses in population' (ibid., p. 310). As a consequence she argues that the conquest of territories with dense populations is the only way to resolve the problem and makes the following argument about Nazi Germany:

> This is also why Nazism, up to the outbreak of the war and its expansion over Europe lagged so far behind its Russian counterpart in consistency and ruthlessness: even the German people were not numerous enough to allow for the full development of this newest form of government. Only if Germany had won the war would she have known a fully developed totalitarian rulership, and the sacrifices this would have entailed not only for the 'inferior races' but for the Germans themselves can be gleaned and evaluated from the legacy of Hitler's plans. In any event it was only during the war, after the conquests in the East furnished large masses of people and made the extermination camps possible, that Germany was able to establish a truly totalitarian rule. (Ibid., pp, 310–11)

Without war, without the conquest of large populations, Hitler could not, then, have established totalitarian government. Again she stresses, 'Only where great masses are superfluous or can be spared without disastrous results of depopulation is totalitarian rule, as distinguished from a totalitarian movement, at all possible' (ibid., p. 311). And again, 'Hitler...regarded the mass slaughter of war as an incomparable opportunity to start a murder programme which, like all other points of his programme, was calculated in terms of millennia' (ibid., pp. 347–8).

Whereas in Germany the insufficiency of population required conquests for totalitarian government, Russia had sufficient population. Nevertheless, for both cases the 'ultimate goal' of the totalitarian leader is 'world conquest', 'since only in a world completely under his control could the totalitarian ruler possibly realise his lies and make true all his prophecies' (ibid., p, 350). Arendt claims that the evidence for these totalitarian governments' aspiration to 'conquer the globe and bring all countries on earth under their domination' is to be found in both Nazi and Bolshevik literature (ibid., p. 415). Yet the preparation for war is not featured in her account of Russia, and even for Germany she fails to make the logical connection between the economy and preparation for war. Arendt does acknowledge that 'the preparation for war itself is not anti-utilitarian, despite its prohibitive costs' (ibid., p. 410), and she acknowledges that Thomas Reveille, in *The Spoils of Europe* (1941), argues that Germany was able to recover from the spoils of the first year of war the whole costs of preparation for war between 1933 and 1939 (ibid.). Pursuing her theme of the economic irrationality of the Nazi system, she argues, however, that 'economic laws of investment and production, of stabilizing gains and profits, and of exhaustion do not apply if one intends in any event to replenish the depleted home economy with loot from other countries' (ibid.). Reinforcing her case for the economic irrationality of the war policy she argues:

> the remarkable thing about this process, however, is that it was by no means checked by such a shattering defeat as Stalingrad, and that the danger of losing the war altogether was only another incitement to throw overboard all utilitarian considerations and make an all-out attempt to realize through ruthless total organization the goals of totalitarian racial ideology, no matter for how short a time. (Ibid.)

In further support of her case Arendt stresses the anti-utilitarian nature of killing Jews, and of removing Jews from armaments manufacturing, pointing out that even high Nazis could not understand it (ibid., fn. 63).

The spoils of war are not, however, the only way in which war policy has economic utility. Just as global domination cannot be achieved without wars, so wars cannot be fought without armaments and military forces. Modern warfare relies on industrialization. If global domination was both Stalin's and Hitler's ultimate goal then both rapid industrialization and increased production to feed the mouths of both the military and the workers in the armaments industry would be required. In Weber's analysis, again as outlined in Chapter 2, however, though designed for economic utility, a 'war economy' as a system of 'substantive rationality' would soon move to economic bankruptcy.

Having adopted the policy of dispensing with a free market in labour and production it followed that economic bankruptcy would threaten while concern for welfare would be sacrificed.

Concentration camps and forced labour

The role of concentration camps remains critical. For Arendt (1958, p. 436) they are the 'laboratories in the experiment for total domination'. They are the 'essence' of the totalitarian regime. Their role is to ensure the destruction of spontaneity so as to achieve total obedience to the leader, total domination. If concentration camps were constructed because they were perceived as having economic utility, even if only in part, then this would seriously undermine not only Arendt's explanation for the origins of totalitarianism but also her argument for the development of the totalitarian regime. Following Weber's position, concentration camps too can be linked to substantive rationality.

Once the policy decision is made to command labour, that is to use coercion over labour rather than the incentives offered by the market, namely pecuniary inducements and job satisfaction, then on Weber's argument, without scope for individual responsibility and without the mechanism for proper accounting, workers perform below expected levels of productivity and the economy functions less efficiently than under a free market. As explained, over time the economy moves towards bankruptcy. Keeping within the chosen policy, increased coercion is the means to increase production: more workers are coerced into work. This fits with Friedrich and Brzezinski's (1965, pp. 245–59) view that an essential element of totalitarian dictatorships is the loss of labour's 'freedom and independence'.

The problem arises in a planned system, a system of substantive rationality, of what to do with unproductive workers. These are essentially of two types: those who hinder work processes, the slackers and the disruptive elements; and those who are physically unfit. The latter might include those worn out by the coerced labour regime or those too young, too old, too sick or too disabled. In a free labour market unproductive workers can be thrown out of employment and left, along with other dependants, to the care of the family, or to the wider community, whether local or national, public or private. Such structures could include guilds, friendly societies, churches, charities, trade unions, insurances or a welfare system.

In a directed labour system where coercion is a policy, punishment will be the natural reaction to the first category of unproductive workers, the slackers and the disruptive elements. Imprisonment with hard labour is a logical reaction. In respect of the second category, the physically unproductive, policies towards these are likely to vary according to circumstances. In an authoritarian system, guilds, friendly societies, churches, charitable organizations and the like will, in any case, be viewed as a threat to political authority. Either a system of welfare run by the state, or the extolment of family virtues to put the burden of financial responsibility on the family, or both, are likely to be developed. However, the less visible these latter unproductive groups are to the wider public and the less 'attached' to them are the wider population, the less concerned with the welfare of the 'unproductive' worker the government needs to be. Faced with declining economic productivity, there will be clear incentives to dispense with compassion if costly.

The cheapest way to deal with workers who have been worn out by hard labour in prison camps is, literally, to work them to death, starve them to death, or to exterminate them at the point where their production fails below their consumption. Shut away in prisons and work camps their fate can be kept more easily from the public. New prisoners can be sent to replace these workers. If necessary, just as Arendt argues, such workers may be obtained through conquering new populations.

Now, nothing in the argument above suggests that the policy to control labour inevitably leads to slave labour, concentration camps, and mass extermination. The argument shows, however, that logically these could follow.

There is no inevitability because policy decisions can be modified as economic productivity goes into decline. On this line of argument, it is not necessary to contend that extermination camps were built for the purpose of economic production but rather that they were developed, at least in part, as a consequence of the low productivity and eventual economic bankruptcy brought about by the policy of a controlled labour market and the move to labour coercion.

Governments lacking the will to push coercion to the extreme, where a secret society is constructed through the organization of terror, would not make the transition to totalitarian government. Governments possessing the will but lacking the necessary pools of potential forced labour would not succeed. This naturally raises the question of war. Pools of workers for forced labour are required. As Arendt points out (though arguing about the needs of mass society and total domination), the necessary large population was available in the USSR and it can be added that the availability of large tracts of land suitable for the siting of labour camps and concentration camps on the outer reaches of the main population areas were also to its advantage. In Germany, however, again in line with Arendt's observation, population size was inadequate and, in Germany's case, therefore, it would follow that war was necessary in order to conquer large populations.

The extent to which it is the pursuit of war which leads to the requirement for forced labour, or the policy of forced labour which, as productivity declines, leads to a need for war, is clearly open to question. Only the examination of the evidence can decide. The answer is likely to be a mixture of the two, though not necessarily the same mixture for each case. It would also be likely that as one goal was pursued, the other policy would become the means to that goal's end and vice versa.

Terror as government: the outline of a new theory

What is to be explained is the development of terror regimes which operate not through the state (as dictatorship) but from behind a state façade and which direct a system of terror deliberately at the objectively innocent. Although Arendt's view of terror as government is accepted in essence, a critique of her proposed origins of totalitarianism in the light of the insights offered by Weber and by Friedrich and Brzezinski has suggested a new theory. This theory, which will be further examined and elaborated through application to cases, is as follows.

A 'dislocated society', brought about by the devastating consequences of large-scale foreign war together with civil war or widespread rebellion, creates the conditions conducive to the rise of a terror regime. This is so for three reasons. First, the rapid social and geographical movement breaks down traditional networks. Second, a recent history of war and rebellion produces 'old enemies' who can be exploited as scapegoats by a terror regime, once in power. Third, such total upheaval brings economic crisis which in turn produces both potential support for extreme policies and governments which view control over the economy as critical to political success. Though conducive to the development of a terror regime, a dislocated society does not make the development inevitable. If a government with the will to develop terror as government is successful in getting into power, then it is that government's consequent policies which are crucial.

Politically, these policies are bound up with the willingness to apply coercion to an extreme. This requires the setting up of a network of police and secret police, and prisons and camps for punishment on a large scale. Economically, these policies begin with the adoption of a system of substantive rationality in which dispensing with a labour market is critical. Following Weber, systems of substantive rationality inevitably lead to economic bankruptcy.

The argument is not, however, that the decision to control the labour market and to make calculations on the basis of projected output necessarily leads to terror as government. Changes in policy, including a move back towards formal rationality is possible. Totalitarian dictatorships, not totalitarian regimes, are to be found with economic systems of substantive rationality. In totalitarian regimes willingness to adapt and change in recognition of failures and mistakes must be lacking. This is why an 'infallible leader', as stressed by Arendt, is essential. Policies can be changed, but where there is an 'infallible leader', changes which indicate that problems encountered emanate from decisions made at the centre will not be countenanced. Where the will of the leader cannot be challenged by the state authorities, the will of the leader is law. This is why actions must be taken to undermine the power of the state and why the leader must rely on a system of terror. As a cover for what is actually economic chaos produced as a consequence of the governments move to a system of unyielding substantive rationality, other people must be found to take the blame – scapegoats. As explained, this process is facilitated by the existence of a dislocated society but the use of propaganda to project such blame is the government's chosen device.

Wild schemes: substantive irrationality

The infallible leader with a developing terror organization does not stop with a system of substantive rationality. It is not planning which leads to terror as government, neither is it specifically production goals based on technical calculations and the labour market under central control. As economic bankruptcy approaches, a consequence of substantive rationality, the infallible leader, whose will is law, moves from plans to wild schemes. No longer a system of substantive rationality, the system is turned into 'substantive irrationality', where the economy is severed completely from the anchor of the market.

As will become clear from the study of both Nazi Germany and Stalin's Soviet Union there is one economic policy on which both Hitler and Stalin were absolutely set: the development of an economy based on the extensive use of labour. In combination with the shared political policy of coercion, it was this utter economic conviction that drove the terror regimes onwards towards their hideous outcomes. Once the decision was made to exploit forced labour, the step from labour camp to death camp became shorter as the logic of what to do with worn-out workers and those unwanted people who consume more than they produce had to be faced. Only the cruellest of systems makes this final step. Logical but not inevitable, the move to camps where people are worked to the point at which their consumption overtakes their production and are then destroyed is the evidence of a fully developed totalitarian regime.

These are not arguments which lend themselves easily to proof, for if Arendt is right, and it is held here that she is, the evidence of policies being prepared is of little relevance, for the chaotic duplication of offices and multiplication of functions constitute a crucial part of the development of a totalitarian regime. Planning might occur and careful rational planning at that, but there would not be just one plan and any final decision made would not be predictable in the rational sense of being based on the most careful reckonings and most sensible deductions from calculations. Wild schemes are the prerogative of the infallible leader. Secrecy is the key to the society. Evidence can only be gathered after the event and with so many lies, so much falsification and so much to hide, the evidence released can never be satisfactory.

As will be shown, both Nazi Germany and Stalin's Russia fit this extreme of substantive irrationality. Contrary to Friedrich and Brzezinski's insistence on their conception of totalitarianism as central control over the economy where planning is the crucial feature, what was characteristic of both Stalin's and Hitler's rule was that decrees and directives overruled 'scientific' plans. Contrary to Arendt's view that policies lacked economic utility, however, in the eyes of these infallible leaders economic policies were essential to their plans and concentration camps played a crucial part in the fulfilment of their wild schemes.

Initially writing so close to events, both Arendt's and Friedrich and Brzezinski's views were necessarily impressionistic to a degree. The evidence for Russia, where the regime had not been overthrown after World War II, was most obviously problematic. In the cold war era of the later editions, not surprisingly, both were concerned to employ their analyses in reflection of recent events: Hungary in the case of Arendt; Cuba, Ghana and China in the case of Friedrich and Brzezinski. The passage of time since these publications, particularly after the events of 1989, have served to generate both new evidence and scope for fresh analysis.

Notes

1. Bauman views social engineering as part of the modernist dream, and the portrayal of Jews
    as vermin and so on is connected to the bureaucratic mentality, but why *Jews* is never
    explained. Arendt takes this on, offering a broad theory of the modern (that is post-French
    Revolution) world with its two new developments: imperialism, which through develop-
    ments and mutations explains both race-thinking and bureaucratic domination; and the
    nation-state with its new party systems and laws of citizenship which prove unable to cope
    with the developing historical changes, not least among them, World War I and its effects.
2. For these events in Germany see Moore (1978, pp. 294–5). For the Russian case see
    O'Kane (1991, pp. 107–13).
3. It is for this reason above all that Burrowes (1969) has criticized Arendt both for ignoring
    the importance of forced modernization (p. 276) in Soviet history and for turning her work
    into 'fantasy' (p. 280).

PART II

THE CLASSIC CASES

Case 1   Russia under Stalin – introduction

Recent analyses of Stalin's Terror lend support to Arendt's conception of a totalitarian regime over Friedrich and Brzezinski's view of totalitarian dictatorship where the party, ideology and bureaucracy dominate. Gill (1990) develops a picture of Stalin's behaviour and passage to domination in the 1930s which is entirely consistent with Arendt's 'leadership principle', with the state a façade.

> Institutional boundaries, prerogatives, sensitivities and traditions, including the established web of relationships between institutions, became of little account as Stalin's leadership style became more idiosyncratic and less regularised. He could search out and accept information and advice from wherever he chose, unconstrained by bureaucratic norms or regulations. His personal position of supremacy, supported by the uncertainty created by the Terror, meant that he shaped institutional contours and processes rather than his working style being shaped by their patterns. (Gill, 1990, p. 305)

On ideology too, Gill shows how Stalin's words became 'ideological orthodoxy' such that ideology itself 'was denied any independent part in the political system' (ibid., p. 306). Daniels (1993, pp. 82–3) concurs: 'for Stalin, the relationship between ideology and power eventually came to be completely reversed. Instead of a source of guidance, ideology was reduced to a mere instrument bent to the achievement, preservation, and extension of power'. In support, Daniels offers, among others' views, Gorbachev's comment on the past use of Marxism–Leninism 'distorted to the utmost to suit the pragmatic purposes of the day' (ibid., p. 83).

As illustration of how Marxism–Leninism was bent to Stalin's purpose, Daniels explains how Stalin's 'theory of socialism in one country', developed in the late 1920s, set the pattern. Derived from a single, old quotation from Lenin, taken out of context and, crucially, supplemented by Stalin's own words, 'the method and machinery of doctrinal reinterpretation' was established (Daniels, 1993, p. 86). This was the method which was used to conjure Stalin's infallibility. First, any *ad hoc* decision taken by Stalin was legitimized by the use of some Marxist doctrine conveniently lifted from anywhere and given only one interpretation. Anyone later questioning the interpretation, attempting to restore the earlier context, would be accused of 'petty-bourgeois deviation' and eventually 'counter-revolutionary wrecking'. Daniels (1993, pp. 86–7) concludes: 'no longer did doctrine set the direction of policy; the immediate needs of policy determined the meaning that would be imputed to doctrine'. Similarly, Gill (1990, p. 305) gives the example of Stalin's pronouncement that class conflict would grow more intense as socialism came closer, a dictum which moved increasingly to the fore as the Terror heightened in the late 1930s.

New evidence, the benefit of *glasnost* and the access to archives which it has brought, has thrown new light on the nature of the Terror, however, which contradicts not only Friedrich and Brzezinski's rationally planned economic system (albeit based on retrogressive rationality) with terror directed at real political opposition, but also questions Arendt's account of the creation of the mass society in the 1930s and her claimed anti-utilitarian nature of economic policies. This evidence, rather, lends support to the new tentative theory outlined above.

5   Before Stalinism to the early years of terror as government

Before Stalinism

A dislocated society

Russia, since 1914, had been embroiled first in foreign war, then revolution, then civil war, then famine. By the early 1920s the country had undergone enormous demographic changes and had experienced dramatic social change. In World War I approximately 1 700 000 Russian soldiers were killed. In the period of revolution and civil war, 1917–21, an estimated 10 million people lost their lives.[1] (See Bullock, 1993 and for comparison of estimates see Rummel, 1990, Table 2A: 50–54.) The number of people living in the cities dropped from 19 per cent of the population in 1917 to 15 per cent in 1920. The population of Moscow fell by half, that of Petrograd by two-thirds (Lewin, 1985, p. 211). The severe drought in 1921 brought famine to the Volga basin, the Southern Urals and areas of the Ukraine. By the end of 1921, 27 million people faced starvation, resulting in 5 million deaths (Levytsky, 1972, p. 43).

During the civil war an economic system developed known as 'war communism' which aimed at central control over distribution and production (Malle, 1985, p. 373). Faced with severe grain shortage the new Bolshevik government introduced a system of food procurement. Grain requisitioning set town against country and worker against peasant. (See Carr, 1966, vol. 2, pp. 152–65.) Under pressure of peasant rebellions, escalating from the autumn of 1920, and faced with serious food shortages in the Bolshevik strongholds, the war communist economy 'collapsed' (Sakwa, 1988, p. 240).[2]

The New Economic Policy: substantive rationality

At the end of the civil war Lenin replaced war communism with a new economic policy introduced at the Tenth Party Congress. This New Economic Policy, NEP, effectively reintroduced the market to the Soviet economy. The NEP was a system based on substantive rationality, The 'tax in kind', the hallmark of war communism, which took all surplus from peasants above what was judged necessary for subsistence, was abolished and replaced by a new tax calculated on the percentage of the crop produced (Carr, 1966, vol. 2, p. 282). By March 1922 this new fixed tax was down to 10 per cent of crop production (ibid., p. 294). This left peasants free to sell their surplus on the market. Significant changes also occurred in industry. Commercialism was reintroduced through the development of leases for non-profitable nationalized industries and small rural industries, and trusts for gathering together small enterprises producing the same goods. These leases and trusts could purchase supplies on the market, not just from the state, and proper accounting was at the centre of their operation. By March 1922 the fuel industry became fully commercial (ibid., pp. 298–309). A free labour market was also reintroduced, compulsory labour gradually abandoned, and a money wage system came back into operation, with wages related to productivity. Wage-fixing was replaced by a minimum wage (ibid., pp. 318–22).

The incentives offered to peasants, along with the good weather, brought rewards in 1922 with the best harvest since the outbreak of revolution. Under NEP enthusiasm for collective farms waned as the workers who had been central to their setting up in the civil war went back to work in the cities (Lewin, 1968, p. 107). Under the NEP cooperatives were viewed as the key to increased production. In 'On Co-operation', dictated in January 1923, Lenin wrote, 'essentially all that we need is that the Russian people should co-operate deeply and widely within the framework of NEP' (quoted ibid., p. 94).

The terror organization and the Bolshevik Party

Shortly after the Bolsheviks came to power, the All-Russian Extraordinary Commission for Combating Counter-revolution and Sabotage, the Cheka, was set up in December 1917. The Cheka was a secret police system which formed an armed combat detachment at the end of March 1918. The Cheka grew through the civil war, reaching its peak of 143 000 personnel by December 1921. (For the above see Leggett, 1981, p. 346.) Following debates in the press over Cheka excesses, its powers were cut in June 1921 (ibid., p. 343). In Moscow the Cheka's 'heavy-handedness' had itself led to disturbances (Sakwa, 1988, p. 242) and the Cheka's violent reactions to demonstrations and strikes also provoked anger in other Bolshevik strongholds, including Kronstadt where rebellion was defeated on 17 March 1921. In February 1922 the Cheka was replaced by the new political police, the State Political Administration, the GPU. With the formation of the USSR in 1923 the GPU became the OGPU, the Unified State Political Administration, though the shorter 'GPU' was soon restored to common usage.

Concentration camps had existed in the Soviet Union (the then RSFSR) during the civil war but these were reformed in 1923 and mostly abolished (Dallin and Nicolaevsky, 1948, p. 157). Prisoners worked as correction for their crimes but, before 1926, their work was entirely directed towards the running of the camp; work was not exacted in order to produce goods for consumption outside the prison camp (ibid., p. 181). For further discussion on the significance of the changes in 1926 see Bacon (1994, pp. 45–6).

At the Tenth Party Congress, with opposition outside the Communist Party suppressed by the end of the civil war, Lenin banned opposition within the Communist Party and party discipline was made compulsory (Carr, 1966, vol. 2, p. 208). From mid-1921, the party organization (Politburo and Central Committee) began to displace the importance of Sovnarkom which had been the centre of the emergency government during the civil war, though it is open to question whether or not this loss of power to Sovnarkom was Lenin's intention. (See Rigby, 1979, pp. 191–213.) Following a series of strokes, the first in May 1922, Lenin died in January 1924.

On 3 April 1922, shortly before Lenin's first stroke, Stalin was appointed general secretary of the Central Committee. At this point he was already a member of the Politburo. After Lenin's death, the general secretary's power grew (Deutscher, 1968, p. 236). In the autumn of 1924, Stalin first developed his ideas on 'socialism in one country' which stood in direct opposition to Trotsky's internationalist theory of 'permanent revolution'. The novel aspect of Stalin's idea was that it asserted Russia's self-sufficiency (ibid., p. 289).

Economic problems under the NEP
Under the New Economic Policy, by 1927 workers' conditions had improved, wage levels were 11 per cent above what they had been in 1913, diets were better, education had progressed substantially and 9 million trade union members had the benefit of social insurance (Siegelbaum, 1992, pp. 203–4). Following the economic devastation of war, revolution and civil war, economic reconstruction was completed between the years 1925 and 1927. Under an economic system of substantive rationality, however, problems were bound to occur.

Though by 1927 official figures indicated that the volumes of both industrial and agricultural production were restored to prewar levels, the levels of efficiency and per capita productivity achieved before 1914 were not reached. Furthermore, heavy and medium industry had declined as a proportion of the national economy. Particularly worrying, new construction was inadequate, with enterprises still mainly housed in old buildings, using worn-out and out-of-date machinery. In November 1927 industrial production was 18 per cent below its projected level and 21.4 per cent below the target in December. At the same time, faced with a large trade deficit, foreign trade, which could have enabled the import of modem goods, was cut. A severe shortage of goods on the market developed, decreasing 15.5 per cent in just one month, December 1927–January 1928. In some provincial cities supplies of basic goods and foodstuffs were so low as to cover only a few days' needs. An increased money supply also led to inflation. (For the above see Reiman, 1987, pp. 4 and 43–4.)

Unemployment was also increasing, with those looking for work pouring into the cities – Moscow, Kharkov, Leningrad and Kiev in particular (Reiman,

1987, p. 5). By 1926 permanent migrants had reached 945 000 with seasonal migrants in addition (Siegelbaum, 1992, p. 205). Reiman (1987, p. 5) estimates that in the latter half of the 1920s urban unemployment approached 2 million. Tensions developed between these newly arrived and established workers and were not helped by the wage scale reforms adopted in 1927 which narrowed differentials between levels of skill. A belief developed that the new workers were bringing piece rates down and damaging equipment. Party and union officials viewed these immigrants as undisciplined and unreliable (Siegelbaum, 1992, pp. 207–8).[3]

Agriculture, like industry, suffered from the lack of good equipment. New farm machinery, tools and fertilizers were completely dependent on imports. The volume of agricultural production had been restored to levels achieved before 1914 by changes in crop management, by increasing livestock and by bringing previously unused land into production. Importantly, however, grain production had not been brought back to prewar levels by 1926–27. Peasants were also consuming a larger share of production and overall, production of agricultural goods for the market, so essential to the towns, was a long way off what it had been before the outbreak of World War 1. (For the above see Reiman, 1987, p. 4.)

In 1927 party officials were shocked by the failure to collect the expected levels of grain. With the level of grain procurement a little higher in July–September 1927 than over the same period in the previous year, in October–December the level fell to 2.4 million tons from the 4.58 million tons it had been in October–December 1926.[4] Most probably a miscalculation had been made in the prices paid to peasants. (For the above see Siegelbaum, 1992, pp. 190–91.) In addition, there were problems of rural population growth, insufficient supplies of manufactured goods to the countryside and recognition by farmers that a good harvest was usually followed by a bad one. (See Reiman, 1987, p. 41.) Furthermore, as Reiman (1987, p. 42) explains, 'Statistics that had been dressed up to please higher authorities gave a false picture of the amount of freely available grain in the silos of the peasantry, as well as the general capacity of agriculture to provide the food supplies needed by the Soviet Union'. By 1928 the Soviet economy was malfunctioning exactly as predicted by Weber's analysis of substantive rationality.

With the economy so heavily dependent on grain exports, in November 1927 the trade deficit grew dramatically, up 8 per cent on the month before, and it continued to climb (Reiman, 1987, p. 43). Stalin used this shortfall in grain to apply force.

1928–29: the move towards substantive irrationality
At the beginning of 1928 the GPU and special party workers were sent to search barns and warehouses. Under these 'extraordinary measures' peasants

were prosecuted for hoarding under article 107 of the criminal code and grain was confiscated from the richer peasants with some of it redistributed to poor peasants at low prices. Tax collections were also made more rigorous and in a few, unconnected, incidents, forced collectivization was attempted. (See Siegelbaum, 1992, p. 193 and Reiman, 1987, p. 45.) In early March special surveillance powers were given to the GPU over economic transactions (Reiman, 1987, p. 49). These measures obtained large amounts of grain but by March–April the levels of grain procured were falling sharply (ibid., p. 53). Widespread disorder broke out in the villages and, in protest, animals were slaughtered and crops went uncultivated (ibid.). Shortages in the cities also led to disorder (ibid., p. 54).

The lessons drawn by Stalin from this initial exercise in force were that market mechanisms had failed and that the party network in the rural areas was unreliable (Siegelbaum, 1992, pp. 194–5). His thinking moved from cooperatives, central to the NEP, to forced collectives. Stalin's idea was to develop large state and collective farms which would be capable of achieving a surplus of half of what they produced. As Siegelbaum (1992, p. 197) explains, 'the trick was finding a device to persuade the producers to hand over the requisite amounts at prices unfavourable to them' – a trick, indeed, that even the most gullible might spot.

Stalin thought that he could achieve his aim of procuring sufficient quantities of grain at low prices through the threat of withholding state subsidies and credits and meeting any resistance 'head on' (Siegelbaum, 1992, p. 197). The resistance he met was not only from peasants but also from the Politburo, with Bukharin dubbing him 'a Ghengis Khan' set on 'military feudal exploitation' (ibid.). In the course of Stalin's battle against Bukharin and the moderates, 'Stalin tore up the scientific plan and ordered his own wild targets' (Daniels, 1993, p. 90).

From plan to wild schemes
Under the NEP considerable effort was put into a carefully calculated system of economic planning by the economists in Gosplan (the State Planning Commission), and this led to the composition of the first Five-Year Plan in 1927 (Daniels, 1993, p. 90). This carefully prepared plan was not formally adopted until the Sixteenth Party Congress in 1929, by which time it had been greatly revised after changes had already been made to it during 1928. Lewin (1968, p. 267) has termed 1928 'a year of drift' and in a later work (1985, p. 100) 'this rudderless year'. This was the year in which calculations at each stage, Bukharin's 'objectivity of statistics', were pushed aside by wild schemes (Siegelbaum, 1992, p. 217).

The dominant economic debates in 1928 centred on the problem of what has been termed 'the wage–goods gap' (Swianiewicz, 1965, p. 239). If industrialization was to be achieved the new industrial workers would need to be fed and urban employment would have to offer incentives if peasants were to be attracted out of the countryside where underemployment existed (ibid.). Bukharin's solution was for light industry to produce the desired consumer goods. Preobrazhensky, aligned with Trotsky, however, argued for the stimulation of industrial investment through adjusting the system of prices. Essentially, his idea was to increase the prices on relatively inelastic state-produced goods so that more would need to be produced in the villages in order to purchase them (ibid., pp. 242–3). Both Bukharin's and Preobrazhensky's solutions were in the spirit of the NEP. Both sought to use market mechanisms within a planning system based on substantive rationality.

Stalin evaded taking a clear position in this economic debate, making statements which contradicted each other but which consistently served to destroy Trotsky's credibility as his rival claimant to party leadership (Swianiewicz, 1965, p. 245). As such, Stalin mostly supported the Bukharinist policy which dominated Gosplan thinking until, in late 1927, Stalin succeeded in having Trotsky arrested and exiled. (See Reiman, 1987, pp. 30–36.) In 1928–29 Stalin came out clearly against Bukharin's slow route to industrialization based on peasant cooperation.

In the second half of 1928, Stalin set the Supreme Economic Council (VSNKh or Vesenkha) to work on economic plans. VSNKh was, in Reiman's (1987, p. 87) words, 'counterposed to the more sober State Planning Commission (Gosplan)'. Plans to increase the rate of industrialization were developed by both agencies and both sets of plans were rejected as inadequate. The arguments put forward for fast rates of industrialization were not carefully calculated on the basis of existing resources but on what was termed the 'deficits in the economy' (ibid.). Calculations of resources available showed them to be inadequate for the proposed faster rate of economic growth. As Reiman (1987, p. 89) explains, 'The planning agencies therefore decided on a not entirely customary measure: to balance the plan by means of resources that the economy did not yet have at its disposal'. As Bukharin expressed the problem in 'Notes of An Economist', published in *Pravda* at the time, VSNKh was trying 'to build present day factories with future bricks' (Siegelbaum, 1992, p. 201).

In agriculture, calculations for the 'plan' were even more contrived: 'Stalin and his supporters denied the real state of affairs in the countryside and greatly exaggerated the results already obtained' (Reiman, 1987, p. 89). The whole scheme was based on an 'imaginary harvest' (ibid.). The state increased its intervention into agriculture. As a consequence state agencies at all levels, from the highest to the lowest, were inundated with work. Administration fell apart as coordination collapsed (see Siegelbaum, 1992, p. 197). By the end of 1928 the level of grain procured stood at only 61 per cent of the target for the year (Reiman, 1987, p. 81). Starvation and social unrest threatened.[5]

At the beginning of 1929 Stalin turned the full weight of his attack against Bukharin, who was ousted from the Central Committee in July. In the middle of 1929, Stalin moved to all-out heavy industrialization and complete collectivization. Both projects were wild schemes, based not on rational calculations directed towards an outcome but on substantive irrationality, lacking calculations on a firm basis. In Ellman's (1989, p. 27) terms Stalin's system was 'production for plan rather than use'. Tsipko (1989) goes further: 'Stalin's general policy was not backed by calculations of any sort.'[6]

In the middle of 1929, going all out for rapid heavy industrialization, Stalin ordered that 3400 million roubles be appropriated for capital investments, five times more than the Commissar of Finance, Frumkin, had budgeted for and four times as much as Stalin had demanded earlier (Deutscher, 1968, p. 321). In June, at the Sixteenth Party Congress, Stalin declared, 'We are on the eve of our transformation from an agrarian to an industrial country' and he announced that industry was to raise output by 50 per cent over the year. As Deutscher (1968, p. 322) remarks, this was 'an exertion which really belonged to the realm of super-industrial fantasy.' Commenting on Stalin further, Deutscher adds, 'He seemed to live in a half-real and half-dreamy world of statistical figures and indices of industrial orders and instructions, a world in which no target and no objective seemed to be beyond his and his party's grasp' (ibid.).

By June 1929 (the end of the agricultural year) only 8.3 million tons of grain had been procured, a fall of 2 million tons from 1927–28, only 14.2 per cent of the total harvest compared with 17.6 per cent for the previous year (Siegelbaum, 1992, p. 201). Panic developed in the cities and rationing was introduced as the country reverted to the crisis situation faced in the civil war, before the introduction of the NEP in March 1921. From the middle of 1929 Stalin moved fully to collectivization, sending 'thousands and thousands of agents' to the countryside to force middle peasants into collective farms and (using Stalin's expression) 'to liquidate the Kulaks as a class' (Deutscher, 1968, p. 324).

The peasants reacted by killing their horses and livestock, destroying crops, and leaving land untended. In Stalin's mind horses could be replaced by tractors, and peasants by machinery, but the factories were not there to produce the machines and the raw materials needed for their manufacture were in short supply. As Deutscher (1968, p. 326) comments, 'The whole experiment seemed to be a piece of prodigious insanity, in which all rules of logic and principles of economics were turned upside down.'

The move to forced collectivization severed the Soviet economy from the anchor of the market. As Siegelbaum (1992, p. 213) concludes, 'By 1930, then, the market mechanisms that had mediated if not guided economic decisions throughout NEP had been sundered, driven underground.' By 1930 the labour market had also undergone a radical transformation.

In January 1929 'socialist competition' became the issue of the day – competition, that is, between firms and workers to increase production at reduced costs. Workers were to be enrolled in 'shock brigades' for the purposes of socialist competition. These specially recruited, technically educated workers had achieved particular success in the autumn of 1928. In April 1929 the role of trade unions was changed to that of fighting for labour discipline and productivity. A system of bonuses, rewards and honours was introduced. The dysfunctions produced by these measures were quickly seen: quantity soon outstripped the quality of goods produced; the production figures for factories competing with each other were statistically inflated; workers contrived to be described as 'shock workers' to obtain benefits; and a build-up of resentment between those benefiting and those not benefiting resulted. Further ill-conceived changes in work practices were also introduced as the year went on, such as the three-shift system and the continuous work week. Both underestimated the time needed for machine maintenance and repair. Quantities increased but productivity fell. Worker discipline was also undermined with increasing absenteeism and disruption of processes; the introduction of work on Sundays and during traditional festivities evoked a particularly angry response.[7]

During 1928–29, Stalin also made a 'chance discovery' (Swianiewicz, 1965, p. 214) – the use in the economy of forced labour. In March 1928 a decree had been issued concerning 'a creative use of penal labour' and in an official circular of the Central Executive Committee of the USSR of May 1928 the purpose of this forced labour was expressed: 'to bring about the realization of a series of economic projects with great savings in expenditure …by means of widespread use of labour of individuals sentenced to measures of social protection'. (Documents quoted in Dallin and Nicolaevsky, 1948, p. 206.) In July the Commissariat of Justice made prison work for all able-bodied prisoners compulsory and this was reinforced by the government in January 1929 (ibid.),

Terror as government begins
The decree on dekulakization was formally introduced in early January 1930. In the same month a new law was introduced which for the first time introduced 'exile combined with corrective labour' (Dallin and Nicolaevsky, 1948, p. 40).[8] In 1930 the OGPU established a new department, the Chief Administration of Forced-Labour Camps, the Gulag.

Forced labour and the Gulag
On 7 April 1930 a decree was issued which made it compulsory for anyone sentenced to more than three years, and anyone sentenced by the OGPU for whatever term, to be sent to a 'corrective labour camp'. Whereas in 1926 14.3 per cent of all convictions were to forced labour, in 1929 the level was 48.1 per cent, rising to 56 per cent in 1931 and then 58 per cent in 1932 (Dallin and Nicolaevsky, 1948, p. 207).

An experiment for the wider use of hard labour, in production outside the camp, began in the Solovetsky Camp in 1926.[9] The Solovetsky Camp, the old Solovetsky Monastery used by the Cheka in the civil war, became the central concentration camp of the GPU in 1923 (Dallin and Nicolaevsky, 1948, p. 173). From 1926, extensive labour was used in the camp for lumbering and timber production, quarrying and loading and unloading of ships (ibid., p. 182). Significantly, too, workers were kept on a minimal diet (ibid.).

With Stalin's turn to forced collectivization the experiment at Solovetsky spread. At Solovetsky itself there had been around 4000 prisoners in 1923 and around 7000 in 1925. In 1928 there were over 20 000 (Dallin and Nicolaevsky, 1948, p. 173). In 1929–30 the Solovetsky camps were expanded to cover a stretch of land from the Arctic Ocean in the north to the border with Finland in the west and to the River Suir and Lake Ladoga in the south. By the beginning of 1930 these camps contained over 100 000 prisoners (ibid.). By the middle of the 1930s it has been estimated that the total number of prisoners had reached 662 000, the greatest number of whom were peasants (ibid., p. 190). By 1930 there were five camps in addition to those on the Solovetsky islands: two on other islands in Onega Bay, one near Murmansk, one near Archangel and one in Turkestan (ibid., p. 52). Between 1935 and 1937 it was estimated that there was a total of 35 labour camps (ibid., pp. 58–9).

Forced collectivization and dekulakization
On Soviet estimates, up to 600 000 farms were dekulakized in 1930 and 1931 alone, with over 240 000 of their owner-families deported, perhaps as many as 381 000. Bacon (1994, p. 56) estimates that 1.8 million were exiled to remote regions of the USSR during 1930–31 alone. Figures produced in *Pravda*, September 1988, estimate the entire number of farms collectivized between 1929 and 1933 to have been 1.1 million. (For the above see Viola, 1993, p. 68.)[10] To begin with, those refusing to hand over their farms to collectives were arrested and their families were deported in cattle trucks under GPU guards to the White Sea area where they were billeted with peasants. As the numbers of deportees increased they were housed in barns and as their numbers rose yet higher they lived in holes in the ground, later constructing their own mud huts (Andics, 1969, p. 93). 'Kulak' came to mean

any peasant who tried to resist the collection agents (Lewin, 1985, p. 150). From 1932, the numbers of peasants arrested, dispossessed and exiled escalated, particularly in the Ukraine, the North Caucasus and the Lower and Upper Volga. These deportees were mostly sent to the far north. From January 1933, mass arrests again increased, particularly in the North Caucasus and purges of party members followed (ibid., p. 155).

This increase in arrests followed the introduction, on 7 August 1932, of the law on 'socialist property', signed personally by Stalin. To give it its full title, it was the law 'On the defence of the property of state enterprises, collective farms and cooperatives, and the strengthening of social ownership'. Conviction under this law brought the death penalty, or ten years in prison, which meant forced labour (Bacon, 1994, p. 51). The accusation of 'theft', even of small items, could result in the harshest of punishments and as the USSR entered a severe famine, following the disastrous harvest in July, the cruelty of this law struck hard. Some 55 000 people were arrested under the law before six months were out (ibid.). Exile for their families soon followed.

Initial makeshift arrangements for deportees gave way to a scheme for exiles to Siberia to develop nearly a million acres of land into collectives, 'special settlements', to provide food for the towns and cites. As Andics (1969, p. 93) comments, 'In practice these Siberian collectives, like the other deportee settlements in thinly populated parts of the country, were simply forced labour camps'. The exact figures on deaths resulting from the journey and labour exploitation can never be calculated precisely. Comparing all the existing figures, Rummel estimates that during the collectivization period, put as 1929–35, around 1 400 000 died as a consequence of deportations and 3 306 000 died in the camps or in transit to them. The range, respectively, is 985 000 to 2 863 000 and 1 566 000 to 6 426 000 (Rummel, 1990, p. 95). Crucially during these years the forced-labour camp system was developed, expanded and established.

Mass society versus economic crisis
On Arendt's analysis, dekulakization began the first of three stages to turn the Soviet Union deliberately into a mass society; it was the necessary condition, 'the absence of classes', for terror as government. This was done, she argues, 'through artificial famine and deportation' with dekulakization and collectivization a 'pretext' (Arendt, 1958, p. 320). Recent evidence, however, has challenged such a view in two ways. First, it widens the group of those terrorized to suggest not only the greater importance of the prior existence of a society dislocated by war, revolution, civil war and famine but also the significance of scapegoating at the local level. Second, recent evidence supports the argument that actions undertaken were in direct response to economic chaos.

On Viola's analysis the clearest victims of repression in the countryside were *byvshie liudi*, people who 'were tied in the popular mind to the political, social or economic system of the ancien regime' (Viola, 1993, p. 70). These included noble landowners, wealthy farmers (kulaks), church elders, owners of land or enterprises of any kind, tsarist officers, cossacks, pre-revolutionary officials and village elders and, in general, members of any groups who had opposed the Bolsheviks in either the revolution or the civil war. Such group- ings included not only white army officers and sometimes soldiers, but also past members of political oppositions such as Socialist Revolutionaries (ibid.).

The classification as a kulak was based not on a precise, legalistic defini- tion but on the basis of social status both before and after the revolution (Viola, 1993, p. 73). Viola argues that at the start of the forced collectiviza- tion campaign the state launched an attack on the *byvshie liudi* 'in an attempt to find convenient scapegoats for the country's grain difficulties' (ibid., p. 71). These were not, however, the only groups which suffered repression. Others targeted, particularly after 1932, were families or individuals who, for one reason or another, were unable to contribute fully to the collective farm. These included the old, the sick, the families of exiled kulaks and Red Army families. It is worth noting that the state was opposed to these persecutions (ibid., pp. 90–93).[11]

The economic crisis which hit the USSR in 1929 with a serious shortage of grain was compounded by each act of collectivization, but as we have seen, the crisis to which forced collectivization was Stalin's wild response was real enough. As Lewin (1985, p. 98) argues, 'the decision to undertake overall collectivization had its roots in the "grain crisis" at the beginning of 1928'. As Nove (1993c, p. 35) comments, 'no one doubts that the motive (or the princi- pal motive) of collectivization was to mobilise a larger agricultural surplus'. Stalin's choice had been coercion and severance from the market.

Following a disastrous harvest in 1932, the Soviet Union suffered a famine of enormous proportions in 1933. Figures recently released, based on the 1939 census data, indicate that the death rate rose from an average of around 20 per 1000 per year in 1925 (at 20.5 in 1932) to 37.7 per 1000 in 1933. This represents around 2.75–3.0 million excess deaths for the year. This was also accompanied by a dramatic fall in the birth rate (Wheatcroft, 1993, pp. 279– 80). The areas worst affected were the Ukraine, where deaths were over three times the 1930 and 1931 levels, an area of the Lower Volga and the North Caucasus. By comparison Moscow and Leningrad fared better, with deaths approximating normal levels.[12] As Viola (1993, p. 75) comments wryly, 'As may be expected, the dangers of the class enemy in those years were per- ceived to be the most acute in the famine-stricken areas of the North Cauca- sus and the Ukraine, thereby indicating the extent to which this wave of repression was an exercise in scapegoating.'

Labour shortages and labour controls
Stalin's move to heavy industrialization required large numbers of industrial workers. In October 1930 the Commissariat of Labour ordered, 'in view of the great shortage of labour', that unemployment benefits be cut. (See Dallin and Nicolaevsky, 1948, p. 194.) Under the Five-Year Plan the state would be responsible for directing all the country's resources, including labour. At a conference in November 1930, the deputy minister for labour declared that 'the words "labour exchange" and "labour market" should be finally driven out of our vocabulary' (Davies, 1993, p. 41). In December a decree was issued against workers who deserted their jobs or changed jobs frequently to improve their working conditions. A series of decrees followed, restricting workers' freedom to change jobs.

In December 1932 internal passports were introduced in which every job undertaken had to be entered. In this way workers' movements were controlled. Crucially, collectivization also provided the means for controlling the supply of rural labour into industry. Under contracts the collectives were obliged to supply workers to the Labour Department agents. Failure to do so resulted in compulsion by the GPU (Dallin and Nicolaevsky, 1948, pp. 196–8). In 1931 alone 4.1 million peasants moved to the cities, as well as seasonal workers, with or without contracts (Lewin, 1985, p. 219). All this movement, which, as Ordzhonikidze exclaimed at the time, turned the country into one big 'nomadic gypsy camp', not only added to social dislocation but also increased worker indiscipline (see ibid., p. 221).

Labour shortages were a particular problem in the building industries and the lumber industry (Dallin and Nicolaevsky, 1948, p. 197). Davies (1993, p. 63) describes the shortages of labour in industry from 1931 as 'endemic'. In 1930, 1 700 000 extra workers were required in the northern lumber industry. The collectives were to provide 900 000 (Dallin and Nicolaevsky, 1948, p. 198). Of these only 50 000 were recruited within the week allowed. These were the circumstances which led to labour control and the discovery that forced labour in camps was ideally suited to Stalin's plans. On Dallin and Nicolaevsky's (1948, p. 199) argument, 'the great network of labour camps emerged as a function of industrialization and the Five-Year Plans.' What was crucial was that Stalin's mind was set on the use of forced labour, and by 1934, irrespective of any dysfunctional consequences, forced labour was intrinsic to the Soviet economic system (ibid., pp. 251–2).

As a solution to the needs of the northern lumber industries the required 1 300 000 workers were obtained, consisting of a small minority of voluntary labourers, and the remainder made up of peasants forcibly recruited for seasonal work, exiled peasants deported to the north but not living in the prisons, and inmates of corrective labour camps and prisons (ibid., p. 202). Under the Gulag system 'hundreds of thousands of kulaks and "wreckers" were turned into lumberjacks by the GPU' (Dallin and Nicolaevsky, 1948, p. 210). The work of the Solovetsky camps expanded into mining, producing coal, lead, zinc and fluorite, and the workforce then began the construction of canals and railways (ibid., pp. 212–15). In 1933 gold mining began in the Kolyma region of Siberia. The number of labour camps in this region grew rapidly.

With collectivization effectively completed, in July 1934 the OGPU was replaced by the new People's Commissariat for Internal Affairs, the NKVD. On 27 October, by decree, all 'places of detention' were transferred to the NKVD (Dallin and Nicolaevsky, 1948, pp. 249–50). The administration of the 'corrective labour camps' under the Gulag remained, as too did the centrality to the whole system of the use of forced labour. The exiles' camps, developed under dekulakization, were also brought under the Gulag's control (Bacon, 1994, p. 56).

Notes

1. In the civil war, armies were led against the Bolsheviks from Siberia, the south, the north-west and from Poland (Bradley, 1975, p. 55). Battles were particularly severe in the Ukraine, Siberia, the Cossack territories and the Tambov provinces to the south-east of Moscow, where rebellions against grain extraction were especially strong (ibid., pp. 163–4). For estimates of deaths in each area, see Leggett (1981, Appendix C).

2. Under war communism a revolutionary tax was developed, calculated on the basis of assessed family need, and everything above this level was requisitioned. Initially it was levied in money and later in kind. This 'tax in kind' was accompanied by price-fixing which, in turn, gave rise to rationing (ibid., pp. 248–50). From the end of 1918 collective farms began to be set up. In industry, with nationalization completed by the end of 1918, wage-fixing began in February 1919. Over 1919 labour conscription developed for both peasants and industrial workers (Malle, 1985, p. 479). During the civil war, the threat of starvation led workers to take flight from the cities (see Brower, 1989). By 1920, rationing gave way to wages in kind and a money economy effectively ceased to exist. Inflation by July 1921 was such that, in real terms, money was worth just over 1 per cent of what it had been worth in November 1917 (Carr, 1966, vol. 2, p. 259).

3. It was the young workers of urban origin who introduced new methods of work. These workers, termed 'core workers', usually Komsomol members, were chosen for education in the engineering schools. One of these workers was Stakhanov. Komsomol 'shock' brigades first appeared in 1926–27, demonstrating how strict discipline and a change in old work practices towards rationalization could achieve increased production (Siegelbaum, 1992, p. 209).

4. Collection was a particular problem in Siberia, the Urals, the Volga regions and the North Caucasus, but not in the Ukraine, and in the central region grain procurement in October–December actually went up on the year before (Siegelbaum, 1992, p. 192).

5. Deutscher (1968, p. 322) argues that the immediate cause of Stalin's move into collectivization was the serious danger of famine which threatened in 1928 and 1929.

6. For these two quotations see Daniels (1993, pp. 90 and 91).

7. For the above see Siegelbaum (1992, pp. 211–13). The three-shift system of production did not survive past 1932 (Siegelbaum, 1992, p. 213).

8. A further decree was issued by the Central Committee in March (Dallin and Nicolaevsky, 1948, p. 40). Essentially dekulakization involved expropriation of property and expulsion from the village. The sentence of 'exile' meant being sent to a specific place in a far distant area. Within the assigned locality the exile was, however, free to move around and seek employment. Exile did not involve sentencing to a prison camp.

9. According to Dallin and Nicolaevsky (1948, p. 181) this experiment was initiated by an inmate, Frenkel, but Bacon (1994, p. 46) has questioned this.

10. On Swianiewicz's (1965, p. 88) estimates there were just over 1 million peasant farms drawn into collectives at the beginning of June 1929; by 20 January 1930 the number of peasant holdings collectivized had reached nearly 4.4 million and by 1 March 1930 they had reached 14 264 300. The recent figures reported by Viola clearly constitute a radical reduction in estimates. Conquest (1971, p. 324) estimated the total number of kulak families to have approximated 10 million people. For comparisons of estimates of earlier works see Rummel (1990, pp. 81–108). Danilov (*Pravda*, 16 September 1988) calculates that a total of 1.1 million households were wiped out in the process of dekulakization (see Nove, 1993c, p. 36). Most of these deaths occurred during transportation (unheated cattle trucks) and in the harsh conditions of the deportation areas; others (a minority) occurred in prison or in the labour camps. Many victims suffered under the cruel decree of 1932, at the onset of famine, which punished theft of 'socialist property' such as grain needed for survival (ibid., p. 37). For further discussion of figures see Ward (1993, pp. 60–61).

11. Viola argues that those picked on fell within the traditional categories of scapegoats in peasant villages in times of crisis: 'The images of the enemy hatched in the minds of peasant officials may have been glossed over with a thin veneer of Marxist–Leninist vocabulary, but their construction was in fact determined less by ideology or state edict than by social realities and battles far older than the Revolution of 1917' (Viola, 1993, p. 97).

12. Wheatcroft (1993, p. 284) finds no clear general pattern of difference between the impact of famine on rural and urban areas or for particular nationalities, though evidence on Kazakhstan is not available in the census.

6   Substantive irrationality and terror under Stalin

In the Stalinist system the accused appeared only rarely before a court of law. Most were sentenced by a committee of the NKVD 'Special Board'. The Special Board (or Special Tribunal) was put in place in 1934 in accordance with the laws of 10 July and 5 November (Conquest, 1990, p. 284). Initially sentences were limited to five years but soon terms of eight or ten years were being imposed. Arbitrariness was a feature of the accusations, as was 'wrecking', essentially circumstantial: a 'non-informer' or an eavesdropper to a conversation seen to smile at the wrong point could also be sent to a labour camp, as could a member of the family of the accused, simply for being related, or equally someone with a past association. Arbitrariness also featured in sentencing; at the end of a Board sentence the prisoner could simply be resentenced. Indeed, the Special Board was given exactly those 'cases for which the evidence was not sufficient for turning the defendant over to a court' and the accused had neither right to defence nor to appeal. Cases were either tried in absentia or in groups at a time. Furthermore, though strictly charges were brought under article 50 of the criminal code, this code was interpreted in the broadest ways. For example a professor whose single offence was to have been a prisoner of war in Austria in 1915 was sentenced under 'suspicion of espionage', and this was a typical case. (For the above see ibid., pp. 284–6 and Gregor, 1982, p. 161.)

On 30 July 1937, though never formally announced, new 'Troikas' were put into operation with Ezhov and the Prosecutor-General, Vyshinsky, at the centre. Under a veneer of legality, Vyshinsky operated terror. The Troikas were established all over the Soviet Union with the local NKVD chief as chairman. As with the Special Board, defendants were not necessarily present at the proceedings. Forty per cent of all cases were held in absentia and in the remaining, the appearance of the accused averaged only three minutes, The Troikas could impose the death penalty and they did so on a grand scale. (For the above see Conquest, 1990, p. 286 and Bacon, 1994, p. 53.)

The Stakhanovite movement
The years 1934–36 saw noticeable improvements in the Soviet economy (see Ward, 1993, p. 83) and the view held generally (Manning, 1992, p. 138) is that during these years Stalin used the Stakhanovite movement to destroy working-class solidarity. This is important to Arendt's position which is that

having destroyed the peasant class, Stalin's next step in the creation of a mass society was the destruction of the working class through the Stakhanovite movement which broke up all solidarity and class consciousness through 'ferocious competition' and the (temporary) creation of a 'Stakhanovite aristocracy' (Arendt, 1958, p. 321). Again, however, analyses based on evidence only recently made available have seriously undermined this view in two ways. First, the movement set not workers against other workers, but workers against management, and indeed, rather than destroying collective interests, the movement asserted workers' over managers' interests. Second, the Stakhanovite movement sought to redress existing problems in the economy and in that sense was utilitarian. The substantive irrationality of the Soviet economic system at the time, however, served to ensure that the new Stakhanovite methods made the economy's problems even worse.

Begun by the worker Stakhanov, the Stakhanovite movement developed dramatically in the autumn of 1935 and spread throughout industry and agriculture (Manning, 1992, p. 138). The problems which the movement sought to overcome were the shortages of skilled workers and foremen, the high turnover of labour, production 'bottlenecks', shortages of equipment, materials and transport, problems in relations between workers and managers and the irrationality of production for output's sake at any cost (Thurston, 1993, p. 143).

The Stakhanovite movement was approved by the government because it was expected to increase productivity by encouraging workers to employ new techniques and technology and to make other workers and managers adopt these new methods. From the end of 1935 to 1937 Stakhanovism was promoted by the government in the form of increasing work norms, the incentive of increased pay differentials and the introduction of self-financing and accountability in a good proportion of heavy industry, state farms and the machine tractor stations (Manning, 1992, p. 138).

According to Thurston (1993, p. 44) the Stakhanovite workers did not constitute a new 'labour aristocracy' with their own exclusive interests, but represented and voiced the common interests of workers against those of managers and bosses, demanding better pay for themselves and lower pay for their bosses, and better management and technicians to ensure supplies of materials so that the workers could carry out their duties. Demands and suggestions were made by the Stakhanovites to the managers, rather than the other way around, and managers' duties were to ensure the supply of materials and tools required by the workers. In some situations the role of managers and technicians became more like that of servants at the workers' beck and call. In one locomotive factory, for example, the Stakhanovites could raise a small flag and the foremen had to attend to their needs (ibid., p. 148). Any shortages of materials and equipment which slowed the workers down were blamed on the management. Seeing the increased incomes and other benefits which Stakhanovite workers gained, other workers wanted to share those benefits and blamed managers for failing to supply the tools and other resources needed if the new norms were to be achieved. When managers and technical staff succeeded in complying with demands suspicions grew over why these new techniques had not been introduced before (ibid., pp. 146–7). Given the extra responsibilities which managers and technicians had, and the years of training in engineering which many of them had undergone, the situation was ripe for friction and resentment.

The increased outputs achieved by the Stakhanovite workers and their new techniques soon, however, hit a number of serious problems relating to diseconomies of scale. In addition, supplies were insufficient, made worse by the demands of the movement and the lack of synchronization between industries. The initiatives produced by pay differentials also added to the problem of labour shortages as workers moved from plant to plant, thereby destroying any remaining chances of factories achieving their goals (Thurston, 1993, p. 153). Lying became endemic. 'Wrecking' was used as an excuse for failure to achieve norms and false accounting was employed to adjust true figures. Managers developed the phrase, 'It's necessary not to work well but to account well' (ibid., p. 154). In this way, an economy calculated entirely on outputs came to have at its disposal only figures with little bearing on reality. This problem was further exacerbated by the target-setting itself being 'talked up' by the production figures available. The economy plummeted into economic crisis – a crisis which was deepened by the further repercussions of the Stakhanovite movement.

As a direct result of the Stakhanovite movement the cost of labour increased. This led the government to raise work norms both in industry and in the machine tractor stations in March 1936 and May 1937, which, in turn, reduced the chances of plant targets being met and put the blame for the shortfall on 'wreckers'. These new work norms could be anything from 14 to 50 per cent higher than previous ones and, not surprisingly, from 9.6 to 44.9 per cent of workers (these percentages differing according to the industry) failed to fulfil their quotas. As a result of these new norms workers suffered cuts in their wages and were turned against managers and technicians for introducing the new targets. (For the above see Manning, 1992, pp. 138–9.)

The number of Stakhanovites dropped and, as they forfeited their Stakhanovite status, their bonuses and perks were lost (Manning, 1992, p. 139). As Manning (ibid.) comments, 'no wonder that charges of wrecking, particularly wrecking the work of Stakhanovites, proliferated each time the work norms were revised upward'. Even with the benefit of *glasnost*, information on the fate of the Stakhanovites and other workers accused of wrecking is as yet inadequate (Thurston, 1993, p. 155). What is clear is that by 1937 the number of people killed in the terror machine reached a peak.

The Great Purges

On Arendt's (1958, p. 321) argument, the third stage of Stalin's deliberate creation of a mass society was the assault on the bureaucracy in the purges of 1936–38. On her account, 'it took Stalin about two years from 1936, to rid himself of the whole administrative and military aristocracy of the Soviet Society' (ibid.). The Great Purges, Great Terror, or 'Ezhovshchina' – as the period is also known after Ezhov who replaced Yagoda as head of the NKVD in September 1936 – have recently raised new controversy. As with interpretations of collectivization and the Stakhanovite movement, this controversy has been revived by new data released as a consequence of *glasnost*. General agreement, hitherto, has held that the Old Bolsheviks were singled out in the Terror. (See, for example, Deutscher, 1968, and Conquest, 1971, 1990.) This view is clearly supported by the show trials. (For details see also Vaksberg, 1990.) Friedrich and Brzezinski (1965) stress that these purges were directed at the Communist Party itself. The purge of the NKVD, when Beria replaced Ezhov in 1938, is also emphasized by Conquest (1971, pp. 275 and 623). In general the view held is that the élite of the Soviet Union, whether intellectuals, educators, managers, technocrats, party officials or administrators of all organizations (including the army as well as the NKVD) suffered the greatest repression in these years (Getty and Chase, 1993, p. 228).

Data on this period remain far from complete, but using the statistical evidence recently made available in a comparison of the vulnerability of élite groups, Getty and Chase (1993, pp. 231–5) have shown that the average age of those purged was actually lower (by three years) than of those who survived the Terror, that those of peasant origin were relatively more likely to be purged than those of urban origin, and the less educated, not the educated intelligentsia, suffered more. Evidence does, though, confirm that party members suffered significantly more than non-party members. By no means all Old Bolsheviks, the 'Leninist Guard', however, were purged. Significantly those who joined the party after 1917 and in particular after the civil war were relatively 'safe' (ibid., p. 236). The evidence also shows that vulnerability ran in direct proportion with seniority in the bureaucracy (ibid., p. 237). However, it is clear that whilst those working in the creative arts and scientific research were relatively safe, those working in the economic administration, the central party and state apparatus (with the exception of foreign affairs) and the military were the most vulnerable (ibid., p. 239). Getty and Chase conclude that 'chaos', terror running out of control, also played a crucial part in 1936–37 and they therefore reject any simple, single causal explanation for the Ezhovshchina (ibid., p. 245). This view has been supported by the analysis of events and documents undertaken by Getty (1993).

The general portrayal of Stalin's planned terror is that it began in late 1934 with the assassination of Kirov, followed by the party purges of 1935, the show trials of Zinoviev and Kamenev in 1936, of Piatkov and Radek in January 1937, the purge of the Red Army in mid-1937 and finally the trial of Bukharin and Radek in 1938. This picture of planned terror, Getty argues, is not borne out by deeper analysis of the evidence. Rather, he argues, the evidence suggests chaos, with Stalin 'zig-zagging' between terror and anti-terror until 1937. Although the evidence is consistent with Stalin clearly supporting the Terror from February 1937 it also supports the view of Ezhov pursuing initiatives which Stalin endorsed (ibid., p. 55). As will be seen in the analysis of Germany to follow, there are parallels here with the relationship between Hitler and Himmler.

The figures
In spite of the recent release of statistics from the Soviet archives on the Terror, controversy over the figures remains. For example, Conquest (1990, pp. 484–9), has reaffirmed his original 'approximations' for 1937–38: 7 million arrests, 1 million executions (mostly by shooting), 2 million camp deaths; this gives about 8 million in the camps at the end of 1938. Nove, in contrast, records the number of shootings following the trials and Special Tribunals as 353 074 in 1937 and 328 618 in 1938 and a total for 1939 of 3 593 000 in NKVD prisons, camps and colonies with 1 360 000 of these in Gulag camps themselves (Nove, 1993a, pp. 270–71). There is no dispute, however, that deaths reached their peak in the years of the Great Purges. Nove's figures on deaths added together for 1937 and 1938 amount to more than the total for the remaining years 1931–53 (ibid.). Thurston (1993, p. 155) confirms that sentencing for 'counter revolutionary crimes' (under article 58) reached a peak in 1938 at 34.5 per cent. What is in dispute is the numbers held within the terror system.[1]

The new evidence suggests that the number of people detained within the Gulag camps was at its peak not during the Ezhovshchina, but in the early 1950s. (See Nove, 1993a, p. 270, Table 13.2; Wheatcroft, 1993, p. 277 and Bacon, 1994, p. 24.) The fact that the highest number of inmates in the NKVD system was found at the end of Stalin's years directs attention away from a purely political explanation for the Stalinist system towards one which, again, stresses the importance of chronic economic crisis.

The depth of economic crisis
In mid- to late 1936, the high economic growth rates reported in the years 1934–36 gave way to what Jasny has termed a 'snail-like crawl, stagnation and even declines' (Jasny, 1961, p. 177, quoted in Manning, 1992, p. 116).[2] Following impressive achievements in industrial production in 1934 and 1935, Stalin and other leaders such as Molotov, Kalinin and the People's Commissar of Agriculture, Chernov, spoke openly and often of the expecta-

tion of 'great breakthroughs' and 'miracles' in the economy (Manning, 1992, p. 128). Indeed, these phrases were used by Stalin at the February–March 1937 Central Committee Plenum in the only major speech that he made during the Great Purges (ibid., p. 139, fn. 69).

With the Ezhovshchina taking place from September 1936 to 1938, this sudden change of economic pace has generally been put down to the effects of the Great Purges, aimed as they were at managers, engineers, technicians and administrators at both national and local levels. Based on fresh evidence, however, Manning (1992) has argued that the sharp drop in industrial production was as much a cause of the purges as their consequence.

Before Kamenev and Zinoviev were arrested in June 1936, the event which signalled the start of the purges, and before Ezhov was appointed head of the NKVD in September 1936, the economy was already entering acute crisis. In the Donbas region production of coal set at a record output in December 1935 by Stakhanovite methods, declined month after month all through 1936 and through much of 1937. For the economy as a whole coal production, which had reached 109.6 million metric tons at 1 January 1935 and 126.8 million metric tons by 1 January 1936, had only increased to 128 million metric tons by 1 January 1937; iron ore production had remained static between January 1936 and January 1937 and declined from then on. Timber fell from 5872 million metric tons in January 1936 to 5454 million metric tons in January 1937. With the high expectations set by output levels in 1935 built into the output targets for 1936, these slowdowns and shortfalls were doubly damaging. Without high growth in these essential fuel and construction materials, the projected expansion of the economy would be impossible. By the end of 1936 the effects of these shortages for the wider economy could clearly be seen. (For the above see Manning, 1992, pp. 125–7.) It is Manning's (ibid., p. 117) argument that 'these economic difficulties contributed substantially to the terror'.

The mass arrests in the summer of 1936 were directed at left oppositionists and their present and past associates but Manning (1992, p. 117) argues that by this time such people had ceased to hold positions of real influence either in government or in the economy. From 26 September 1936 the purges changed. Following the Kemerovo Coal Mine explosion three days earlier, Ezhov, head of the Party Control Commission and of the Industrial Department of the Central Committee, was installed by Stalin as the head of the NKVD. Ezhov was someone who 'tended to heed worker complaints against managers and regard economic troubles as manifestations of wrecking' (ibid., p. 139). Ezhov had himself worked in the Putilov armaments factory before the outbreak of World War I (Starkov, 1993, p. 21). Under Ezhov, the Terror expanded increasingly to include industrial managers, engineers and administrators. The main accusation against the victims of the Great Purges also changed from conspiracy to kill Soviet leaders to economic sabotage – 'wrecking' (ibid., p. 117).

Through 1937, as economic problems grew worse, similar charges were also brought against administrators of agriculture and Communist Party leaders in charge of overseeing the economy at the provincial and district level. Manning (ibid., p. 118) quotes Zaleski (1980, pp. 248–9) at length on the accusations levelled at the trials:

> ...the chronic defects of the Stalinist planning system were simply presented as sabotage: incorrect use of equipment, failure to carry out capital repairs, reluctance to introduce new techniques, delays in installations of imported equipment, ordering equipment not corresponding to needs, failure to declare real productive capacities, frequent changing and poor drafting of specifications, dispersion of resources on multiple construction projects, extension of construction schedules, reduction of investment efficiency, disproportions among various workshops and putting into operation blast furnaces not completely finished.

Zaleski (ibid.) concludes: 'these facts appear to be confirmed and indisputable. The accusations of sabotage and the language of repression, however, make it impossible to discuss true responsibility'.

What is notable here is not simply that economic sabotage and 'wrecking' came to form such an important basis of accusation against victims but that the accusers may well have believed such accusations to be genuine. Today the inefficiencies of centrally planned systems are recognized but in the 1930s the system was relatively new and against the evidence of the recent high production growth rates, the sharply reduced growth rates experienced in 1936 lent themselves to a conspiratorial explanation. With the upheavals in Russia's recent history – revolution, civil war, collectivization, famine – willingness to accept ideas of conspiracies and sabotage could be easily understood. Indeed, there is evidence that the entire Soviet system in the 1930s was gripped by a feeling of 'omnipresent conspiracy' (Rittersporn, 1993, p. 99).

Secrecy as policy: the harvest of 1936 and 1937
Lying behind these feelings of conspiracy was secrecy. The harvest for 1936 was as poor as the 1932 harvest which had led to the famine of 1932–33. In practice, the Soviet government coped well, using food reserves to bring famine relief and making loans for animal feeds to collective farms on very reasonable terms. Nevertheless, food was in short supply and in the industrial areas bread rationing was introduced. In the Donbas coal-mining region both the quality and quantity of food supplies became so low that by the end of 1936, 450 of the region's 860 workplace canteens were closed. As discontent grew so too did fears for the outbreak of rebellion. (For the above see Manning, 1992, p. 123.)

What was extraordinary was that the 1936 harvest failure was kept secret. Only in retrospect was the harvest discussed in the press which, at the time, was full of Stakhanovite achievements in areas such as the Ukraine, where crop failure did not occur (Manning, 1992, p. 121). Reports of shortages in 1936 were kept back for a year and then combined with the reports of the 1937 harvest, which was exceptionally high (*Pravda*, 21 August 1937 and 24 August 1937; see ibid., p. 123, fn. 25). Animal deaths from malnutrition and disease were blaimed on provincial and district party leaders and local and national agricultural administrators who were reported as having 'wrecked' the collective farms by deliberately infecting the animals with diseases.

Discontent was real enough in 1936, but shortages could be coped with, just, through the use of existing reserves, but if the 1937 harvest proved little or no better or even worse than the 1936 harvest then the economic crisis threatened to become so severe that the resulting discontent would be uncontainable. Even after it became clear how good the 1937 harvest was, worries expressed in the press about the 1937 harvest were far greater than they had been for the really disastrous 1936 harvest (Manning, 1992, pp. 125–6, fn. 32). Blame had to fall somewhere. From June 1937, it fell on local government officials and administrators and specialists within the Commissariat of Agriculture. As Manning (1992, p. 124) explains,

> Policy makers, administrators, and specialists responsible for policies and practices that contributed to the short 1936 harvest – like the absence of any crop rotation whatsoever on most collective farms, the chronic inability of the MTSs [machine tractor stations] to balance their account books and keep their tractors and combines in working order, and foul-ups in the production and distribution of selected seeds – began to be arrested en masse for wrecking agriculture and/or creating food shortages in order to increase popular discontent against the government.

The pattern of the purges in 1937 followed that set by events in the Ukraine and Northern Caucasus.

The Donbas region

The Donbas, or Donets Basin, which covered the Donets region of the Ukrainian Republic and the Northern Caucasus of the Russian Republic, was an area which suffered particularly badly both in the Ezhovshchina and before. The Donbas was the main coal-producing area and also the area which was particularly hard hit by shortages. The fact that Soviet economic expansion was so dependent on coal combined with the civil war history of the area offer the key to the particularly high level of repression found in the region.

The Donbas produced 77.3 per cent of the country's coal in 1929 which by 1938 had gone down to 60.8 per cent (Kuromiya, 1993, p. 216). The area was also badly scarred in the civil war, with terror perpetrated by both Reds and Whites and even in the years of the NEP, show trials of 'wreckers' from the mines had taken place. 'The Shakty Affair', the arrest and trial of 53 mining engineers from Shakty in the eastern part of the Donbas in 1928, led, by mid-1931, to the arrest of over half the Donbas engineers and technicians. The area as a whole was hit gravely by collectivization and dekulakization leading to dispossession, deportation and execution of peasants. During the famine of 1932–33 the population of the area suffered extremely harsh punishments.

Following the slump in coal production and the effects of the Stakhanovite movement, between the summer of 1936 and the autumn of 1938 arrests, deportations and executions reached their peak. Of the 76 members of the Obkom in May 1937 only six remained by June 1938 (Kuromiya, 1993, p. 218). In September 1937, Kaganovich, the People's Commissar of Heavy Industry, went personally to visit the trusts and mines in the Donbas to expose 'wrecking activities' and went back to the area again in May and June of 1938 to 'unmask' these 'enemies', 'wreckers' and 'saboteurs' (ibid., p. 20). With members expelled from the party at such a high rate and engineers and managers arrested in such alarming quantities, criticisms of the excessive use of repression appeared in *Pravda* in 1936 and 1937 (Manning, 1992, p. 124, fn. 28).

In 1936, in addition to production shortages, a disastrous harvest and a slowdown in economic growth, Russia's economic crisis was heightened further by the pressure of increasing military expenditure.

Military expenditure and the official purge
From the middle of the 1930s the economy became burdened by military expansion. Down from 5.5 million troops at the end of the civil war, the armed forces stood at 562 000 between 1924 and March 1934. At 1 January 1935 the number had jumped to 940 000, a year later to 1.3 million and 1.433 million by 1 January 1937.[3] As a percentage of the total government budget, defence expenditure had fallen between 1929 and 1933. In 1934 defence expenditure (at 9 per cent) came close to its 1928–29 level of 10.2 per cent and continued to increase from then on. At 11.1 per cent in 1935, it jumped to 16.1 per cent in 1936, reaching 18.7 per cent in 1938 and jumping again as war broke out, with the figure at 32.5 per cent in 1940. Overall Soviet military expenditure was four times greater by 1940 than it had been in 1936. This was not expenditure according to plan. Planned defence expenditure for the year 1936 in the official second Five-Year Plan was 4.3 billion roubles; actual expenditure was 20.2 billion roubles, still wildly above the 14.9 billion roubles listed at the beginning of 1936. (See Manning, 1992, p. 135, fn. 58.)

As defence expenditure rose as a percentage of the budget in the 1930s so investment fell. With investment at its peak in 1932 at 65.2 per cent, by 1936 it was down to 45.3 per cent and 33.4 per cent by 1940. (For the above see Manning, 1992, Tables 5.9–5.11.) The effects on the economy of the slowdown in output of essential materials for industrial production which hit Russia at the end of 1935 were exacerbated once the armed forces and armaments industries took prior claim over civilian industries. Military needs also took priority over the already overstretched transport system (Manning, 1992, p. 135). With too many people chasing too few goods inflation escalated.[4] Declining terms of trade on the world market also reduced the quantity of imports that the Soviet Union could trade for exports in 1936 and 1937 (ibid., p. 129).

The growth in military expenditure was itself a reaction to international developments. War threatened on both the Asian and European borders, from Japan in Manchuria and Germany and Italy respectively (ibid., pp. 136-7). The fear of foreign enemies added to the general feeling of conspiracy already present at home. With war threatening, one of the mysteries of the Stalinist era has always been the decision to purge the military on the eve of the outbreak of war.

The purge of the military has been seen as an event which supports the view that the primary aim of policy was to construct a mass society. Recent evidence challenges this view. Rather than the estimates of up to 50 per cent for officers purged in 1938, the figure was actually around 7.7 per cent. Significantly, too, of the total 34 301 military personnel arrested and expelled from the force by May 1940, 11 596 were later reinstated, though not usually to the same rank. In total, 22 705 (13 000 of these from the army) were executed, sent to the Gulag or dismissed from the army in disgrace. (For the above see Reese, 1993, p. 213.) Although the incidence of purging is reduced on this evidence, judged in terms of loss of experience these military purges remain irrational. Nevertheless, the fact that a significant proportion of personnel were reinstated undermines the image of the total destruction of a potential power group and puts the events rather more in line with the wider purging of engineers and managers as saboteurs in 1938.

The military reinstatements went some way to correct the excesses of the Ezhovshchina (ibid., p. 214). After 1938, and the dismissal of Ezhov, hardly any repression took place within the military (ibid.). Furthermore, in contradiction of the image of the destruction of social networks within the army, the evidence suggests that the greatest protection against denunciation was achieved exactly where groups had strong group ties: 'Our party group held together. We did not look for "enemies of the people" among ourselves and firmly resisted all attacks from outside'; 'Now these are fine communists in the cavalry section! A close-knit bunch, they held together'. (Comments made by officers quoted by Reese, 1993, p. 208.)

From war to Stalin's end: forced labour and the growth in camps

With the replacement of Ezhov by Beria, the number of executions fell sharply but regulations on worker absenteeism, lateness and so on became more punitive and a new kind of camp appeared especially for workers who broke labour regulations. These camps were located all over the Soviet Union rather than concentrated in the remoter areas where the forced-labour camps were located. Mostly sentences of one year were imposed. This new, harsher legislation began to be imposed in 1940 (Swianiewicz, 1965, pp. 155–6). In June 1940 a decree introduced the seven-day working week and along with it harsh new laws on worker absenteeism and indiscipline. Under this decree arrival at work more than 20 minutes late became a criminal offence. By the beginning of January 1941, under this decree alone, 28 995 people had been sent to the Gulag (Bacon, 1994, p. 51).

From 1940 non-Russians came to form an increasingly large proportion of the labour camp inmates. First Poles, Balts and Bessarabians then, during the war, Germans, Italians, Rumanians, Hungarians and Japanese. Ukrainians, Tartars and other non-Russian Soviet citizens also formed a growing proportion (Dallin and Nicolaevsky, 1948, p. 263). Members of nationalities viewed as a threat to national security were arrested under the NKVD decree of June 1941 (Bacon, 1994, p. 145). Deportations began with Poles in 1940. Train- and truck-loads of people, grabbed from the streets by agents of the NKVD, were taken to north and east Russia. Around 25 per cent of these were sentenced to labour camps, the rest to special settlements (Dallin and Nicolaevsky, 1948, p. 263). With the outbreak of war with Germany in 1941, these 'deportations' became 'a repetition of the mass deportation of kulaks in the early thirties with all the ominous consequences' (ibid., p. 277). For example, from Crimea every Crimean Tartar was exiled (Nove, 1993a, p. 273). As these new prisoners were added to the camps, so prisoners were being 'released' into the army.

Bacon (1994, p. 103) estimates that during the first three years of the war an additional 1.8 million people entered the camps and colonies while 2.9 million were removed, around 1 million of these being due to death in the camps and a further 1 million due to transfer into the army. Some nationalities, for example, Poles, Czechs and Slovaks, were also released and some prisoners, under the cloak of war, managed to escape.

At the end of the war, large numbers of new forced labourers were sentenced to the labour camps, with large numbers of German and Japanese prisoners of war among them. They were set to a variety of work including cutting trees, building concrete coastal fortifications, ammunition stores and rebuilding factories and other buildings destroyed in the war (Dallin and Nicolaevsky, 1948, p. 278). The Russian workers and prisoners of war returning from Germany were 'screened' by the NKVD in verification and filtration camps. Nearly 80 per cent were sent to forced labour (Bacon, 1994, pp. 94–5). Some were given 15 to 25 years of 'corrective labour'; others were sent off to hard labour. All were categorized as 'socially dangerous' (Dallin and Nicolaevsky, 1948, p. 293). A purge of Soviet officials also took place in August 1946.

The Five-Year Plan for 1946–50, designed for economic reconstruction, again produced wild targets. As Dallin and Nicolaevsky (1948, p. 298) concluded at the time, 'The fulfilment of this great plan is, under present Soviet conditions, contingent upon the existence and expansion of the system of forced labour.' By 1945–47, Dallin and Nicolaevsky's (1948, pp. 62–71) calculation of the number of camps in the Soviet Union had expanded to 125. With the benefit of access to records only recently made available, Bacon (1994, pp. 84–5) stresses that these camps were camp groupings and differentiates between those camps under direct central NKVD control and those under local NKVD control, 53 and 78 camp groupings respectively. Bacon (ibid.) also adds 475 colonies to the list and a further 667 labour camps which were subdivisions not included in the 131 camp groupings. Crucially, Bacon (ibid., p. 151) finds that it was economic requirements which underlay the rapid development of the Gulag system.

During the war, industrial labour camps were moved into the production of armaments with the NKVD producing between 10–15 per cent of all ammunition during the war years. Within the Gulag system a whole range of goods for the war effort was also produced, from timber to gas masks and uniforms. (For the above, see Bacon, 1994, pp. 134–7.) In the agricultural camps, essential foodstuffs were also produced and construction work was undertaken (Bacon, 1994, pp. 137–40). During the war, outside of agriculture, forced labour constituted 10 per cent of the workforce (ibid., p. 143). By 1940, fully 8 million names had been entered in the Gulag record of prisoners (ibid., p. 111).

The increase in the use of forced labour during the war years, however, was part of a rising trend, a trend which had begun years before the war with Stalin's move to forced collectivization and heavy industrialization, and it was to continue through to Stalin's end. The number of inmates contained within the Gulag system reached its peak in the years shortly before Stalin's death. Analysing the latest figures made available and, crucially, examining both the inflow and outflow of prisoners year by year, Bacon (1994, p. 24) calculates that while the highest figure for any year in the 1930s is 1 881 570 (1938) and for the 1940s 1 356 685 (1949), in 1950 the figure was 2 561 351 falling to 2 468 524 in 1953. These figures are in line with both Nove (1993a, p. 270, Table 13.2) at 2 561 300 for 1950 and Wheatcroft (1993, p. 277) at 2 526 402 for 1953. For the years 1934–52 as a whole, Bacon calculates that the number of prisoners entering the Gulag camps and colonies was more than 18 million (ibid., p. 37).

Labour camps and economic utility

Although Conquest may have overestimated the numbers held within the Gulag system as a whole during 1936–38, his assessment of the inmates' economic utility, over a longer period, remains salient: 'The millions of slave-labourers at the disposal of the Gulag played an important economic role, and indeed became accepted as a normal component of the Soviet economy' (Conquest, 1971, p. 481). A United Nations report in 1953 confirmed the 'considerable significance' to the economy of this forced labour (ibid.). Bacon (1994, p. 40) confirms this importance. As early as 1940, the NKVD was fulfilling 13 per cent of the volume of capital work, with 2 million forced labourers involved in construction. On the basis of new evidence Bacon does not simply reinforce the importance of Stalin's scheme for all-out industrialization for the expansion of the Gulag system, but actually reverses the usual direction of causation. Even in the 1930s he argues that '...the economic tasks assigned to the NKVD influenced the number of inmates in the camps to a greater extent than the size of the camp population influenced the setting of plan targets' (Bacon, 1994, p. 50). The setting of targets was itself based on predictions about the future numbers of forced labourers. Bacon (ibid.) concludes:

> Against the background of a plan-centred industrialization campaign, coupled with the increased possibility that those officials whose organizations failed to meet their targets would suffer some form of repression, the motives for the NKVD to tailor arrests to fit economic needs are apparent.

Through this mechanism mass arrests served both political and economic ends (ibid., p. 15).

As the size of the Gulag system increased so the balance of political ideological versus economic ends tipped more and more towards the economic (ibid., p. 160). For example, by the early 1940s, Bacon argues, the archives show that the reorganization of the camp administration 'was motivated solely by the desire for economic efficiency' (ibid.). The political ends, however, always retained a weight in that balance. As Bacon (ibid., p. 161) stresses, 'the level of executions and deaths in the camps suggests that the simple provision of a large labour force, although the main factor behind the maintenance of the Gulag, existed alongside a more complex array of circumstances involved in the subjugation of Soviet society to the ideals and person of Stalin.' Indeed the numbers of executions fell sharply at the end of the Ezhovshchina, exactly at the point at which the labour shortages were acknowledged and the future need for more work hours was recognized as the war threatened and the consequent need for soldiers, taken out of economic production, became evident. The centrality of labour power to the

Stalinist economic system has also been demonstrated through analysis of Soviet economic data.

Khanin's economic analysis
In his recent analysis of Soviet statistics, G.I. Khanin, a Soviet financial economist, has not only exposed the myth of rapid economic growth achieved under Stalin and revealed the falsification of statistics, he has also blown apart the Soviet claim that the growth achieved under Stalin was based on modern methods. (For exposition and analysis of Khanin's work see Harrison, 1993.)

Growth can be achieved in a number of ways. The 'modern' method is to increase output through improved and innovative technology and procedures. As well as better machinery the workforce will also be more skilled and better educated. The modern method is capital-intensive, replacing workers with capital, either employing fewer workers or employing them for fewer hours or both. Output can also be increased by employing increasing numbers of workers or extending work hours. In these ways, existing machinery can be used more fully. This was what the 'shock workers' and then later the Stakhanovite workers essentially undertook in industry, working extra shifts, and keeping machinery in operation for as long as possible. Sheer labour power can also be substituted for machinery. Picks and shovels used by miners in sufficient quantities can still produce a great deal of coal or ores, equalling or even surpassing output by modern mechanical extraction processes if enough workers are set to work. Similarly, large numbers of workers with basic tools can be used to construct long stretches of roads or quarry stone at production levels equal to capital-intensive methods.

According to the official figures produced at the time, the productivity of the Stalinist economy between 1928 and 1940 grew largely through increased capital investment. On official figures it is claimed that from 1928–40 the 'stock of fixed assets' (machinery and the like) grew on average by 8.7 per cent per year, 'capital productivity' grew on average by 4.8 per cent and 'output per worker' increased by 11.9 per cent. (See Harrison, 1993, p. 149.) On these official figures the Soviet economy was, during these critical years, primarily intensive, the consequence of investment in modern machinery and production methods (ibid.).

Khanin's data, however, contradict this claim significantly. Production increases, he shows, were essentially extensive, that is they were achieved by increased labour power. While the 'stock of fixed assets' did increase substantially between 1928 and 1941, at an average of 5.3 per cent per year, capital productivity actually declined by an average of 2 per cent and output per worker was increased by an average of only 1.3 per cent per year. (See Harrison, 1993, p. 151, Table 3.) Labour was the fundamental building block of the entire Stalinist economic system; labour shortage was the factor which most threatened to bring its collapse. It was a shortage greatly exacerbated by the decision to go for 'heavy industrialization' in 1930 and made worse by the military expansion of the late 1930s.

Forced labour

Forced labour held great appeal for Stalin. As Dallin and Nicolaevsky (1948, pp. 88–9) argue, it has two great 'virtues': it is cheap and it holds 'the possibility of employing prisoners almost entirely without investment of capital'. Its attraction appeared particularly clear for lumbering, canal and road building, mining, basic building and the like. In addition it had the attraction of discipline (ibid., p. 91). Though control over labour was increased in the 1930s, particularly through the use of internal passports, labour shortages had meant that both under the experiment in 'socialist competition' and during the Stakhanovite period, with its increased pay differentials, workers could be attracted away from one factory to another. Though wages and prices were fixed, workers could move too freely (Davies, 1993, p. 63). Forced labour was a means for controlling worker discipline.

Swianiewicz (1965, p. 95) argues that given shortages of supplies in consumer goods the removal of workers to labour camps also helped to control inflation. Fewer consumers would be chasing the same quantity of goods. This would be true, of course, only if the camp inmates kept consumption down. The closer to a minimum consumption is kept, the more economically attractive forced labour appears. Equating camp labour with slave labour throughout history, Swianiewicz stresses the importance of the lowest expenditure on each worker: 'The economic prerequisite of slavery is the ability of a man to produce more than the minimum he requires for living' (ibid., p. 93).

While in theory forced labour has advantages, in practice it has numerous disadvantages, not least among them the breaking of the human spirit and the sacrifice of human lives. In terms of the production process, the practice of labour coercion develops a lack of interest in work and consequent reductions both in productivity and the quality of goods produced (Swianiewicz, 1965, pp. 99–107). In addition, forced labour incurs all the costs of running camps, the employment of (non-productive) guards and agents and the expense of weaponry.

Stalin thought that he had overcome the recognized problem of lack of incentive, which would reduce both the quality and quantity of goods produced, by relating the level of rations to output (Conquest, 1971, p. 483). Norms were set and evidence suggests most camps were run with allocation of bread (though not soup) according to performance: 700 grammes or more for 100 per cent fulfilment of norms, 400–500 for non-fulfilment and for under 50 per cent (punitive) only around 300 grammes (ibid., pp. 486–7). Swianiewicz (1965) has concluded that, at best, the savings made through the use of forced labour over the economy as a whole were 'marginal'. There were some clear successes. For example, coal from Karaganda, produced with forced labour, was cheaper than that produced from the Donets Basin (Conquest, 1971, p. 485). Conquest also draws attention to the inordinate costs of free labour in some situations, such as the mines and roads of north-east Siberia (ibid.).

Poignantly, and crucially, Conquest argues, 'in any case, to start examining the economics of the operation in an abstract way is clearly a mistake. A man killed by squeezing a year or two's effort out of him is of more use than a man kept in prison' (ibid., p. 485, fn. 1). The case of the camp at Koltas is a telling one. There a group of prisoners, made up of invalids and old people, were refused by all the camps for their lack of economic worth. Gradually the problem solved itself as, one by one, they died (Conquest, 1971, p. 486). Those enduring the harshest labour rarely lived longer than two years. Once worn down by their labours they were transferred to lighter duties: 'This was the last stage in the camps. When worn down, debilitated to the degree that no serious work could any longer be got out of them, prisoners were put on sub-starvation rations and allowed to hang around the camp doing odd jobs till they died' (ibid., p. 492). The famine of 1933 and the harvest of 1936 may well have nourished Stalin's ideas.

Conclusion: inexorable logic
When economic projections went awry, for whatever reason, two rules governed the Stalinist regime's behaviour: conceal what can be concealed and for what cannot be concealed, be sure to direct attention away from the possibility that economic mismanagement emanated from the centre. What lay behind the conviction that this combination of concealment and scapegoating would work was a belief that if enough force were applied then production levels would be improved. As the shortage of labour increased, exacerbated by the growth of military personnel, the conviction that the economy could be put right by forcing people to work harder became the central tenet of the entire system.

The emphasis put on the Great Purges of 1936–38, taken as symbolic of the terror of the Stalinist system, has obscured the wider nature of the system. In stressing the show trials it has drawn attention away from lawlessness, what Lewin (1985) has termed 'extra legality'. In highlighting executions it has cast a shadow over the more drawn-out excesses of the Gulag system, in which the number of inmates reached its peak not during the Ezhovshchina, but at the end of Stalin's reign. In the Stalinist system the secret police in collusion with Stalin was elevated above the party and became a powerful economic empire with terror its basis of rule. Echoing Arendt, Lewin (1985, p. 283) has summed up the Gulag system in the following terms: 'the essence of the Gulag system…is arbitrariness', and the 'masses of innocent people crammed into the camps' a microcosm ('a test case') of Stalinist society as a whole, totally lacking the rights and duties of the citizen.

Under the cloak of secrecy in a system of terror, an economic system of substantive irrationality based on coerced labour and wild targets developed under Stalin. Set, immovably, on the conviction that forced labour was the route to economic success and political mastery, the logic of the Stalinist system moved to concentration camps and the highest levels of human exploitation to deaths on a large scale. The number of people executed under the Stalinist regime, especially during the Ezhovshchina, 1936–38, demonstrates that terror as government cannot be explained in purely economic terms – the response to economic crisis escalated by wild schemes in a system of substantive irrationality. The choice of victims and the public language of class conflict in which they were vilified cannot be understood without taking into account the fact that it was a communist regime with a history of revolution and civil war. Equally, however, the Stalinist system cannot be understood in purely political terms. Stalinism did not follow inevitably from the logic of communist ideology, as Bukharin and Preobrazensky's plans clearly showed. The decision to move to terror and forced labour was not politically inevitable but neither was it economically necessary. Though the problem of labour shortage presented a severe threat to the system, in moving to coercion and pushing for wild schemes 'not based on calculations of any sort' Stalin threw away rational plans, Bukharin's 'objectivity of statistics'.

Stalin clung to the value of extensive labour and the use of coercion as a substitute for the incentives of the market. Having made the discovery of the use of forced labour within camps, Stalin, the infallible leader, remained set on it right through to his end. The attraction of the system most probably came from the fact that it essentially offered the neat coincidence of two solutions for the price of one. Economic crisis could be blamed on political enemies while camp labour could be used to right the economy's ills. Although Arendt may be right to argue that, on the basis of results, Stalin's Terror lacked economic rationality, she is wrong to reject the view that economic utility was at the heart of the Stalinist system. In the mind of the infallible leader, the use of forced labour was the key to economic success. In a system of substantive irrationality no objective evidence could be produced to contradict his view.

Notes

1. Conquest (1971, p. 708) estimates the number in jail or in the camps by the end of 1938 to be 8 million plus 1 million who were executed and a further 2 million who died in the camps between 1937 and 1938. In addition to the figures offered by Nove, Fitzpatrick (1993, p. 249) notes that the discovery of mass graves at Kuropaty and elsewhere probably indicates that more summary executions of people took place in 1936–38 without their entering the Gulag system. Rather than the estimated 7–15 million in prisons and the Gulag system by the end of the 1930s (see Rummel, 1990, for comparison of figures in the literature) at the outbreak of World War II, calculated on the basis of more recent data, Thurston (1993, p. 155) argues that there were only around 1.5 million people in the labour camps and a further 0.8 million in prisons or exile. By adding the special exiles to the figures, Wheatcroft (1993, p. 277) approximates Nove's estimate for 1939, giving 4 million people in the entire NKVD system.
2. With access to records made available since 1987, Khanin, a soviet economist specializing in finance, has argued that the economic crisis in Stalin's USSR was even worse than western observers suggested, putting the average rate of growth between 1928 and 1941 at only 3.2 per cent, actually below the long-run average for the Soviet Union between 1928 and 1987, This figure contrasts sharply with the official Soviet figures for 1928–41 of 13.9 per cent and even falls below conservative western estimates of 6.1 per cent. (See Harrison, 1993, Tables 1 and 2.) Furthermore, on Khanin's analysis the entire economic growth achieved from 1928–41 was actually concentrated on the years of the second Five-Year Plan (1933–37). This corresponds with Jasny's 'three "good" years, 1934–36' (ibid., p. 145).
3. With the outbreak of war, the number reached 4.2 million by 1 January 1941 (Manning, 1992, Table 5.9).
4. On Khanin's estimates for 1928–34, inflation averaged 18.5 per cent as compared with the 8.8 per cent in official Soviet estimates. In addition Khanin suggests a further 8.9 per cent of 'hidden inflation'. Though generally supportive of Khanin's calculations, Harrison considers Khanin's figures on hidden inflation to be overestimations. (See Harrison, 1993, p. 157.)

Case 2 Germany under Hitler – introduction

The comparison of Germany with Russia as totalitarian dictatorships has foundered on the differences between their economies – the command economy in Russia but the continuation of private enterprise in Nazi Germany. The argument developed in Chapters 5 and 6, however, has moved the debate on, for Russia under Stalin has been portrayed not as a centrally planned economic system but as a system of 'substantive irrationality'. Such an economic system is one cut loose from the anchor of market mechanisms and most markedly so in respect of the labour market where workers are not only not free to bargain wages but where forced labour becomes an integral part of the economic system. In such a political economy decisions are not based on technical calculation, that is calculation based on the real costs of production inputs (both resources and labour), or assessment of actually available materials and carefully calculated future requirements. Rather, economic systems of substantive irrationality are based on wild economic targets, on decisions taken 'on the hoof' and in such systems the 'infallibility' of the leader is preserved through concealment, sacrificing scapegoats for evident contra-indications. Such preservation of infallibility becomes ever more pressing as the system of substantive irrationality is drawn rapidly into deep economic crisis, spun round by statistical fabrications and downright lies.

The economic crisis produced in a system of substantive irrationality could be relieved even by partial reconnection to market mechanisms (that is a return to substantive rationality) through serious efforts to calculate the true prices of inputs, both labour and resources, and outputs. The chosen policy of labour compulsion, the costs involved in the use of force which the policy entails, and the rejection of planning based on technical calculations, could be reversed. The 'infallible leader', however, knows best and in his invincibility he believes that the policies will work. He also knows the dual advantage of secrecy which preserves both the illusion of the leader's infallibility and the conditions under which the chosen policies will succeed. Such utter conviction, which in reality brings rapid economic crisis, requires scapegoats to take the blame. While potential scapegoats can be found in any society, only in some can the necessary accusations be made to stick. Such a society, it has been argued, is a 'dislocated society', one which has experienced great social upheaval. In Russia it was the *byvshie liudi*, outsiders, a group with both pre- and post-revolutionary connections, who were blamed for the economic crisis. In Germany it was the Jews and communists. Jews in Germany were a group traditionally blamed for economic problems (see Moore, 1978, p. 414). From the 1870s waves of anti-Semitism pounded the German Reich (Pulzer, 1992, p. 345).

7 Background to Nazism and Nazi dictatorship

A dislocated society

Following the foundation of the German Reich in 1871, rapid industrialization took place in the 1870s and 1880s. Industrialization required increasing numbers of workers in the towns and cities, so many rural workers migrated to urban areas. As the rural workers moved out, so landowners replaced the migrating workers with seasonal foreign labour, particularly in Eastern Germany. By 1914 half a million foreign agricultural workers were seasonally employed in Germany. A few came for longer and were employed in mines and factories. (For the above see Homze, 1967, p. 3.) The outbreak of World War I brought important changes. Following a brief period of unemployment, by 1915 the Germany economy was suffering a labour shortage. This problem was judged to be the country's main weakness and a policy of attracting foreign workers and using prisoners of war was introduced. By 1916, there were 600 000 prisoners of war and 348 917 foreign civilian full-time workers in Germany (Homze, 1967, p. 4).

Defeat in war in November 1918 brought both economic chaos and social disorder to Germany. The loss of soldiers in the war is estimated at 1 808 545, the highest figure of any of the countries involved (Bullock, 1993, Appendix 2). Following a mutiny at Kiel on 2 November 1918, spontaneous revolts began to break out elsewhere and, along lines similar to the soviets in Russia, workers' and soldiers' councils were formed. By 9 November this revolutionary impulse had reached Berlin. The Kaiser abdicated and a 'revolution through reform' was instituted by Ebert, leader of the German Social Democratic Party, SPD, to whom government of the Republic was handed. Whether because of the effect of this peaceful transfer of power or because conditions were inadequate, revolution never developed fully. Between late 1918 and March 1920, with two subsequent outbursts in March 1921 and 1923, Germany experienced a series of revolts and strikes which were put down, with increasing violence, by the Freikorps, formed especially for the purpose. These revolts and strikes were concentrated in the industrial areas, particularly in the Ruhr, and though essentially spontaneous, they were led by the Revolutionary Shop Stewards (formed from the Berlin Metalworkers' Union) and the Spartacists (formed from the Independent Social Democratic Party), who wanted proletarian revolution. The Ruhr had its own Red Army, which was defeated in March 1920. (For the above see Moore, 1978, pp. 287–313.)

Against this background of revolution and counter-revolution, communists and socialists were ripe for exploitation as scapegoats by the Nazis once in power. The economic problems which were to beset the country while the socialists were in power until 1923 provided further evidence, later to be used against them. With the return of unemployment for German workers, all the foreign workers ceased to be employed (Homze, 1967, p. 4) and the presence of dispossessed foreigners in times of economic hardship gave substance to racist scapegoating.

Convinced of their victory, the Imperial Government had not financed the war through increasing taxes but by loans which foreign powers (the Germans certain of the defeat of their enemies) were intended to pay. In the event of Germany's defeat the consequence of this policy was runaway inflation. By 1919 the Mark was worth only one-third of its value in 1914. Balance of payments problems developed and as the reparation payments demanded by the Allies further increased government expenditure over revenues, by June 1922 the value of the Mark had dropped to just 1 per cent of its value in 1914. (For above see Balfour, 1992, p. 44.) After Belgian and French troops occupied the Ruhr, the major industrial area, and further undermined production, output in 1923 was little over half what it had been in 1913 (ibid.). It was in this year that Hitler, as head of his growing National Socialist German Workers' Party (NSDAP, Nazi Party), made his first attempt to take power, proclaiming a revolution on 8 November.[1] Loans from the USA brought relative economic stability, though with five new cabinets in the same number of years, politics was less firm. The SPD returned to a 'Great Coalition' government in 1928.

The Great Crash of October 1929 and the economic policies pursued in reaction to it from 1930 by Heinrich Brüning provided the immediate economic background to Hitler's election to power as chancellor in 1933. By the winter of 1930–31 unemployment reached 5 million, putting intolerable pressures on the new system of unemployment pay and strains on the Great Coalition government. By the following winter the unemployment total had reached 6 million (Balfour, 1992, p. 49). On 27 March 1930, the socialist chancellor resigned and Brüning (Centre Party) was given the task of forming a new government. In an effort to solve the economic problems he embarked on a policy of deflating the economy through cutting expenditure and wages in an effort to balance the budget, with the longer-term aim of reviving foreign investment in the German economy. Following the high inflation of 1918–24, a reflationary policy looked dangerous but in practice the deflationary policy reintroduced the harsh conditions of those years. Political crisis ensued in July 1930. President Hindenburg invoked article 48 of the Constitution, a provision for emergencies under which rule became by presidential decree.

In the Reichstag elections of September 1930 the NSDAP polled 6 409 600 (18.3 per cent) of the votes, moving from 12 to 107 seats (Broszat, 1966, p. 138; Frei, 1993, p. 32). Following Brüning's resignation in April 1932 and two further elections that year, in July when the Nazis took 37.4 per cent of the votes cast and November when they took 33.1 per cent, on 30 January 1933 Hitler became chancellor with a nationalist coalition cabinet in which Nazis were a minority.[2] The coalition was designed to ensure control over the Nazis but as Balfour (1992, pp. 52–3) observes,

> The plotters failed to realise that with Frick as Nazi Minister of the Interior, with Goering doubling the newly created post of Air Minister and that of Prime Minister of Prussia and with the Reichswehr under the charge of the crypto-Nazi General von Blomberg, the Nazis effectively controlled the police and troops.

Control over the police and army was exactly what Ebert had lacked in 1918 and, critical to their hold on power, the Nazis quickly built up their own coercive forces in the form of the Stormtroopers (the Nazi paramilitary organization), SA, and its subsection, the SS (the 'Protection Squads' of the NSDAP, headed by Himmler). In February 1933, 40 000 SA and SS members were made auxiliary policemen (Broszat, 1966, p. 141).

Nazi dictatorship, 1933–38

The dictatorship is put in place
In protest at the Nazi rise to power the communists called a general strike for 31 January. It failed and the Nazis exploited this failure to the highest degree. When a fire broke out in the Reichstag, it was interpreted (in spite of lack of evidence to support the claim) as the start of a communist revolution. The fire opened the way for the German Communist Party, KPD, to be destroyed and a systematic persecution of the communists began immediately (Frei, 1993, p. 36).

An election was called for 5 March, the third in eight months, and from his new position of power within the system Hitler could strengthen his campaign to the full. With the 40 000 Nazi police auxiliaries, the SA and SS launched their violent campaign on the streets, and the airwaves carried Nazi broadcasts. In the event, the NSDAP failed to gain an overall majority, winning only 43.7 per cent of the votes cast out of an 88.7 per cent turnout, with the Communist Party losing only 19 seats (representing a loss of 1.1 million votes) and 13 million of the 32 million votes cast for the democratic parties. Votes for the SPD held firm. Support from the German Nationalist Party gave the Nazi Party the necessary majority, with 51.9 per cent of the vote (Frei, 1993, p. 38).

The Nazis immediately set about constructing a dictatorship. On 13 March Goebbels was appointed 'Minister for Popular Enlightenment and Propaganda'. On the same day the Länder governments (the fifteen German provinces with local control) were dissolved, to be reconstituted to reproduce the Reichstag election results – to reproduce, that is, a Nazi majority everywhere. On 7 April Nazi Federal Commissions (Reich governors) were appointed to run the Länder governments. (For the above see Broszat, 1966, pp. 142–3.) On 21 March special courts were set up for the prosecution of 'political enemies'. Prisons soon proved inadequate to contain all the political prisoners and concentration camps were set up which, as Balfour (1992, p. 55) comments, 'though not yet slaughterhouses, soon earned an ugly reputation'. Buildings such as disused warehouses and factories were used (Noakes, 1986). On 26 April 1933 a secret police, the Gestapo, was set up to deal with political crimes (Broszat, 1966, p. 146). The police force was made subordinate to the SS (Balfour, 1992, p. 55).

On 23 March the Enabling Act was passed by the Reichstag, with only the Social Democrats voting against it. By then the Communists were proscribed. This Act enabled the government to rule by decree until April 1937 (when it was renewed). The bill turned Hitler into a dictator. It authorized him to issue laws without reference to the president or regard to the Constitution.

On 14 July, the NSDAP was declared the single legal party. On 22 September the Reich Chamber of Culture was established under Goebbels to control the press and all other forms of media. On 12 November the Reichstag elections, the last to be held by the Nazis, returned 95.2 per cent of votes to the NSDAP, giving the Nazis 661 deputies. (For the above see Broszat, 1966, pp. 142–4 and Frei, 1992, pp. 32-49.) On 30 January 1934 all the remaining independent powers of the Länder were abolished, so completing the centralization of power.

In the early months of coming to power, in addition to their political policy of setting up a dictatorship and destroying the Communists in particular and all political opposition in general, the Nazis made a start on the two areas of social and economic policy which, in the movement of their ideas, were to remain constants: the different treatment of people according to racial group – racialism – and control over labour. Racial thinking was fundamental to their behaviour and in their economic thinking, extensive use of labour was seen as the lynchpin of the economy. These two constants were to be crucially entwined. The level of coercion applied to workers was in accordance with their classification of racial group.

On 1 April, just nine days after the Enabling Act, a boycott of Jewish professional and business people began. On 2 May, the German Labour Front (DAF) replaced the trade unions. Racial thinking permeated Nazi philosophy but racial policies as well as labour policies were directed both at political opponents and at reducing unemployment.

Nazi racialism: 1933–38

Legislation against Jews in employment began in April 1933, with 'Restoration of the Civil Service'. It was both anti-Semitic and anti-communist in design. Similar measures then followed to cover other professions and students. Further legislation then discouraged Aryans from employing Jews in private as well as public spheres. In 1935 the Military Service Law made 'Aryan' ancestry compulsory for the armed services. Definition of who counted as a Jew became essential. In September 1935, the Nuremburg Laws were introduced, forbidding intermarriage or sexual relations under any circumstances between 'Aryans' and Jews and officially defining Jews as 'subjects', not 'citizens'. In November the Reich Citizenship Law was supplemented by a decree to define 'Jew' by religion. (For the above see Burleigh and Wippermann, 1991, pp. 44–5.)

Along with these anti-Semitic laws other legislation and decrees directed at 'alien' races and 'racially less valuable' members of the population, such as the mentally ill, those with hereditary diseases, alcoholics and dangerous habitual criminals, were introduced. Actions to be taken included sterilization, castration, abortion as well as committal to asylums and prisons. Marriage loans, introduced in June 1933, could be refused 'if one of the prospective marriage partners is suffering from an hereditary or mental or physical illness which renders their marriage undesirable to the whole national community' (translated from the legislation by Burleigh and Wippermann, 1991, p. 46). These loans were not offered to Jews. A month after the legislation was introduced a supplementary decree required all applicants for the loan to be medically examined (ibid.). The Reich Citizenship Law of September 1935 not only deprived Jews of citizenship but also deprived welfare measures from families with 'hereditary mental or physical illness' (ibid., p. 48).

The last of such legislation was the Law on the Punishment of Juvenile Offenders of 22 January 1937 under which a 'racial–biological' examination determined the length and nature of the sentence, This was also applied to adult offenders and 'criminal biological research centres' were set up for the purpose. A similar law was projected for the 'asocial'. As Burleigh and Wippermann (1991, p. 49) remark,

> However, like its analogue – a law on 'Gypsies' – no comprehensive law on the 'asocial' was ever promulgated. This was due not to the collapse of the Third Reich, but rather, as was the case with the Jews, to the fact that the regime preferred to solve the 'question' without resorting to formal legislation or decrees.

Labour control: 1933–38

In the campaign for the March elections Hitler told the finance minister that 'all exact details regarding an economic programme were to be avoided' (Frei, 1993, p. 49). His justification entered in the minutes of the cabinet meeting was that 'the Reich government had to gather 18–19 million votes behind it. Nowhere in the world did there exist an economic programme which could find the agreement of a mass of voters of this size' (ibid.). The one economic issue which featured in the Nazi electoral propaganda was that of mass unemployment (ibid., p. 50).

Policies towards labour, which along with racialism prove ot fundamental importance to the Nazi system, began with control over trade unions. Given that in the early part of 1933, 46.3 per cent of trade union members were unemployed, and 25.9 per cent of all employees as a whole were unemployed, the removal of the trade unions addressed both political and economic needs. (For figures see Frei, 1993, p. 72, Table 2.) Inextricably linked with the Social Democratic Party, the unions were abolished on 2 May 1933. Their leaders were arrested, their funds, properties and newspapers taken over by the Nazi-controlled German Labour Front (DAF), headed by Robert Ley. Workers were organized into specialized unions: farms into the Reich Food Estate, schoolmasters into the Teachers' League, women into the Frauenshaft, youth into the Hitler Jugend and so on (Balfour, 1992, p. 55).

As Frei (1993, p. 53) argues, 'At first and above all, however, the DAF was an instrument for the regimentation of workers'. Officially founded on 10 May, on 19 May the Law on Trustees of Labour ended negotiated wage rates and moved to compulsion (ibid.). In practice, the thirteen 'Reich Trustees of Labour' were more in tune with employer rather than employee needs and the Law on the Regulation of National Labour of 20 January 1934 formally confirmed the balance. The law gave to the employer the role of 'leader' (Führer) and to employees only that of 'retinue' (Gefolgschaft). The German Labour Front was explicitly denied the role of acting on any individual's behalf (For the above see Frei, 1993, pp. 54–5.)

In its containment of actual and potential opposition the destruction of the trade unions was clearly a politically motivated policy but, crucially, control over labour also enabled the Nazis to tackle unemployment. Employers were encouraged to employ as many workers as they could (Homze, 1967, p. 6) and getting the employers to agree to this meant that trade unions had to be destroyed and wages controlled. On I June 1933, on the initiative of big business, companies began to donate one five-thousandth of their annual wages and salaries bill to the government (Frei, 1993, p. 55). Large wage cuts occurred. In the upper Palatinate, for example, wages in the porcelain and glass industry fell by half within a year (Frei, 1993, p. 4). Other policies in the Nazi recovery programme, wanted by the manufacturers, were stabilization of the Mark at a high exchange rate and price as well as wage controls (Homze, 1967, p. 7).[3]

Not only were employers encouraged to create new jobs, which helped to achieve the dramatic cut in unemployment in 1933, but young workers were kept out of the labour market through the National Labour Service. Under this system young men aged 18 to 25 were made to undertake six months of community work in activities such as tree planting and land drainage, all unmechanized and reliant on large numbers of workers (Balfour, 1992, p. 61). This was made compulsory in June 1935 (Homze, 1967, p. 7, fn. 9). Reduction in working hours for employees was also encouraged and retirement at pensionable age was made mandatory (ibid., pp. 7–8).

To cut unemployment further, on I June 1933, the Law for the Reduction of Unemployment was introduced which instituted interest-free marriage loans to be given to newly-weds where, on marriage, the woman gave up employment (Burleigh and Wipperman, 1991, p. 46). The loans were to be a maximum 1000 Reichsmarks (Frei, 1993, p. 73) and a quarter of this loan was cancelled after the birth of each child (Homze, 1967, pp. 8–9). In just 1933 there were 200 000 more marriages than in 1932 and of all married couples more than half were given the loan, representing a substantial number of new jobs for the unemployed (Frei, 1993, p. 73). A significant cut in unemployed was further achieved by the introduction of conscription into the armed forces (ibid.).

In addition to the German Labour Front programmes, the National Labour Service, the reduction in working hours, compulsory retirement, the loan scheme to remove married women from employment, and conscription into the armed forces, the large drop in unemployment in 1933 was also achieved through the huge numbers of people swelling the prisons and overflowing into the new concentration camps, mostly around Berlin.[4] New posts were vacated too as Jews were removed from their positions and Jews did not figure in the official unemployment statistics. The statistics were managed in other ways too. As Frei (1993, p. 4) remarks, 'many of the long-term unemployed must have discovered that the impressive official figures were based on biting reductions in social expenditure and massaged statistics'.[5]

In 1934, free movement of labour was halted and voluntary movement from jobs was stopped. The Reich labour offices became the sole authority for allocation of labour within their designated areas (Homze, 1967, p. 8). In February 1935, the work book law was introduced. Every wage earner had to register with the local labour office and obtain a work book, one copy of which was to be held at the labour office and the other to be given to the employer. Later regulations enabled the employer to keep the work book for the length of a contract. The book was lodged with the employer, so that any worker breaking a contract would be unable to obtain another job. The work book contained personal information about the workers, such as age, name and so on and also a record of training, previous jobs, wage and 'rating' and any history of 'disciplinary measures' taken against them (Homze, 1967, p. 10 and fn. 5).

These work books afforded the potential for the government to have total control over labour mobility and the information contained within the books could be used in planning. By the beginning of 1936 employment in a large number and wide range of jobs could not be obtained without presenting a book. By 1939 every German wage earner was required to have one (Homze, 1967, p. 11 and fn. 16). Regulations were also passed which ensured that skilled workers could not leave the Reich (ibid., p. 11 and fn. 17).

In June 1938, the Compulsory Labour Decree was passed. Under this decree anyone living in the Reich had to accept any job anywhere within the Reich or undergo the vocational training ordered by the labour office. In addition, under the Emergency Service Decree of October 1938, the police authorities (under Himmler) could conscript people to deal with emergencies.[6] Homze (1967, p. 13) remarks that, before the outbreak of war, 'Germany had a far more comprehensive system of labour control than any other country in Europe with the possible exception of the Soviet Union'.

Substantive rationality to economic crisis: 1933–38
When Hitler entered office in 1933 the economy was already showing signs of recovery (Frei, 1993, p. 30). In reversal of Brüning's deflationary policies, a public spending package of 600 million Marks had already been agreed by the previous cabinet, in which Schleicher had been chancellor (ibid., p. 50). This was implemented under Hitler, with the only modification to ensure that the army be the first to benefit from the public investment. This capital investment was directed at rearmament, expansion of industry and public works, such as the construction of the autobahns, with as much propaganda as possible milked from these schemes (ibid., pp. 32–3). In reaction to the high levels of unemployment and also in reflection of Nazi thinking about production, work programmes were designed for extensive use of labour, For example, the autobahns were to be built not by increased mechanization but by 'pick and shovel' (ibid., p. 73).

The control over labour which began in the very early days of the Nazi government and grew more complete as the Nazi system developed was an intrinsic and fundamental aspect of Weber's classification of an economy based on 'substantive rationality'. In such a system, as explained, calculations are made in terms of the outcome of economic actions, oriented to 'ultimate ends of some kind'. A system based on 'substantive rationality' contrasts, therefore, with one based on 'formal rationality' which depends on numerical calculations (money in modern societies) at each stage of production. The consequential problems of substantive rationality soon began to be revealed.

In controlling the labour markets neither efficiency nor productivity could be maximized. For workers there was neither the wage incentive nor the inherent satisfaction of doing a job most suited to an individual's talents. For the employer, in the absence of a labour market, it was impossible to ensure that the most appropriate employees got the job and, therefore, that the most cost-efficient workforce was achieved.

Even accepting statistical massaging, however, remarkable evidence of economic recovery had been achieved by 1936. Unemployment had almost returned to the pre-Depression level of 1928 (1 593 000 in 1936, 1 391 000 in 1928) and industrial production was higher than it had been before the Great Crash (Homze, 1967, p. 10). Nevertheless, as James (1987, p. 424) points out, 'unemployment was "solved", it is true, but largely at the expense of incomes'. In spite of reducing unemployment, wages fell as a proportion of national income. At 56 per cent of national income in 1933, wages fell steadily, down to 51.8 per cent in 1939 (ibid., p. 416). Crucially there were also serious shortages of skilled labour in key industries. The metal industries, in particular, needed more workers and demand for skilled labour began to outstrip supply. The work books had been introduced exactly to deal with these problems of labour shortage, of skilled labour in particular.

In addition to dramatic reductions in unemployment, official figures also showed rapid economic growth. By 1937 GNP per capita was 10 per cent higher than in 1929 (Balfour, 1992, pp. 60–61) and industrial production by 1936 was 7 per cent above what it had been in 1928 (Frei, 1993, p. 140). As James (1987, p. 424) concludes, however:

> We should be sceptical about other Nazi claims to have worked an 'economic miracle'. Controlled prices, worsening qualities and artificial foreign exchange rates meant that published figures on the rise of national income during the 1930s are misleadingly high (this is a notorious problem in measuring output changes in any controlled economy).

The problems relating to shortages of foodstuffs supplies for industry, declines in quality of goods and foreign exchange began to grow in a way similar to those felt in Russia in the late 1920s.

The Nazis were concerned not only with controlling labour and wages but with fixing the prices of commodities generally. The Reich Food Estate (RNS), a marketing organization which fixed prices for each agricultural good and standardized sales, was set up (after the good harvest of 1933 threatened to reduce prices) to increase farmers' profits and to end the 'tyranny of free prices' or 'liberal materialism' (James, 1987, p. 357). Instead it provoked anger over incompetence (Frei, 1993, p. 5). The Reich Entailed

Farm Law, which was intended to keep workers on the land (rather than migrate to the towns), in fact infuriated landowners who felt it undermined property rights and freedom of decision-making (ibid., p. 5; James, 1987, p. 357). The one benefit that farmers derived was the lorry-loads of unemployed brought in as auxiliary agricultural workers, likened to a 'slave-market' at the time (Frei, 1993, p. 6).

Shortages of supplies were a problem even as early as 1934. For consumers, dairy products and cooking oils were in particularly short or erratic supply. The low-wage economy and price controls also meant a steady worsening of qualities in consumer goods, particularly noticeable in textiles (James, 1987, p. 417). For industrial producers, the supply of rubber and fuel oils fell far short of production needs. For both consumers and producers a search for substitutes was recommended, but with foreign exchange reserves low, imports were not offered as a solution (Frei, 1993, p. 6). Import control rather than price mechanisms was the Nazi policy for cutting consumer demands. In September 1934 a 'New Plan' was introduced, in place of the Four-Year Plan announced on 1 May 1933, for the control of foreign trade through the allocation of foreign exchange (James, 1987, p. 395). From the spring of 1935 exports were subsidized through a general levy on German industry. After the 'New Plan', however, foreign exchange problems continued to worsen and increasing world market prices contributed to food shortages (Frei, 1993, p. 75).

From 1934–35 rearmament also took a larger and larger proportion of state expenditure, whilst other sectors benefited from only small increases and for some, such as house building, state investment decreased, falling below the 'good years' of the Weimar Republic (Frei, 1993, p. 74). In 1934, military expenditure took 18 per cent of the total public budget, reaching 58 per cent by 1938, over 20 per cent of national income (ibid.). As James (1987, p. 382) points out, however, statistics on rearmament, its definition and its relationship to the economy as a whole, are unreliable.[7]

On 18 October 1935 the minister of war suddenly abolished all restrictions and budget restraints on military expenditure. The immediate reaction was to complain that military planning would now no longer be based on economic rationality (James, 1987, p. 386). Schacht, the Reich Economics Minister, led the attack, arguing for an export market to be developed in the armaments industry, for Germany to move away from its policy of autarky.

Until 1938, much of this military expenditure was financed through loans from big business, some 12 billion Reichsmarks (RM) in all. The bill of exchange, the mefo-bill, set up for the purpose, was concealed from the money supply. The inflation that this threatened led to Schacht's resignation as Reich Economics Minister in 1937 and as Reichsbank president in 1938. In that year, the mefo-bill was replaced. (For the above see Frei, 1993, p. 74.)

Government debt at a total of 11 342.2 million RM in 1931, rising to 11 792.8 million RM in 1934, escalated to 19 098.3 million RM in 1938 (James, 1987, p. 375, Table XXXVI). In 1937 government borrowing rose to 6.1 per cent of GNP (ibid., p. 376, Table XXXVII).

The problems of labour shortages continued to grow through 1936 and in November 1936 the second Four-Year Plan was introduced which aimed to overcome the problems of both labour and supply shortages and reversed much of the original policy directed at cutting unemployment. Wives who had been given marriage loans could now obtain work. The 40-hour work week was ignored (becoming a 48-hour week in August 1938). Restrictions on foreign workers were also reduced. (For the above see Homze, 1967, p. 11.) With wages steadily falling as a proportion of national income from 1934–35 incentives for higher productivity were introduced, which (as was the case for the Stakhanovite movement in the Soviet Union) were particularly popular among the young. (For the above see Frei, 1993, pp. 79–80.) Neither real nor money incomes, however, returned to the levels attained before the Great Crash until 1937 (ibid., p. 79, Table 3).

The Four-Year Plan, with Goering its 'Commissioner', set up 'business groups' for each of the four problematic areas of shortage – raw materials, foreign exchange, labour, agricultural production – and also for price controls (Frei, 1993, p. 76). Under the Four-Year Plan Goering had full control, through the labour offices, over the allocation of workers in industry, even in individual factories (Homze, 1967, p. 13). A 'General Council of the Four-Year Plan' was set up at the same time with an increasing number of important posts given both to industrial managers and officers of the armed forces (*Wehrmacht*). As Frei (1993, p. 76) remarks, 'any remaining illusions about a proper demarcation between the state administration and private business were finally dispelled' when, in 1938, Carl Krauch was appointed 'General Plenipotentiary for Chemicals'. From that point, the Four-Year Plan became, in effect, an I.G. Farben plan (ibid.). Krauch, the foremost scientific expert on synthetic fuels and rubber, was a member of the board of I.G. Farben, the German chemical cartel which had a monopoly on the production of both synthetic fuels and rubber and later produced Zyklon B for use in the gas chambers. (In 1940, Krauch became the chairman of the board of directors of I.G. Farben – ibid.)

Production continued to be concentrated on armaments and the economy continued to be distorted as a consequence. Agricultural policy remained highly problematic, particularly subject to labour shortage. Approximately 1.4 million agricultural workers were employed in industry, and in particular in armaments production, by the outbreak of war. (For the above see Frei, 1993, pp. 76–7.)

The high level of unemployment which had won votes for the NSDAP had by the outbreak of war been turned into a labour shortage of half a million workers (Schoenbaum, 1967, p. 96). As Frei (1993, p. 77) remarks,

The notorious lack of agricultural labour, which the regime sought to counter with the introduction of young people (Hitler Youth Land Service, Honest Help, the Land Year) instead of with decisive mechanization, rationalization and land reform, was a source of discontent for years and only began to abate when prisoners of war and foreign forced labour could finally be brought in.

The terror organization and the Nazi state

During the years 1933–38, the SS organization with Himmler at its head developed as a terror system outside state control, while the state itself lost power, subordinated to the will of the Führer. With its parts multiplied the state became a façade behind which the expanding terror organization operated, ready (in 1938) to become the source of 'real power'. In short, during these years of totalitarian dictatorship, exactly as Arendt portrays, preparations were underway for the eventual transformation into a totalitarian regime, with terror as government.

In January 1933 the SS under the command of Himmler had 52 000 men and was subordinate to the SA leader Röhm (Burleigh and Wippermann, 1991, p. 60). The SA had by 1931 a strength equivalent to the 100 000-strong Reichswehr, the state army (Frei, 1993, p. 9). By the spring of 1934, the Stormtroopers numbered nearly 3 million men, not counting their reserves (ibid.). On 30 June 1934 the leaders of the SA were shot on Hitler's orders and in the changes which resulted, the SS ceased to be commanded as a section of the SA and was made an independent agency of the NSDAP on 20 July 1934, when the SS 'Reichsführer', Himmler, came under Hitler's 'personal and direct' command (ibid., p. 26).

By this act against the SA Hitler not only began the development of the SS as a state behind the state; he also subordinated the law to his will. On 13 July 1934 Hitler stood before the Reichstag and made the following declaration: 'I gave the order to shoot the main culprits in this treason...and every man should know, and for all time, that if he raises his hand to strike at the state, his fate will be certain death' (quoted in Frei, 1993, p. 24). Assessing Hitler's speech, Carl Schmitt, the academic authority on constitutional law at the time, confirmed the prominence of the leader's will as follows: 'The true Führer is always also judge. The status of judge flows from the status of Führer...the Führer's deed was, in truth, the genuine exercise of justice. It is not subordinate to justice, rather it was itself supreme justice' (Schmitt quoted in Frei, 1993, p. 26.)

On 1 August 1934, in anticipation of the aged President Hindenburg's imminent death, Hitler passed a law to merge the offices of president and chancellor and under this law the title 'Führer' became official. The following day Hindenburg died, the title of 'Reich president' was abolished, and command of the army, hitherto under the President of the Reich, came under Hitler's command. On 19 August, Hitler's new position of supremacy as head of state, government, party and of the army was confirmed in a referendum with 89.9 per cent of the votes in favour, with a 95.7 per cent turnout. From that point on ministers no longer swore allegiance to the 'constitution and to the law' but to the 'Führer of the German Nation and People'. (For the above see Frei, 1993, p. 27; Broszat, 1981, pp. 282–3.)

By the end of 1933 Himmler had achieved control over every German state police force except the Prussian police, which remained a separate agency – the Gestapo – organized under Goering (Burleigh and Wippermann, 1991, p. 60). The Gestapo, set up to deal with political opposition, held an estimated 60 000 to 100 000 communists in prisons and concentration camps by the end of 1933 and had virtually destroyed the communist resistance by the mid-1930s. On 20 April 1934, Goering appointed Himmler 'Inspector of the Gestapo' and while Goering remained its chief, in practice, Himmler was in control of the SS in its entirety. The difference between Goering and the Gestapo and Himmler and the SS was that, as Frei (1993, p. 101) explains, 'While Goering strove for a political police that would indeed be separate but still organised within the state administration…the ideologue Himmler's aim from the outset was the radical removal of all competence concerning the political police from the aegis of state power in favour of the SS.'

On 30 June 1934 Hitler gave Himmler total responsibility for all concentration camps. By 1937 the small prisons and camps maintained by the SA had been replaced by large concentration camps: Sachsenhausen, near Berlin, established in 1936, and Buchenwald, at Weimar, established in 1937. Both were modelled on Dachau, the concentration camp set up near Munich in March 1933 (Broszat, 1968, p. 445; Frei, 1993, pp. 103–4). While Dachau held mainly political prisoners, Sachsenhausen and Buchenwald became increasingly filled with 'asocials'. To be classified as 'asocial', it was not necessary to have breached any law, and the SS had already perfected the practice of taking people off to concentration camps immediately after they had been acquitted at trial or had served their sentence (Frei, 1993, p. 104). Eicke had been camp commandant at Dachau before his elevation to 'Inspector of the Concentration Camps and Führer of the SS Guard Units'. These SS Death's Head Units, which guarded and ran the concentration camps, numbered 5000 in 1937 (ibid., p. 101). The Hitler Bodyguard Regiment, recruited from the SS and formed in 1933 (strengthened in 1938–39), constituted the third area of Himmler's control (ibid., p. 102).

On 17 June 1936 Hitler gave Himmler the new official title of 'Reichsführer SS and Chief of the German Police in the Reich Ministry of the Interior'. From this point the criminal police began to be taken over completely by the SS and the power of the Minister of the Interior, Frick, passed, in practice, to Himmler (Frei, 1993, p. 102).

New categories of arrests and committals to concentration camps came in waves in 1937–38. On 23 February 1937, Himmler instructed the criminal police to 'take into protective custody about 2000 professional and habitual criminals who are a threat to public morality' and to arrest them on 9 March 1937 'with lightning speed everywhere in the Reich' and commanded that they be 'transferred to the concentration camps of Sachsenhausen, Sachsenburg, Lichtenburg and Dachau'. (Instructions quoted in Broszat, 1969, p. 448.) On 26 January 1938, Himmler circulated instructions for a 'single, comprehensive and surprise swoop' on the 'work-shy', arrests to be carried out between 4 and 9 March. The local labour exchanges were instructed to draw up lists of those who were physically fit but had refused work on two occasions or accepted work only to abandon it. (Instructions cited in Broszat, 1968, p. 450.) In June 1938, after a 'crime prevention campaign' in the newly annexed Austria, 'at least 200 male persons capable of work' (asocials) and in addition 'all male Jews with a previous prison record' were to be arrested in each police area . These were all to be sent to the Buchenwald concentration camp (Frei, 1993, p. 104). These 'asocials', in addition to those with 'numerous' previous convictions, included anyone without a fixed address and 'gypsies and persons travelling about in the manner of gypsies, if they have shown no willingness for regular work or have rendered themselves liable to legal penalty'. (Instructions quoted in Frei, 1993, p. 104.)[8]

This 'asocials operation', as it was called, was not only racial but also economic in design. The second Four-Year Plan was introduced in September 1936. It made explicit that the plan required full employment and 'cannot permit asocial people to evade work and thereby sabotage the Four-Year Plan' (quoted in Frei, 1993, p. 105). Frei adds: 'Meanwhile, in fact, the key issue had become the recruitment of forced labour for the first SS-owned enterprises.' These included brickworks (Deutsche Erd und Steinwerk GmbH) and granite quarries at Flossenbürg and at Mauthausen, and these enterprises were referred to at the time as the 'Führer's construction projects' (ibid.). New concentration camps were built alongside these forced-labour enterprises. In 1938 the Flossenbürg concentration camp was established, to be followed by the camp at Mauthausen in 1939 (Broszat, 1966, p. 146). In the Basic Decree of December 1937 the SS concentration camps were specifically given the function of 'state correction and labour camps'.

As the real power of the SS had grown the ostensible power of the state had declined. This had begun with the Nazification of the civil service and, most importantly, the growth in influence of administrative departments 'directly responsible to the Führer' which ran either in tandem with the state authorities or acted in direct competition with them. This 'decline and deformation of traditional government', as Frei describes it (1993, p. 90) began in regard to employment and economic policy and then spread into other areas.

For example the Ministry of Economics had to compete, after 1936, with Goering as commissioner for the Four-Year Plan (Balfour, 1992, p. 56).

Within the organization of the NSDAP duplication of offices and multiplication of tasks abounded, There was the German Labour Front (DAF) and the Reich Organization Leadership. Under the latter there were five separate sections: organization, personnel, training, National Socialist factory cell, and craft and commerce. In addition to this there was also the Reich Labour Service under the Ministry of the Interior. There were numerous other dual organizations: the Reich Food Estate and the Reich Office for Agricultural Policy; the National Socialist Judges' League and the Reich Law Office; the Head Office for Municipal Policy and the German Municipal Congress; the Head Office for Civil Servants and the Reich League of German Civil Servants; the Head Office for Educators and the National Socialist Teachers' League; the Head Office for War Victims and the National Socialist War Victims' Support Organization; the Head Office for Public Health and the National Socialist German Physicians' League; the Head Office for Public Welfare and the National Socialist German Technical League. There were other dualities, subsidiary to the Nazi Party, besides. For example, as well as the Hitler Youth there was also the German Young Folk. Along with the League of German Girls there was also Young Girls in the Hitler Youth. (For the above cases see Frei, 1993, Appendix 2, pp. 244–6.)

Though in a large number of cases each pair of these duplicated organizations of the NSDAP was headed by the same person, this weakened, not strengthened, the head's position because each organization produced two outcomes, two policy proposals, each attached to the same person. Proposals, therefore, required an independent arbiter. As each member of the Reich leadership was entirely responsible to the Führer, only Hitler could exert his will.[9]

Over the years from 1933 the number of times the cabinet met declined sharply, In 1935, it met only twelve times, its sole function to pass laws prepared elsewhere. In 1936 it met four times; in 1937, six times. In February 1938 the Reich cabinet met for the very last time (Broszat, 1981, p. 280).

Notes

1. Using his trial as an occasion for propaganda he wrote *Mein Kampf* while in prison in 1924 (Balfour, 1992, p. 45).
2. In the September 1932 election the Communist Party (KPD) had their best results ever with 17 per cent of the votes and the Social Democrats (SPD) won 20 per cent of the votes, with the centre parties losing heavily (Frei, 1993, pp. 32–3).
3. For discussion of the controversy over the relationship between the leading German industrialists and the Nazis and the extent to which Nazi Germany could be considered capitalist or not see Kershaw (1989; pp. 42–60). While accepting that the large industrialists could make a handsome profit under Nazism Kershaw argues both against the Marxist view that Nazi Germany was driven by capitalist economic laws (the primacy of economics) and

against the 'liberal' view of Hitler's political (totalitarian) control over the economy (the primacy of politics). Policies such as the transportation and extermination of Jews were not economically rational, he argues, and the view of Germany as a command economy is greatly oversimplified. These views are supported here.

4. The concentration camps around Berlin were set up in March 1933, and in the city itself 'private prisons' were set up with the SS Columbia prison the most hellish of these torture chambers (Broszat, 1968, p. 408). The Dachau concentration camp set up near Munich in March 1933 and run by Eicke from June became the model upon which the later established concentration camps were based. Dachau aside, the older camps were gradually reduced and replaced by the new large camps, the first – Sachsenhausen – beginning operation in 1936. (See ibid., pp. 429–46.)

5. Local welfare support was also often cut or impossible to secure. Requirements were imposed, such as proving unsuccessful application for work, in person, at 25 firms every week (Frei, 1993, p. 4),

6. See Homze (1967, pp, 11–12). Further Labour Decrees in September 1939 made the Reich Labour Service compulsory for all men between the ages of 18 and 25 and for unmarried women aged 17–25.

7. See Lorrell (1976, p. 9, Table 1-1) where the different statistics offered in the literature on military expenditure are compared. For example, for 1933–34 estimates range between 4 and 9 billion RM, in 1936 between 6 and 13.5 billion RM and in 1938 from 16 to 26 billion RM.

8. A system of triangles sewn to prison uniforms was used to distinguish the various prisoners. Red, political prisoners; purple, Jehovah's Witnesses; black, anti-socials; green, criminals; pink, homosexuals; blue, emigrants; a yellow triangle added to the above to form a Star of David, Jewish prisoners. 'Recidivists' who had been sent back to the concentration camp had a crossbar above the triangle and were sent for hard labour. Later nationality was added, P for Pole, F for French etc. (Broszat, 1968, p. 452).

9. To capture Hitler's power position, Hiden and Farquharson (1983, p. 60) use the analogy of 'a net, where the strands were not of equal length nor of equal thickness, and may have changed their interrelationship from time to time, but which had one thing in common: the ends were all in the hands of Adolf Hitler'. For the debate over Hitler's 'centralized or polycentric dictatorship' see Hiden and Farquharson passim. They argue that personal relationships with Hitler were very important and that he allowed events to develop until he considered it the right point to intervene. Although Hitler had decisive control at key moments, the system was to all appearances chaotic. It is the argument here, however, that Nazi Germany (in line with Arendt and Broszat) changed crucially in 1938. In line with Hiden and Farquharson's position, however, it is also argued that though Hitler had control in the sense of making the final decisions, it does not follow that he had control in the rational sense of actually being fully aware of the 'knock-on' effect of the decisions he made.

8   Germany 1938–45: substantive irrationality and terror as government

In 1938, the German dictatorship transformed itself into a terror regime. It was a transformation marked by 'Crystal Night', the night of shattered glass, 9–10 November, when Jews were beaten and murdered, synagogues burnt, shops and homes belonging to Jews destroyed and 25 000 Jews arrested and sent to concentration camps at Sachsenhausen, Buchenwald and Dachau (Landau, 1992, p. 144). The night, signifying the grip of terror over the whole society, came at the end of a year in which large-scale changes had taken place within the state's coercive forces, each strengthening the position of Hitler, Himmler and the SS. In January and February the army command was changed, a change which removed resistance to the increase in the armed SS and opened the way for the development by October of an entirely separate SS domain. At the same time as the change in the army command, Ribbentrop replaced von Neurath as Reich Foreign Minister and Schacht was removed from control of economic and fiscal policy through the creation of the Organization for the Four-Year Plan (see Broszat, 1981, pp. 294–300).

Ribbentrop's appointment as foreign minister opened the way for closer cooperation between the Foreign Office and Himmler, which was later to be important in the movement of the SS into occupied territories and the transportation of Jews. In the shorter term, through 1938, Hitler got his way in annexing Austria in March, and taking the German area of Czechoslovakia (the Sudetenland) in the Munich Agreement of September (Kaiser, 1992, p. 184).[1] Both Schacht and Fritsch (one of the three dismissed from command of the army) were regarded as political moderates who upheld the rule of law (Broszat, 1981, p. 294). The changed relationship between the army and the Foreign Office released the possibilities for wild schemes in respect of both warfare and movement of peoples. The removal of Schacht, who as minister of economics and president of the Reichsbank had introduced the New Plan in 1934, signified the move from substantive rationality, planning anchored to the market, to substantive irrationality, a rudderless economy. From 1938 wild economic schemes supplanted planning.

Economic crisis to substantive irrationality
The 1934 plan had aimed to balance the economy, but in line with Hitler's wishes imports for rearmament had taken precedent over foodstuffs. This had contributed to the shortages which by late 1935 had brought the economic

crisis of 1936, lack of butter the primary consumer complaint, and lack of fuel and rubber the main complaints of producers in industries unconnected with armaments. To close the import–export gap, Schacht had proposed measures to bring Germany back to rational calculation. Wishing to take advantage of the world economic recovery, he proposed removing exchange controls, reducing the pace of rearmament, encouraging export production and possibly devaluing the Reichsmark, to bring it into line with the pound and dollar. Schacht's aims were in line with those of the Weimar Republic and, in the mould of normal politics, he saw his economic proposals in tandem with a foreign policy of a negotiated return to Germany's geographical boundaries and world position of 1914. (For the above see Kaiser, 1992, p. 181.) Hitler's rejection of these plans and Goering's appointment in charge of the Four-Year Plan led to Schacht's resignation as minister of economics in 1937. In 1938, he was ousted as president of the Reichsbank. Goering, as explained, in complete opposition to Schacht's position, pressed on with rearmament and pushed for self-sufficiency through development of synthetic products such as oils, rubber and fats.

Wild schemes, 1939–42: war and foreign workers
Under Goering's Four-Year Plan rearmament increased but so too did shortages. The economic hardship was blamed in Goebbels's propaganda on an international Jewish conspiracy (Kaiser, 1992, p. 182).

Having annexed Austria in March 1938 and gained the Sudetenland in the Munich Agreement of 30 September through diplomacy, in 1939 Hitler adopted different tactics. He manipulated a means to destroy the remainder of Czechoslovakia, occupying Prague in March and annexing Bohemia–Moravia and Memel from Lithuania. After signing the Nazi–Soviet pact he then invaded Poland in September 1939 (ibid., p. 184).

Germany's economy, in serious crisis by 1937, had survived as well as it had only because of the booty brought by the annexation of Austria, the Sudetenland and Bohemia–Moravia in 1938. In 1939 resources and production levels in Germany had reached their limits. Foreign exchange had run out and labour shortages had reached 1 million (Kaiser, 1992, p. 188). In Mason's (1968, pp. 178–85) view these labour shortages, along with shortages of raw materials, were critical in destroying the independent power of industry. It has been estimated that at the start of the war, in September 1939, stocks of oil in Germany were sufficient to last only between three and six months and stocks of ferrous-based metals were little better (Klein, 1959, pp. 56–9). Hitler informed his generals on 22 August 1939 that 'because of our restrictions [*Einschränkungen*, or bottlenecks] our economic situation is such that we can only hold out for a few more years. Goering can confirm this' (Hitler quoted in Kaiser, 1992, p. 188).

In their attack on Poland the Nazis adopted *Blitzkrieg* tactics, short sharp attacks by armoured army divisions with the close air support of the air force. Debate over the *Blitzkrieg* concentrates on two issues: whether war was planned, Germany developing a war economy in peacetime, in preparation; and whether the strategy's main impetus was to obtain the raw materials and supplies which Germany so sorely needed. (For a summary and discussion of the debate see Lorrell, 1976, pp. 1–39.) The evidence of lack of oils and ferro-alloys counts against the view of a war economy in peacetime for, in September 1939, Germany was not adequately prepared for war. On the other hand, this evidence is consistent with the view of a deliberate short sharp attack not intended to be a prolonged war. That the Nazis thought that they could get away with it without Allied retaliation is itself indicative of a wild belief in invincibility. It was a gamble, not a plan.

Considered within these debates but given far less prominence overall than the shortages of materials, is the importance of foreign labour. This is understandable because, in contrast to plans drawn up by German army leaders to obtain raw materials from occupied areas, no master plan for obtaining and using foreign labour has ever been found (Homze, 1967, pp. 13–14). In the secrecy of a terror regime, outside the normal planning procedures of governments, however, this does not rule out its importance and the sheer scale of foreign labour is proof enough that its use was close to Hitler's heart.

At the end of May 1939, before the outbreak of war, less than 1 per cent of the total workforce were foreigners and 'foreigners' were defined to include 'Jews of all nationalities'. (See Homze, 1967, Tables 1, 11, VI.) By the end of 1944, 35 per cent of all those employed in armaments and armaments-related industries were foreign workers (including 'all Jews and prisoners of war' [see ibid., Table XVII]) and as a percentage of all industry, 29.2 per cent were 'foreign workers' (ibid., p. 236). These firms included the massive giant of the chemicals industry, I.G. Farben (headed by Krauch), which supplied the chemicals for the concentration camp gas ovens. By October 1944, 46.1 per cent of all those employed by I.G. Farben were 'foreign workers', including prisoners of war and, of course, 'Jews of all nationalities'. As Homze (1967, pp, 237–8) points out:

> ...in Farben's new synthetic gasoline plant at Auschwitz, built entirely during the war, foreign workers reached 55.1 per cent of the total employed by 1 October 1944. Moreover, this infamous plant, built in an unfavourable location in order to exploit the labour supply of the big concentration camp nearby, had on the same date 26.6 per cent concentration inmates, including foreigners and Germans, and only 18.3 per cent regular German workers.

The other huge employer of foreign workers was the Goering works, where by June 1944 fully 58.7 per cent of all workers were 'foreign workers'. Even as early as December 1941, the score had already reached 42.4 per cent (ibid., p. 238). By the end of 1944 there were 7–13 million foreign workers and prisoners of war (the total 'including Jews of all nationalities') working in Germany, fully 20 per cent of the total workforce in Germany (ibid., pp. 233–4).

Hitler is recorded as mentioning foreign labour for the first time in May 1939 when, in a meeting with Goering, Raeder and Keitle, representatives of the military forces, Hitler made it clear that he intended to attack Poland at the first opportunity, arguing, 'We shall be able to rely upon record harvests, even more in time of war than in peace, the population of non-German areas will perform no military service and will be available as a source of labour'. (Minutes quoted in Homze, 1967, pp. 16–17.) On his part, Goering, as chief of the Four-Year Plan, who by 1939 had taken over most of the power of the Ministry of Labour, sent instructions to the army command on 28 January 1939 for, in the event of war, the employment of prisoners of war in camps of over 10 000 prisoners (Homze, 1967, p. 16). As explained, by the end of 1938, Germany was suffering serious shortages of labour, particularly in agriculture. These shortages were to be exacerbated by conscription into the army.

Between May 1939 and May 1940 4.4 million workers were drafted out of the economy into the army (Homze, 1967, p. 19). The shortage of agricultural workers posed an immediate threat to the economy but also to Hitler's hold on power. Foodstuffs were needed urgently both for the domestic population and the army. The 'emergency solution' was foreign labour.

The problems of labour shortage can be tackled in a number of ways, The modern way would be to increase mechanization, developing or importing labour-saving machinery. Increased production might be achieved through worker incentives and plant might be used more efficiently if working hours were increased for existing workers or if workers outside the labour market such as married women and pensioners were brought into it. Labour compulsion, wage fixing and shortages in essential materials had, however, by the end of 1938, destroyed the vestiges of a competitive market, whether for goods or labour, under which these incentives might have worked.

Labour compulsion had marked a decision to develop the economy through the extensive use of labour rather than mechanical power, and the move away from a competitive labour market together with a move away from market pricing in goods had brought the economy towards the crisis predicted by Weber in any economy based on substantive rationality. The cost-effectiveness of production might be improved through decreasing the costs of inputs. Where labour is the greatest input then cutting wages, keeping 'wages' near subsistence level or removing some workers from the wage market altogether could have the desired effect. Such was Nazi thinking.[2] The centralized system for the exploitation of coerced labour was in place. So too was the racial thinking which in the Nazi view meshed so well with their economic approach.

'Untermensch' philosophy

The categories of workers chosen for exploitation were based on Nazi racist views of superior and inferior peoples. Inferior peoples (*Untermensch* meaning literally 'sub-human' [Homze, 1967, p. 39]) were intended, by nature, to be the slaves of the superior, German 'master race' (the *Herrenmenschen*), so long, of course, as these Germans were in mental and physical good health and had no proven record of 'asocial' behaviour such as criminality, homosexuality, communism, being Jehovah's Witnesses, being work-shy, or being without fixed abode. Crucially, foreigners could be graded on a scale of superior and inferior races. Jews and gypsies were 'foreigners', whether German-speaking or not and irrespective of the number of generations for which their families had been living in Germany. Certainly, there could be no disputing that workers in occupied territories were 'foreign'. The particular attraction of Polish workers was that as East Europeans they were considered racially inferior to Northern Europeans.

In the Nazi philosophy of *Untermenschen* Poles were almost at the bottom of the racial scale with only Jews and gypsies lower. According to Hitler the Poles were 'especially born for low labour...There can be no question of improvement for them. It is necessary to keep the standard of life low in Poland and it must not be permitted to rise' (quoted in Homze, 1967, p. 39).[3] Ranked beneath the Slavs, at the lowest rung of inferiority, Jews and gypsies would be treated with even greater inhumanity and levels of exploitation. Whilst supplies of labour were kept high by foreign workers, the economic worth of these 'sub-humans' would be negligible and they would, therefore, be expendable.

Poland and Slav labour

In September 1939 the German army invaded Poland.[4] Before the month was out, Poland had surrendered. According to Homze (1967, p. 23), 'the entire Polish Army, numbering nearly a million, fell captive to the *Wehrmacht*. A vast labour pool of both war prisoners and civilians was ready for exploitation. The Germans were not slow in using it'. As the German army swept across Poland, even before Warsaw surrendered, indeed within days of first crossing the border, Poles began to be recruited for work in Germany.

The speed with which the Poles were organized and employed was so great that it seems unnecessary to argue that there was any more pressing reason behind the Nazi decision to attack Poland than the desire for Slav (slave) labour. The attack was launched at the height of the German harvest and the shortage of agricultural labour was critical. Within three days of the attack being launched labour offices were operating in the Polish towns of Rybnik and Dirshau. By 18 September there were 30 such offices operating in Polish towns (Homze, 1967, p. 23). Circulars providing for the employment of Polish prisoners of war were issued by the Reich Ministry of Labour on 26 September, the day before Warsaw surrendered, and by the Food Ministry on 4 and 5 October. With close cooperation between the German army and labour offices, newly set up in the Polish towns, 110 000 civilian Polish workers were in the Reich by October 1939. These Polish workers were to be used in agriculture; later some were to be used in mining and construction. In 1940, 300 000 Polish prisoners of war were used in harvesting crops. (For the above see ibid., pp. 23–4.)[5]

So successful was this foreign labour programme that by May 1940 there were 847 000 more foreign workers in the Reich than in the year before, an increase from less than 1 per cent to 3.2 per cent of the working population (Homze, 1967, p. 24). Of this total 1.1 million workers, 344 000 were prisoners of war; of the civilian workers 19 per cent were women and of the total around 700 000–800 000 were Polish workers with around two-thirds of these being prisoners of war (ibid., p. 25). Yet, to stress again, in spite of these dramatic increases and vast movements of people, there was no master plan, no open, laid down programme on record. The employment of foreign labour was, in important part, to be kept secret.

The speed with which Poland was taken confirmed, in Nazi eyes, the inferiority of Poles and the superiority of the German race. In October 1939, Hitler made it clear to General Keitel that the living standard of the Polish people was to be greatly reduced and Poland was to be an *Arbeitsreich* for the *Herrenvolk* (Homze, 1967, p. 26). The western section of Poland became part of the German Reich. Poles were evacuated out of this area, so that Germans could be moved in. The rest of Poland came under the 'General-Government' headed by Frank, to be turned into a 'great Polish work camp' (Hitler's description, see Browning, 1992, p. 21).

Immediately upon German occupation all Polish trade unions were banned and new decrees were issued on wages and work conditions. One of the first of these decrees was the *Arbeitspflicht* which introduced compulsory public labour for all Poles aged 18–60, later extended to 14–60, excluding only those who could prove 'permanent employment useful to the commonwealth'. Compulsory public labour included working in agriculture, building and so on. At first voluntary, by the end of 1939 recruitment was through force. Importantly, it excluded Jews, stating that 'a special decree will be issued with regard to Jews' (quoted from the decree, Homze, 1967, p. 29). On the same day, 26 October, special regulations for Jews stipulated forced labour (*Arbeitszwang*) (ibid.).

In January 1940 a request was sent, by Goering, for the 'supply and transportation of at least one million male and female agricultural and industrial workers to the Reich...among them at least 750 000 agricultural workers of which at least 50 per cent must be women in order to guarantee production in the Reich and as a replacement for industrial workers in the Reich' (quoted in Homze, 1967, p. 30 from the Nuremberg Trials). At first Frank, the head of the General-Government, continued to try to use persuasion rather than force, but by 10 May 1940 only 160 000 Poles had been recruited for work. So began a campaign of snatching people from the streets and the Polish POWs were redefined, through contracts, as civilian workers (Homze, 1967, p. 36). The exceptions to these arrangements were the Polish officers, and in addition Jews, other minorities, the physically infirm, the lazy or other 'asocial' workers (ibid.). By October 1940, 880 000 Poles were working in Germany. By the spring of 1942 there were 1 080 000, and this out of a population under the General-Government of approximately 16 million (ibid., p. 37).

Blitzkrieg west: skilled workers
By June 1940 Hitler's *blitzkrieg* tactics had taken Denmark, Norway, the Netherlands, Belgium, Luxembourg and France. These conquests brought a wealth of new sources of raw materials and also new pools of labour. With western Europeans higher up the racial scale, in these countries selection concentrated on skilled workers. On 20 June 1940 a decree in France prohibited any increases in salaries or prices (Homze, 1967, p. 50). Western foreign labour brought into the Reich was on a voluntary basis until 1942 when force was applied (ibid., pp. 46–7). Prisoners of war, in any case, provided a ready source of new labour. By October 1940 there were 1 million western POWs working in Germany, mostly in agriculture. Again, of course, exception was made for Jews and officers. These were sent to special camps (ibid.). In addition to workers from these western occupied countries, workers were also recruited from Germany's allies, the bulk coming from Italy. Italian workers were not, however, well regarded.[6] By May 1941 there were 3 020 000 foreign workers in Germany, an increase of over 263 per cent on a year earlier, The largest increase was in occupations related to the war industries (Homze, 1967, p. 68).

The attack on Russia: 'The Green File'
In June 1940, Hitler began the attack on Russia, 'Operation Barbarossa'. The Barbarossa campaign was intended to be the war which would provide all the material and human resources for the perpetuity of the Reich (Geyer, 1984, p. 217). The *blitzkrieg* strategy was again employed, the war intended to be concluded within three to five months (Jacobsen, 1968, p. 508).

In the spring of 1941, General Thomas issued a plan, the Oldenburg Plan, for the seizure of captured materials, such as oil and iron ore. The plan had a stated aim of maintaining the structure of Russian industry. Along with this army plan, however, there was also a secret set of directions, 'The Green File', which completely contradicted the Oldenburg Plan. 'The Green File', issued on 22 May 1941, from Goering's Four-Year Plan office, sought to destroy both Russian industry and society totally. Homze (1967, p, 71) quotes the following section:

> Many tens of millions of people in the industrial areas will become redundant and will either die or will have to emigrate to Siberia. Any attempts to save the population in these parts from death by starvation through the import of surpluses from the Black Earth Zone would be at the expense of supplies to Europe. It would undermine Germany's and Europe's power to resist the blockade. This must be clearly and absolutely understood. (Goering, The Green File.)

In December 1940, Hitler had ordered preparations for the war against Russia whose 'natives' he classed 'of inferior race' and whose fate according to Himmler was to become 'a people of leaderless slave labourers'. (Quotations from Hitler and Himmler in Jacobsen, 1968, p. 509.) On 6 June 1941, orders went out to kill Russian prisoners of war, the 'General Instructions for the Treatment of Political Commissars', the Kommissarbefehl (Jacobsen, 1968, p. 519). In mid-July 1941 Himmler committed two SS brigades (a total of 11 000 men) – the Einsatzgruppen – to operate behind the Gestapo and SD Force. By 19 September, 85 000 Russians were dead. On 29-30 September, the massacre at Babi Yar occurred with 34 000 Jews killed (Browning, 1992, pp. 80–81). Up to the spring of 1942, 3 900 000 Soviet prisoners of war had been taken by the German army, far too many to be coped with. Through a combination of genuine shortages and deliberate starvation, forced marches, disease and general abuse, by the spring of 1942 only 1 100 000 Soviet POWs were left alive (Homze, 1967, p. 81). So what had been predicted in 'The Green File' had come to pass.

Russian labour in Germany: changes in policy
In July 1941, just as the Einsatzgruppen began their operation, Hitler, though he had initially ruled against Russian labour being used within Germany, relaxed his position, allowing Russian POWs to be brought in – so long, that was, as these POWs were neither Asiatic nor Mongolian and their only language was Russian (in order to avoid communist propaganda being spread in German). The Ukrainians and Balkan peoples, defined as racially close to Germans, were to be released, if their homes were in occupied areas, on condition of reporting to local police and labour offices. Of the remaining groups, however, as the massacres suggest, treatment was very different. The Asiatic, Jewish and German-speaking prisoners of war were intended to be kept in the fighting area and to be used by the army to do any work needed.

(For the above see Homze, 1967, pp. 74–5.) Of the remaining three groups the Red Army political officers were to be eliminated by the SS and the Red Army officers and NCOs were put to work behind the operational areas. (For details of the scale of executions and liquidations see Jacobsen [1968, pp. 528–31].) The Russian POWs were also only to be employed in heavily guarded large groups.

The army was notified that half a million Russian prisoners of war were needed. By late August preparations were being made for their 'recruitment' (Homze, 1967, p. 74). French POWs were shifted out of the armaments industries in order to receive the Russian POWS. The transfer of French POWs was to be completed by 1 October 1941. Russian POWs were to be used in harsh work such as mining. From September 1941 the recruitment of Russian civilian workers also began. Wishing to capitalize on cheap Russian labour, Goering wanted to remove 'the little-producing but much-eating workers from other states' (quoted ibid., p. 77).

The Russians were to work entirely separated from other nationalities and to be 'fed lightly and without serious inroads upon our food balance' (Goering quoted in Homze, 1967, p. 78). Russian civilian workers were to receive some money but, as for the Polish workers, wages were not to be equal to German wages and a 'social equalization tax' was applied. These poor conditions were in line with the Nazi view of Eastern Europeans as 'a mass of born slaves, who felt the need of a master' (quoted ibid., p. 79), Germans being, of course, the 'master race'.

By February 1942, however, only 400 000 Russians were employed in the Reich, the problem being, according to Mansfeld of the Reich Ministry of Labour, 'exclusively a question of transportation. It is insane to transport these labourers in open or closed unheated box cars, merely to unload corpses at their destination' (quoted in Homze, 1967, p. 81). Of 500 Russian POWs assigned to work at the I.G. Farben factory in January only 185 (37 per cent) were fit enough to work. A month later only 158 could work, 107 were dead and 200 sick. Elsewhere they were reported to have arrived in a completely starved and exhausted condition. At the Herman Goering plant at Regensburg Russians were found capable of working at only between one-third to one-half of German workers' production levels (ibid., p. 82).

Forced labour and extermination
The 'liquidation' of Jews and the execution and harsh treatment of Russian POWs, such as letting them starve to death, was causing a dangerous level of hostility among the local population (Homze, 1967, p. 81). It was also upsetting the German soldiers who objected particularly to the killing of women and children. Indeed Eichmann was himself convinced that the methods employed by the Einsatzgruppen were having a bad psychological effect on

the men involved (Landau, 1992, pp. 174–5). A more undercover operation was required.

In the winter of 1941–42 the concentration camps were developed as an 'SS-owned arsenal of compulsory labour' (Broszat, 1968, p. 483). This occurred at the same time as the policy of extermination of 'undesirables' (Jews in particular) was put into operation. From the summer of 1941, German and European Jews under German occupation were deported to the east and exterminated in the camps at Auschwitz, Chelmo, Treblinka, Belzec, Majdanek and Sobibor. Because Himmler wished to make increasing use of concentration camp labour in the war industry, some of these Jews were kept from extermination, at least for the short term. In a telegram of 26 January 1942, Himmler instructed that provision be made for the arrival within a month of '100 000 Jews and up to 50 000 Jewesses in the concentration camps'. (For the above, see ibid.)

The use of Jewish concentration camp labour was essentially restricted to Auschwitz.[7] Auschwitz was, however, by far the largest camp; it became a huge source of forced labour and, with its large gas chambers, also became one of the biggest centres for extermination (Broszat, 1968, p. 485).

The final solution

'A masterpiece of secrecy'
At the Nuremburg trials, General Jodl described the plan to eliminate Jews, 'the final solution' to the 'Jewish Question', as 'a masterpiece of secrecy' (Fleming, 1986, p. 2, quoted in Steinberg, 1991, p. 201). Codes were employed to refer to it and Martin Bormann gave strict instructions that 'the Führer's Chancellory must under no circumstances be seen to be active in the matter' (Fleming, 1986, p. 22, ibid.). Where there is secrecy, analysis can never be final. Although many documents relating to the 'final solution' survived, many were lost or deliberately destroyed. For example, little is known about the Führer Chancellory and virtually all the records of Auschwitz and Birkenau were destroyed (Breitman, 1992, p. 200). In general, records for the Nazi era were better kept at the lower and middle level bureaucracies than the top (ibid., p. 201). Controversy remains over the exact nature of Hitler's role in the decision to eliminate Jews, over the date on which the plan was first conceived and over the importance of the Nazi scheme to eliminate Jews, in relation to other goals. (See Kershaw, 1989, pp. 82–106; Browning, 1992, pp. 86–121.)

The lack of records at the top reflects the nature of decision-making in the Nazi regime. The Nazi regime did not act within a normal decision-making framework. Browning (1992, pp. 120–21) explains the way the system worked as follows: 'Hitler would give signals in the form of relatively vague statements that established the priorities, goals, prophecies, and even "wishes" of the Führer. Others, especially Heinrich Himmler responded to these signals with extraordinary alacrity and sensitivity, bringing to Hitler more specific guidelines for his approval.' Up to the point at which Hitler's will 'decided', in practice this system gave considerable scope for local control over policy. From 1938, decisions essentially taken 'on the hoof' took over. As Broszat (1981, p. 357) concludes, 'The mass murder of the Jews was no more planned from the outset than the preceding and progressive use of legal discrimination against Jews.' Schemes, competing against each other, were running wild. As Homze (1967, p. 44) comments, by early 1940,

> Someone had to determine which was more important, be it the resettlement programme, the SS racial programme, Frank's occupational programme, or the foreign labour programme. To allow each individual and organization to run its own programmes in its own way without considering other factors was tantamount to chaos.

The equation of labour with death

An understanding of how the 'final solution' was reached can only be understood in the light of developments between 1939 and 1942: the changing fortunes of war; the (related) labour situation in Germany (whether perceived as sufficiency or shortage); and the capacity of the SS, in the light of progress in construction of concentration camps, to either eliminate or employ Jews on a large scale.

Analysing the treatment of Jews in Poland between 1939 and 1942 through comparison over time between the Łódź and Warsaw ghettos, Browning (1992) demonstrates the importance of decisions taken locally rather than centrally. For example, he argues, 'In short, *sealed* ghettos of *prolonged* duration were not part of any policy imposed by Berlin on local German authorities in September 1939' (Browning, 1992, p. 31). Initially Jews were stripped of their assets: their homes, their farms, their wealth. Deported from their livelihoods they were forced into the ghettos where they were used as a source of skilled labour. In accordance with the two crucial prongs of Nazi thinking – racialism and forced labour – the Jews were kept on 'hunger wages' (quoted ibid., p. 63). It was essential that the cost of keeping Jewish workers alive did not exceed the value of output. Jews in Łódź, by early 1941, were fed on just 23 Pfennigs per day, less than half that spent on prisoners' diets (ibid., p. 44). In this crucial economic equation some argued that productivity would be increased by improving the food, which counts against a claim for planned genocide at this point (ibid., p. 72).

The success of the *Blitzkrieg* in Western Europe had offered a new 'solution' to the problem of the shortage of skilled workers. The skill of Jewish workers would become surplus to requirements with the conquest of the northern European nations, classified as superior. From mid-1940 to mid-1941, Germany appeared to have its employment needs fully met. In 1941–42, extermination camps were set up in Poland: Auschwitz II (Birkenau), Belzec, Kulmhof, Maidenek (Lublin), Sobibor, Trawniki and Treblinka (Broszat, 1966, p. 153).

In September 1941, however, the serious shortage of labour was registered, which had led to Hitler's relaxation of his previous hostility to the employment of Russian prisoners of war, of any kind, in Germany. With the invasion of Russia promising victory, the plans for the operation to liquidate the Łódź and Warsaw ghettos were first conceived (Browning, 1992, p. 54). Significantly the building of the death camps at Chelmo and Belzec was begun in October 1941. The possibility of extermination on a large scale away from the public gaze could not begin until the camps were in place.

On 20 January 1942 the Wannsee Conference was held in Berlin to decide the 'final solution' of the 'Jewish Question'. Head of the department which dealt with the 'Jewish Question' within the Reich Security Head Office, RSHA, was Adolf Eichmann. His role was to make the preparations for the meeting and write the minutes. In his pre-trial interrogation in 1961 Eichmann interpreted these minutes. On page 7, Heydrich's comments are recorded as follows:

> In pursuance of the Final Solution, conscript Jews should now be used in an appropriate fashion, and under appropriate leadership, for labour duties in the East. Jews capable of work will be escorted in large labour columns, separated by sex, on road-building duties in these areas, whereby, no doubt, a large number will drop out as a result of natural decline.

'Natural decline', Eichmann explains to his interrogator, is 'a technical term for normal death'. To this the interrogator replies, 'I can imagine that when a person has to perform heavy physical work, doesn't get enough to eat – he becomes weaker – he becomes so weak that he has a heart attack!' Eichmann agrees and confirms that such a death would be registered in the RSHA as 'natural decline'. The interrogator then drew Eichmann to page 8 where Heydrich continues: 'Those who might possibly still remain, and they undoubtedly will be the toughest amongst them, still have to be treated accordingly, because, representing a natural selection, they would, if released, have to be considered as the seed of a new Jewish reconstruction.' 'Will have to be treated accordingly', Eichmann explains to the interrogator, originated from Himmler, as too did 'natural selection'. On prompting from the interrogator to explain the meaning in the document of 'will have to be treated accordingly', Eichmann answered 'killed, killed, certainly…'. (For the above see Frei, 1993, Document 9, pp. 190–91.) In July 1942, the liquidation of the Łódź and Warsaw ghettos in Poland began.

Sauckel and Speer: the battle between substantive irrationality and rationality

The 'final solution' was a wild scheme. Transportation would be a major factor to be considered, yet transportation was inadequate for the other demands being put upon it, for example, growing reliance on foreign workers made huge demands. Transport was needed for the resettlement programme which gave Germans the farms and properties 'vacated' by Jews and other Poles. Transport was, of course, also sorely needed for the war effort, in the delivery of supplies and ammunition and, indeed, in the movement of soldiers. Transport was also needed for supplies for both consumers and producers in Germany. Transport was also needed by the SS.

All these programmes were based on the belief that victory was at hand and that it would be achieved not through technical planning, new technology and modernized methods but through the oldest methods of 'civilization', the increasing use of labour power. At the Wannsee Conference Nazi thinking on the exploitation of *Untermenschen* labour was confirmed. In March 1942 Sauckel was appointed to the newly created post of special 'Plenipotentiary General for the Utilization of Labour'. By the end of 1941, contrary to expectation, Germany had failed to defeat Russia. Between 22 June 1941 and 20 February 1942 very nearly 1 million German soldiers were lost through death (199 448), wounding (708 351) or going missing (44 342), a total of 952 141 (Goebbels's Diaries and Army Reports; see Homze, 1967, p. 131).

Hitler conveyed his analysis to Sauckel immediately after Sauckel's appointment as plenipotentiary general. Hitler pointed out that the lesson to be drawn from the defeats suffered by the German army in the harsh Russian winter was that new technology was not the way to win. Mechanized army units had been rendered useless by the harsh conditions; trains, planes, tanks and mechanical weapons had failed and German soldiers had suffered and died as a consequence. There was no time for new workers (such as women) to be trained, or working methods to be rationalized. Trained workers had to be used immediately, even those taken from the occupied areas in the east; Hitler dismissed any concerns about the international laws on foreign workers. He also made reference to Stalin's forced recruitment of foreign workers, including 3 million Chinese. (For the above see Homze, 1967, pp. 111–12.)

Sauckel understood the point exactly. Force would be used where necessary and the central point of his plan was that 'All men must be fed, sheltered and treated in such a way as to exploit them to the highest possible extent, at the lowest degree of expenditure' (Sauckel quoted by Homze, 1967, p. 113).

A system run on forced foreign labour could not achieve high productivity and efficiency. There would be no mechanisms for getting the best people for the jobs, no incentives to make people work hard and well. With wages and conditions set low for Eastern Europeans, recruitment of foreign workers, on a voluntary basis, could not be made attractive, and workers were needed. The use of force against workers was costly, as too was the expanded bureaucracy required to administer the labour system and the increased size of the terror organization. The more Germans employed in the terror organization and labour administration, the fewer were available for productive employment.

Speer, appointed as Reich minister of munitions after the death of his predecessor Todt in an air crash, was acutely aware of the economic crisis being experienced by the German war economy. Production had dropped from the summer of 1940 to the winter of 1941 and stocks of raw materials were decreasing very quickly. Speer made clear after his appointment that the German war economy needed modernization. Inefficient plants needed to be replaced by new plants. German women workers needed to be employed. This position clearly contradicted Sauckel's brief and the Nazi leadership kept firm to their belief that victory was within grasp and that such modern armaments factories would be unnecessary in peacetime (Homze, 1967, p. 89).

In April 1942 Speer got Hitler's permission to set up the Central Planning Board (Zentrale Planung) and Speer endeavoured to introduce rationalization. (See Milward, 1965, pp. 72–99 for a full account of Speer's policies; see also Homze, 1967, pp. 204–29.) Behind the state, however, the economy continued to become ever more reliant on coerced labour. The state was woven with yet greater complexity to conceal reality.

Sauckel's newly created post in charge of foreign labour, plenipotentiary general for the utilization of labour, added to the multiplicity of offices rather than streamlining them and Sauckel was far from Speer's personal preference. Strictly under the authority of Goering's Four-Year Plan, the foreign labour section which Sauckel headed was made up from three sections of the Labour Ministry which was headed by Seldte, not Goering. This new post added to the confusion by making Sauckel responsible for domestic as well as foreign labour. This meant that there were now four ministers of labour: the minister of labour, the Reich labour leader, the chief of the German Labour Front and the special plenipotentiary of labour (Homze, 1967, p. 104).

Both the establishment of the new post and the appointment of Sauckel signalled the decline of Goering's influence. Placing Sauckel, and indeed Speer, within the Four-Year Plan was, as Goering's chief deputy remarked after the war, just 'a cover for the outside world' (Homze, 1967, p. 106). Whilst Speer pushed for modern economic reform, to be built on technical efficiency and modern labour-intensive technology using trained workers (a move that is back to substantive rationality), Sauckel pursued the path taken by the ancient economies, production built on the coercion of foreign labour. Whereas Speer's actions took place fully within the outward state (at the Nuremberg Trials, Speer was acquitted of complicity in the organization of slave labour and received a prison sentence of 20 years, not death [Milward, 1965, p. 190]), Sauckel's actions were more shadowy, in a half-world between ostensible and real power.

Initially, at least, recognizing the costs of attracting further voluntary recruits, Sauckel sought to correct the poor diets and harsh treatments meted out to eastern workers (Homze, 1967, p. 122). He achieved a slight improvement in June 1942 but it was clear that Hitler, and Goering, were not simply set on the policy of exploitation of foreign labour, but were mightily impressed by it. Given the low wages paid to eastern workers and the below-subsistence conditions in Russia, they were not convinced by market arguments. In their view, with such cheap and desperate foreign labour available, its exploitation had to be the best policy. These eastern workers were not only employed at low wages, but the tax brought in billions of Marks to the Reich Treasury.[8] Hitler felt that he had scored over professional economists in this. On 4 May 1942 he boasted in the following way:

> ...integration of twenty million foreign workers at cheap rates into the German industrial system represents a saving which, again, is greatly in excess of the debts contracted by the state. *A simple calculation, which curiously enough seems to have escaped the notice of the majority of our economic experts, will show the correctness of this contention*: the foreign worker earns approximately a thousand marks a year, in comparison with the average earnings of two thousand marks by German workers. Work out what this comes to in toto, and you will see that the final gain is enormous.
>
> In the assessment of the national wealth *I had to explain to Funk, who, after all, is Economic Minister of the Reich*, how the standard of living of the German people had been considerably raised by the system of employing foreign labour which we had introduced. One has only to compare the cost of local labour with that of German labour abroad to see that this must be so. (From *Hitler's Secret Conversations*, p. 372, quoted in Homze, 1967, p. 126.) (Italics added.)

Hitler clearly entertained neither the relevance of productivity in his calculations, nor the costs of transport, administration and policing.

Hitler was also absolutely set on fixed wages. The order for a general wage freeze issued in 1939 was to be taken as a principle. Ideally Hitler wanted Sauckel to stabilize wages, in the Reich and Europe, based on the 1942 wage scale, for two reasons. It would reduce the chances of inflation; and it would produce an incentive for volunteer, foreign workers. Real wages in Germany compared favourably with those in France. For eastern workers, however, with wages set so low in Germany, at around subsistence level, voluntary labour from the east was simply too unattractive. (For the above see Homze, 1967, p. 125.) Hitler rejected or simply did not comprehend the incentive of wage increases for increased productivity, The logic of the wage incentive, of course, contradicted his platform on abandonment of a labour market. Whilst nominal wages increased a little during the war, real earnings changed hardly at all (Homze, 1967, p. 245).[9] In 1944, real earnings based on the weekly wage were actually lower than in 1939 (see Frei, 1993, p. 79, Table 3).

With close to 1 million German soldiers lost by the spring of 1942, more foreign workers had to be conscripted to work in Germany. Between 1 million and 1.6 million foreign workers had to be found to replace them, 1 million of these from the east. Coercion was to be used if necessary in the east, though not, at first at least, in the west. Sauckel followed the instructions in 'The Green File': 'I have received my mandate from Adolf Hitler and I will bring millions of eastern workers into Germany without considering whether they want to or not' (quoted in Homze, 1967, p. 134).

By June 1942 Sauckel had 'recruited' around 800 000 workers from the east, some voluntary, some by force, but the more were recruited the more were demanded. The SS estimated a need for 2 million foreign workers. By July, Sauckel claimed to have 'recruited' 1 639 794 foreign workers, 1 300 993 of these from the east. At this point 30 per cent of all foreign labour in the Reich were from Russia. (For the above see Homze, 1967, pp. 136–9.)

Russia remained undefeated and Hitler saw labour supply as crucial to Germany's war effort in August 1942 (Homze, 1967, pp. 140–41). At the end of September, Sauckel's powers were broadened and, on 15 March 1943, Hitler issued a decree giving Sauckel total control over the Department of Labour. By the end of December a further 1 million foreign workers had been raised. By this point Sauckel's office was also to handle the POWs in the prison camps, the *Stalags*, By December, Sauckel also had control over the location of these workers to each individual factory, according to the requirements of the armaments economy. Again this confirmed that Sauckel was not under the authority of the Central Plan.[10]

By the end of 1942 there were nearly 6 million foreign workers and POWs in the Reich (Homze, 1967, p. 144). Sauckel promised to recruit a further 1.6 million in 1943 (ibid., p. 146). By May 846 511 had been recruited but, faced with resistance, Sauckel had 'recruited' only 1 427 680 workers by the end of the year, so falling short of the target. Furthermore, the number obtained was only as high as it was because of the internment of the Italian army in September (ibid., p. 218). For 1944, at a conference held by Hitler in January, the target for the year was set at 4 050 000 new workers of whom over 3.5 million would be foreign workers (ibid., p. 149). Even Sauckel saw that it was impossible.

Speer had originally supported Sauckel's outward policy for the recruitment of foreign labour but he began to perceive the use of foreign labour as a 'crutch' which distorted the economy. (See Homze, 1967, pp. 214–15.) It led, in his view, to firms inflating their demands for labour, lulled the German population into expecting normal peacetime production of goods, worked against the introduction of modern capital-intensive techniques and hindered the full utilization of German labour including that of women. As increasing numbers of workers were introduced into Germany it also, Speer argued, increased pressure on the food supply. In the spring of 1943, Speer was successful in getting more German women into part-time work, but from 1943 the war began to take a serious turn for the worse.

In January 1943, the German army surrendered at Stalingrad. The much heralded German offensive was countered by Russia. In July, Mussolini was deposed from office and arrested. In September Italy signed an armistice with the Allies (Steinberg, 1991, p. 267). Speer worked to address the crisis with a rationally calculated plan for total war which aimed to release German factories for armaments production, with consumer goods produced in 'S-plants' in the occupied areas. By this means the number of foreign workers to be recruited to work inside the Reich was to be reduced. On 4 January 1944, Hitler approved Speer's plan.

Sauckel, however, worked to undermine Speer's plan. The number of workers was never produced on the scale required (Homze, 1967, p. 224). In the first half of 1944, instead of the 1 million to be recruited from France, Sauckel produced 33 000. Instead of the 1.5 million workers required from Italy, Sauckel produced 37 500 (ibid., p. 150). Speer blamed Sauckel and Sauckel blamed Speer's plan for the difficulties in recruiting workers from the occupied territories. In June 1944, the Allied invasion began into France. In July 1944, Goebbels was appointed as 'Plenipotentiary for Total War', the position coveted by Sauckel. It signalled his imminent demise (ibid., p. 226).

Speer immediately put forward a proposal to Hitler for the Reich to split into seven or eight 'armament commands', under Speer. These armament commands would have control over the labour offices, factories and all other party structures related to economic production. Under this scheme the SS would no longer be allowed to take or arrest anyone in post without the permission of the armament command. These proposals were vehemently opposed. On 11 July, a special meeting was held to address the problem of labour recruitment. Speer's moderate suggestions to recruit labour without violence, which were at first upheld, were reversed following the assassination attempt on Hitler on 20 July. On 24 July, Sauckel instructed his labour staff that the army and police were to seize labour wherever they could. (For the above see Homze, 1967, p. 151.)

The records, such as were found for the period after July 1944, indicate that only 400 000 new foreign workers were recruited by these means during the latter half of the year. Based on the estimate produced by Speer's statistical office, there were, in total, some 8 102 000 foreign workers and POWs at work in the Reich at the end of 1944 (Homze, 1967, p. 151). Taking account of expiring contracts, deaths and so on the actual number of foreign workers brought into Germany was probably 10 million, possibly 12 million, in total (ibid., p. 153). All these figures on foreign workers, include, of course, not only prisoners of war but 'Jews of all nationalities'.

The SS, the real power behind the ostensible state
From as early as September 1942, agreement had been reached between the SS and Speer's Ministry that between 3 to 5 per cent of the production of SS plants were to go directly to the Waffen-SS divisions, Unknown to the German economic leaders, however, the SS, ostensibly there to police absenteeism amongst foreign workers, was actually creating the problem of absenteeism: instead of returning workers to their employers the SS was sending them to SS-run concentration camp factories. As Homze (1967, p. 255) explains, 'the SS, the state within a state, was rapidly developing an economic base for its Waffen-SS units'. From mid 1943–44, for certain, the SS were engaging in mass arrests, mostly of foreign workers, in order to expand their concentration camp production. (See ibid., pp. 255–6.)

Complete statistics on SS arrests of foreign workers during the war have never been found but they are available for the first half of 1944. During this time the SS arrested 19 000 Germans (for 'political and religious offences'), a further 13 000 for labour offences and nearly 204 000 foreign workers were arrested for similar offences. When asked by Speer in May 1944 about the huge drain of foreign workers to the SS, Himmler replied that concentration camp food rations were better and therefore the foreign workers were more productive there (Homze, 1967, p. 256). Speer was not impressed and told Hitler so, spelling out that the armaments industry could not take a loss of 30 000 to 40 000 workers a month to the SS (half a million a year) and maintain production (ibid.). Along with these workers captured from within Germany, Jews were being brought in from outside under a cloak of secrecy.

The concentration camps: 1942 to the end
After the shortage of labour was revealed in the winter of 1941–42, the process developed whereby when Jews arrived at Auschwitz-Birkenau SS doctors and officers selected those who were to be sent straight for extermination and those who were to be exploited for labour in the neighbouring camp. Essentially those chosen were young and middle-aged men and fit women without children. The old, the infirm, children and mothers were exterminated, with the relative sizes of the groups assigned to labour or extermination dependent on current needs and the particular levels of debilitation caused by the journey (Broszat, 1968, p. 484). This change towards economic concerns in the functioning of the concentration camps was signalled on 16 March 1942 by their general administrative reorganization under the SS Economic and Administrative Office (headed by Pohl), the WVHA. It

had been within days of this economic turn, on 21 March, that Hitler had appointed Sauckel.

As the war developed it became the practice of the police to send ever larger groups (Poles and eastern workers in particular) to the concentration camps. The concentration camps 'represented the form of forced labour which seemed appropriate to groups regarded as inferior, undesirable or politically dangerous' (Broszat, 1968, p. 485). Firms involved in the armaments industry, or mines or other war-related industries, made requests for prisoners to the Inspector of Armaments in Berlin who passed on the request through the WVHA (ibid., pp. 487–9).

At first the inmates worked 9–10 hours a day. From 1943 it became an 11-hour day right through the winter (Broszat, 1968, p. 492). After 1942 mortality increased and productivity deteriorated (ibid., p. 493). In the latter half of 1942 alone, of an approximate total of 95 000 prisoners, 57 503 died. Between January and August 1943, 60 000 more concentration camp prisoners died; from 26 May 1943 statistics on deaths were concealed (ibid., pp. 498–500). In a memorandum from the inspector of concentration camps of 21 November 1942 it was made clear that final reports on Jewish prisoners' deaths were 'superfluous' (ibid., p. 501).

While instructions went out to reduce camp death rates, SS doctors were, at the same time, encouraged to kill prisoners too ill or too weak to work in order to make the camps 'fit for action'. From his notes written in Cracow jail before his execution Höss, Commander of Auschwitz 1940–43 and WVHA top administrator 1943–45, it is clear that SS doctors in Auschwitz regularly selected 'for extermination…in Auschwitz and Birkenau and in the labour camps, Jews no longer able to work and who were unlikely to be fit again within four weeks'. (Quoted by Broszat, 1968, p. 501.) Höss continues, 'Jews suspected of epidemic diseases were also exterminated.'

By August 1943 the total of concentration camp prisoners had risen from 88 000 at the end of 1942, to 224 000. Roughly a third of these (74 000) were in the three Auschwitz camp units – Auschwitz (I), Birkenau (II) and Monowitz (III). The second largest camp, Sachsenhausen, had 26 000 inmates, Dachau and Buchenwald 17 000 each (Broszat, 1968, p. 503). By 5 April 1944, there were 20 concentration camps with, in addition, 165 labour camps attached. Whilst Birkenau was the main extermination camp with gas chambers, Auschwitz I was the main administrative camp and there labour was used to produce armaments, and at Monowitz the labour camp produced synthetic rubber and petrol.

Other camps were also attached. An agricultural camp, a poultry camp, a market garden camp and chemical laboratories came under Birkenau and under Auschwitz III came coal mines and cement works in surrounding areas (Kraus and Kulka, 1966, p. 8). Above the main entrance to Auschwitz I hung the words *Arbeit Macht Frei* (literally, 'work makes free'). With the plans to move important branches of the armaments industry underground and the huge and dangerous building work this involved, concentration camp labour was viewed as particularly suitable. In May 1944 Hitler instructed that the Jews to be deported from Hungary should be used (ibid.). During 1944, 458 000 Hungarian Jews were deported to Auschwitz, of whom 350 000 were gassed and 108 000 were condemned to the concentration camps as slave labour (Herbert, 1944, p. 256), what Herbert (p. 257) refers to as 'annihilation by labor'.

In a WVHA report of 15 August 1944 the total number of inmates was recorded as 524 286 (145 119 of whom were women). In the last months of the war, Jews and other forced labourers swelled the camps further. By 15 January 1945 there were 714 211 inmates controlled by 40 000 SS guards. Around a third of these prisoners lost their lives in the suffering following Hitler's directive to evacuate camps and transfer prisoners to camps further from Allied invasions. Estimates suggest that not less than half a million prisoners died in the concentration camps from disease and physical collapse (Broszat, 1968, p. 504).

The twisted logic of the two constants: forced labour and racialism
Hitler, as we have seen, consistently clung to his conviction that labour, cheap labour, was the key to economic success and therefore the plank upon which victory in war would be built. He was both infallible and invincible; he must be right, he must win. But not only was the whole enterprise flawed from the start as the basis of a system of substantive rationality; by the end it had become a system of substantive irrationality, not based on firm calculations but on will. Speer questioned Sauckel's statistics over and over. Whereas Sauckel claimed that almost 2 million new workers had joined the war economy between the spring and the end of 1942, the statistics compiled by Speer's ministry from individual factory reports suggested only a few hundred thousand new workers had arrived in armaments factories over this period (Homze, 1967, pp. 208–9). The dispute over numbers continued through 1943 (Homze, 1967, pp. 221–2). One possible explanation is the difference between the number of foreign workers loaded on to transport destined for Germany compared with the number who got off (Milward, 1965, p. 97).

It is doubtful that Speer's figures were much to be relied on anyway. Whilst Speer's ministry claimed that productivity per worker went up in the armaments industry during the war, Wagenfuehr, the chief statistician, admitted, 'it is no fairy tale that even in 1944 nobody in Germany really knew how many working hours were required to produce one Tiger tank, and that at a time when labour was the bottleneck in the German war economy' (quoted in Homze, 1967, p. 261).

The whole conception of a war economy built on foreign labour was, in any case, a wild scheme, as counterproductive as it was productive. Exactly as Speer argued, the use of foreign workers for production distorted the economy, contradicting his modernizing push for more efficient techniques and the use of skilled workers. The whole logic of the system led to deliberate inflation of factories' demands for foreign workers. In terms reminiscent of the problems faced in Stalin's Russia, Speer had argued that, pressed by quotas and new products, it would naturally follow that in order to ensure production, labour demands would be inflated. With a constant supply of foreign labour there was no incentive to devise new technically efficient methods of production, Last, but not least, Speer argued that this addition of millions of foreign workers in the Reich was counterproductive in respect of the food supply. (For the above see Homze, 1967, pp. 215–16.) As Kehrl, head of the Planning Office, stated at the Nuremberg trials:

> In my opinion there was no increase in working capacity because every new worker had to be fed, which happened at the expense of the workers who were already there. That decreased their output. Therefore, it was merely a self-delusion that this would increase the output. (Quoted in Homze, 1967, p. 216)

The low productivity of concentration camp workers employed in industry in particular required more workers to be employed to achieve the same output and with the increase in prices paid to the WVHA for employment of prisoners in 1942–43, the financial incentive for their employment disappeared (Broszat, 1968, p. 493). Added to this, the foreign workers had to be housed and clothed. Being kept separate from the German population meant that special barrack accommodation had to be built for them which represented a large expense for factories.[11] There were additional counterproductive aspects to the treatment of foreign workers. Not only did the treatment of eastern workers under the *Untermensch* philosophy reduce the chances of voluntary recruitment, but the combination of propaganda and coercion made the workers not only docile but also indifferent and careless, resulting in losses in production. (See Homze, 1967, p. 259, reporting on a psychological study undertaken by Shils at the end of the war.)

Hitler, however, as his secret conversations quoted above make clear, thought he knew better than all the economic experts. 'Cheap rates' were the answer – 'the final gain is enormous'. To repeat, it was a simple calculation 'which curiously enough seems to have escaped the notice of the majority of our economic experts'. The key to the calculation lay in the cheapness with which the workers could be maintained. Sauckel, as quoted above, had understood that 'all men must be fed, sheltered and treated in such a way as to exploit them to the highest possible extent, at the lowest degree of expenditure'. What this would mean in practice, how it was to be applied would, of course, depend on the racial classification of the worker. The foreign labour programme was the ideal state policy behind which the absolute experiment of forced labour at the lowest possible expenditure could be carried out in the concentration camps where those without value (the ill, the old, the young, the 'asocial', the politically objectionable and the racially 'inferior') could simply be gassed at no further expense to the economy. There too human beings could also be used for horrific experiments, in line with ideas of the inferior being used in the service of the superior.

Conclusion: relentless logic

This is not a straightforward argument that the Holocaust took place in order to exploit Jews for their economic utility.[12] Nazism was racist to its core and however history had unfurled under Nazi domination Jews and other 'sub-human' races would have been abused and separated from Germans and deaths would have occurred as a consequence. Of this there can be no doubt. But there was also another firm, immovable aspect to Hitler's and therefore Nazi thinking: the utter conviction of the importance of labour compulsion, low wages and the absolute advantage of a labour-extensive economy. Whenever labour was in short supply Jews could be used at the lowest possible expenditure. When not needed they, at the bottom of the racial pile, were expendable and action could be taken in line with racial thinking within the limits of the latest means available. Thus, in a system of wild schemes, labour camps became intrinsic to the system and death camps the depository for the valueless, just as Arendt describes. Her error, however, was to confuse the objective assessment of the system as anti-utilitarian and Hitler's immovable belief that the extensive use of cheap labour, indeed the cheapest possible labour, was the key to economic success.

Terror as government in Germany had a purpose beyond the creation of a mass society where people had stopped thinking and were perfectly obedient, a society in which for the infallible leader everything was possible. Terror as government concealed the reality of economic chaos and provided both the screen behind which wild schemes could be put into operation and the means through which they were pursued. In the mind of the infallible leader the combination of racialism with his chosen labour policies was absolutely rational. The Holocaust was the logical consequence of unnerving belief in the rightness of these two principles; but only so long as these principles remained constant. In that sense, the Holocaust was neither inevitable, for human action could have changed it, nor the product of goal-displacement. Racialism and the extensive use of forced labour were not goals; they were the immovable fundamental convictions upon which the system of substantive irrationality was built.

Notes

1. The Army, Navy and the Foreign Office's opposition to Hitler's wishes to take Austria and Czechoslovakia and then conquer further living space (*Lebensraum*) to the east was revealed at the Hossbach Conference of 5 November 1937 (Kaiser, 1992, p. 183). Kaiser (ibid., p. 184) argues, however, that the path actually taken by Hitler was not that outlined by him at the conference.

2. It is also the case that incentives to German workers to work harder were introduced in the form of improved work conditions and increased holidays at prices that ordinary workers could afford. Mobilization campaigns such as the 'Joy to Work' were also introduced for this purpose. (See Schoenbaum, 1967, pp. 110–13.)

3. From 8 March 1940, Poles in Germany were required to wear badges with a violet 'P' on a yellow triangle, and Himmler sent directives to his police units. Failure to wear the badges carried stiff penalties. Sexual relations with Germans were also forbidden (on penalty of death for the Pole) and Poles were restricted in the use of public transport, attendance at social functions and so on. They were also, as mentioned, paid lower wages than Germans, but to avoid the natural consequences of the labour market (employers preferring the cheaper labour) employers paid the same wages but the Reich took a special 15–20 per cent 'social equalization fee' from the Poles. The Polish workers were also excluded from the majority of the German workers' benefits (Homze, 1967, p. 42).

4. Contrary to Bauman's argument that *Lebensraum*, more room for Germans, was the goal, Browning (1992, p. 8) argues that 'specific plans' for racial policy and *Lebensraum* in Poland took shape only during September 1939 and not before the invasion. Browning argues that this specific plan was essentially Himmler's and that it was developed in the 'euphoria of victory'. Homze (1967, p. 26) argues that the Nazis had three competing goals: *Lebensraum*, labour and material, and race theory.

5. In gangs of upwards of 50 prisoners of war, under the control of the German army, the employers of the POWs had to pay the army camp 60 per cent of normal wages and 80 per cent for piecework minus the cost of room and board. The labour and food offices arranged the work (Homze, 1967, pp. 23–4).

6. For full details of these foreign workers see Homze (1967, pp. 56–64). A relatively small number were also recruited from neutral countries.

7. All other camps in the east, with the single exception of Lublin–Majdanek, had been set up solely for liquidation (Broszat, 1968, p. 484).

8. At this point, the ghettos were economically viable, producing consumer goods. These ghettos Browning (1992, p. 53) likens to 'warehouses' storing Jews. They were never intended to be permanent.

9. The tax deducted from each worker's wages meant that no eastern worker obtained more than 6.50 RM and the average was only 4.6 RM. Sauckel, nevertheless, managed to improve eastern workers' wages (excluding the wages of POWs and Jews, of course). By 1944, they were comparable to western foreign workers' wages. Homze (1967, p. 245) points out, however, that these improvements in eastern workers' wages proved the one exception to the 'prevailing Nazi philosophy' to hold the general level of wages down.

10. Even so Sauckel never came even close to achieving supremacy over labour. The army controlled drafting policies, the German Labour Front had control over the welfare and training of German workers, the Zentrale Planung had charge of distributing labour to industry, the Food Ministry had charge of agricultural Labourers, and Himmler, the SS Reichführer, had complete jurisdiction over worker security, concentration camp labour, and racial policies relating to workers (see Homze, 1967, pp. 305–6).

11. See Homze (1967, p. 266). Conditions within these camps ranged from good to appalling. The Farber and Krupp camps were particularly bad. (For details see ibid., pp. 267–71.)

12. This is an argument which has been made by Mayer (1989). His argument has been criticized, however, for ignoring the fact that for Jews alone, the old, the children and mothers were sent for extermination to Auschwitz along with the Jewish able-bodied for forced labour, and that the (smaller) camps at Chelmo, Belzec, Sobibor and Treblinka were not used for forced labour (Browning, 1992, pp. 82–5). Herbert (1994) tips too far in

the opposite direction, viewing the deployment of forced labour as the 'camouflaging cover' (p. 258) for the 'final solution' and the use of Jewish labour related to the necessity produced by the German defeats in war from 1944. As explained above, this conflicts with Homze's (1967) more extensive investigation of the same sources. Herbert makes no reference to Homze's definitive work. In general, there is a tendency for investigations of the 'final solution' to occlude analysis of others who perished under the Nazi regime, such as asocials, the 'hereditary ill', gypsies, communists, homosexuals and, not least, foreign workers snatched from the streets, and prisoners of war. In the secret society of Nazi Germany it is impossible to know the total number of victims exterminated or worked to death by the regime. The painstaking efforts made by researchers of the Holocaust have produced the following figures on the Jewish dead: 3 million exterminated in the concentration camps; 1.5 million shot by the Einsatzgruppen in Russia; 900 000 died in the ghettos, under transit and in labour and concentration camps; plus tens of thousands of others, for example those dying in the forced marches and transportation near the end of the war. In all, a total of 5 978 000 of whom 2.8 million were Poles, 1.5 million were Russians and 1.032 million were from other Eastern European countries (see Landau, 1992, pp. 180, 316).

PART III

GENERALIZATION
AND THE
CASE OF CAMBODIA

Introduction

Terror as government is conducted in secret, the whole system of terror an elaborate concealment. As a consequence, and as Germany and Russia have shown, it is only possible to separate out these totalitarian regimes from the less exceptional totalitarian dictatorships after the regimes have fallen. Even then, as the cases have also shown, there is neither guarantee that the evidence later released will be adequate nor that it will be sufficiently impartial. The very shadowy nature of these totalitarian regimes, where terror is government, puts them at the furthest reaches of political science. Totalitarian dictatorships at least provide clear structures to examine, state systems ready for analysis. In totalitarian regimes 'real power', to use Arendt's term, operates behind the state and the employment of the normal tools of political science therefore misconstrues the true nature of such regimes. Indeed, analysis of political structures, organizations, policies, or statements will actually mislead understanding.

Any classification as a totalitarian dictatorship – that is dictatorship through the state, aimed at substantive economic changes and using the instruments of terror to stop people carrying out proscribed acts – runs the risk that the case may actually be a totalitarian regime. Whilst the government remains in position, rumours of terror used as a deliberate policy against the innocent, resulting in the extermination of large numbers of people, will be the best pointer to the likelihood of terror as government. Today, the likeliest candidate for classification as a totalitarian regime rather than a totalitarian dictatorship is Iraq. Iraqi policies against Kurds offer the clearest sign, though such conduct is not incompatible with nationalistic dictatorship. At the earliest, accurate analysis cannot be carried out until after the fall of Saddam Hussein. The possibility of Iran developing into a totalitarian regime while Khomenini remained alive, or of Ethiopia had Mengistu stayed in control has been considered, tentatively, elsewhere (O'Kane, 1991). Since the end of World War II, genocide has also been reported in China–Tibet, Rwanda, Indonesia, Sudan, Pakistan–Bangladesh, Burundi, Uganda, Paraguay, Cambodia, Guatemala, Afghanistan and Sri Lanka. (See Fein, 1993, p. 87.) The evidence produced following the fall of governments in Eastern Europe after 1989 has confirmed both the importance of differences between cases and the inappropriateness of comparison, for similarity, with the exceptional cases of Nazi Germany from 1938–45 and Stalin's Russia from 1930–53. There is, however, one case which, following the fall of its government, has revealed the true distinctiveness of a secret society and a system of totalitarian terror.

9 Terror as government and its causes, Cambodia, April 1975–January 1979

The 'zero years' in Cambodia began with the defeat of General Lon Nol's government and the entry of the Khmer Rouge into the capital, Phnom Penh, on 17 April 1975. On entering Phnom Penh the Khmer Rouge forced the city's population to migrate to the countryside to work on the land. In other towns, similarly forced evacuations occurred. The zero years ended after the Vietnamese army, together with the Cambodian National United Front for National Socialism, formed from the refugees who had fled to Vietnam over these intervening years, succeeded in defeating the Khmer Rouge in seventeen of the nineteen provinces and established a People's Revolutionary Council in Phnom Penh on 8 January 1979 (Sagar, 1989, pp. 37–8).

Out of a population of up to 7.7 million, estimates put on the number of people killed as a direct result of Khmer Rouge policies over these zero years, based on interviews with survivors, have been put as high as 3 million (*Keesing's*, 1984, p. 32672). Earlier estimates such as Ponchaud's (1978, p. 92) at between 800 000 and 1 400 000 and Barron and Paul's (1977, p. 206) at 1 200 000, however, have been criticized for using unsubstantiated statistics (see Chomsky and Herman, 1979, ch. 6). In reaction to Barron and Paul's estimates, Vickery (1985, pp. 184–8) offers a cautious and carefully calculated figure of 400 000 for the decrease in population over those years. Of this 400 000 some would have been accounted for by a decrease in the birth rate and deaths due to the war. Vickery argues that it is impossible to know the actual number of deaths through execution. Sagar (1989, p. 34) puts the death toll, the figure above the normal death rate, as 'substantially under 1 000 000'. Mass graves and evidence of atrocities continued to be found throughout the early 1980s. (See *Keesing's*, 1981, p. 30671; 1982, p. 31418; 1984, p. 32672.)

Background to the zero years: a dislocated society

Before the fall of Phnom Penh, Cambodia had a severely dislocated society. The prelude to 'year zero' involved a civil war which took place within a society torn apart by foreign war. The country had been ravaged by war, the economy was devastated and millions of people had left the countryside in order to escape both the indiscriminate bombing and the starvation which threatened as a consequence of the destruction of agriculture in the war regions.

Guerrilla forces first appeared in Cambodia in 1946 in the fight for independence from the French. These guerrillas re-emerged in 1958 in a somewhat different guise and challenged Sihanouk at various times over the years to the mid-1960s. In 1967, following a peasant revolt, the new 'Khmer Rouge' had grown to sufficient strength for the 1967 revolt to spread in 1968 to eleven of the nineteen provinces in Cambodia (*Keesing's*, 1975, p. 27154). In 1970 a *coup d'état* overthrew Prince Sihanouk's government and brought to power a government, under General Lon Nol, more acceptable to the USA. The war with Vietnam followed.

After the 1970 coup, Sihanoukist forces joined with the Khmer Rouge in the formation of the National United Front of Cambodia, NUFC, to bring down the Lon Nol government. A government in exile, headed by Prince Sihanouk with a Sihanoukist prime minister, was also set up in Peking. Khieu Samphan, who was the deputy prime minister and minister of defence in the government in exile and a member of the Khmer Rouge, returned to Cambodia along with the other two Khmer ministers to continue active engagement in the fight. As Sihanouk explained, 'This war is not a civil war, but a war of aggression and colonisation against Cambodia by the United States' (*Keesing's*, 1975, p. 27149).

Whereas the NUFC was supplied by the Vietcong, the Republican Army was supplied by the USA. Strictly, US air raids ended in 1973 but the US continued to play a crucial role in supplying arms and supplies to the Republican areas. In June 1974, for example, the US Defense Secretary stated that 690 missions to parachute ammunition and provisions were being carried out each month. US aircraft also continued flying missions from Thailand. (For the above see *Keesing's*, 1975, p. 27149.) Chomsky and Herman (1979, p. 165) quote comments made by Richard Dudman, a US war correspondent captured after the fall of Phnom Penh:

> The constant indiscriminate bombing, an estimated 450 000 dead and wounded civilians, to say nothing of military casualties, and the estimated 4 000 000 refugees were almost inevitable results of the short US invasion of Cambodia and the consequent proxy war that ended in defeat for the United States as well as for its client regime in Phnom Penh.

Vickery estimates the deaths incurred during that war at between 500 000 to 1 million, and it has also been estimated that between March and August 1973 alone 40 000 tons of bombs fell every month (Vickery, 1985, p. 25; Ponchaud, 1978, p. 191). Bombing and fighting combined to destroy crops, forests, transport systems and factories and led to massive movements of people out of the rural areas into the towns and cities. An estimated 3 million people, mostly refugees from the fighting zones, had moved into the towns, the majority of them into the capital, Phnom Penh. Of these most were living in the areas controlled by Lon Nol and had been subsisting on rice supplied by the USA (*Keesing's*, 1976, p. 27758).

The Khmer Rouge takes over: April 1975–April 1976

Between 1970 and 1975 the Khmers Rouges came to dominate the Sihanoukist forces. The establishment of a functioning partial 'government in exile' within Cambodia, in which Khmer Rouge representatives dominated, played an important part in this. Whilst the combined Sihanoukist and Khmer Rouge forces, the NUFC, defeated Lon Nol, it was the Khmer Rouge which in April 1975 took the victory. From the takeover in April 1975, the Khmer Rouge worked to consolidate their control and over the months the Pol Pot faction strengthened its position (Sagar, 1989, pp. 28–9). Prince Sihanouk himself was to return to power temporarily, tendering his resignation officially on 2 April 1976. He expressed his position on 14 April 1975 in the following way: 'After victory I will be head of state and there will be an entirely communist government and administration. So either I am a puppet of the Khmer Rouge, or I remain independent and there will be trouble'. (For the above see *Keesing's*, 1975, pp. 27149–54.)

In January 1976 a new constitution came into force, naming the country 'Democratic Kampuchea' and creating a 250-seat 'National Assembly' for which elections were held in March. In April 1976 Saloth Sar, in his new name – Pol Pot – became Prime Minister and Khieu Samphan became President of the State Praesidium. Sihanouk and the Sihanoukist Prime Minister Penn Nouth had been officially displaced.

The initial estimates of deaths for the year April 1975–April 1976 ranged between 80 000 and the evidently exaggerated 1 000 000 (*Keesing's*, 1976, p. 27758).

Wild schemes

Fierce debates have raged over the reasons behind the forced evacuations of cities and towns. The fundamental political–economic ideas of Khmer Rouge policy were to be found in Khieu Samphan's doctoral thesis, submitted to the University of Paris in 1959. In it he argued that the Cambodian economy could overcome its dependency only by initially extricating itself from the international economy ('self-reliance') and expanding agricultural production to provide a basis for industrialization. On his analysis, over 80 per cent of the urban population were unproductive and he recommended that they should be transferred into productive sectors, into agriculture in particular, in the form of cooperatives (*Keesing's*, 1979, p. 29581).

Khieu Samphan's thinking was evidently behind the policies put into immediate operation in April 1975 but there were highly practical considerations too. With agriculture devastated by war and an estimated 3 million people recently moved into the urban areas and dependent on rice supplied by the USA, the immediate consequence of the capture of Phnom Penh by the Khmer Rouge meant that this supply of rice was at an end. All the inhabitants faced starvation unless a new rice harvest could be planted. As Chomsky and Herman (1979) argue, the Khmer Rouge had to get the peasants back into the countryside in order to feed the population and in that light they argue that the Khmer Rouge probably saved lives in forcibly moving people out of the towns into the countryside. They also point out that the forced long marches were necessary in the face of insufficient transport. They concede, though, that the forced evacuation was 'heavy handed'.

Reports have suggested that rice production achieved in November 1975 was exceptionally high, yielding double that needed to feed the population for the year (*Keesing's*, 1976, p. 27758). Though the claims about the 1975 harvest and the fairness of its distribution have been questioned, good harvests seem to have followed both in 1976 and 1977, though not in 1978 when freak weather conditions brought a 10 per cent loss (see Sagar, 1989, p. 33 and Twining, 1989, pp. 143–5). On balance, then, the evidence seems to support practical interpretations. At the same time, the speed with which the initial operation was undertaken fits more the description of a 'wild scheme' than a calculated plan. Wild schemes may 'pay off' in the short term, but as Nazi Germany and Stalinist Russia have shown, in the longer term they produce ever wilder extremes. As in Nazi Germany and Stalinist Russia it is also clear that in Cambodia a dislocated society gave rise to an economic system in which forced labour was the essence.

Terror as government
The Khmer Rouge government operated not through the state but behind the state. After the March 1976 elections the Assembly quickly 'dropped into obscurity' (Carney, 1989, p. 90). Apart from the January 1976 constitution, the Khmer Rouge issued neither laws nor decrees. As Carney (1989, pp. 95–6) comments, 'they seemed deliberately to ignore the administrative and legal frameworks that make up most states'. In 'Democratic Kampuchea' government was carried out through terror and in the autumn of 1976 Pol Pot himself dropped out of the public eye to operate under complete conceal-ment. On 27 September it was announced that Pol Pot had resigned for 'health reasons' and Nuon Chea, Chairman of the Standing Committee of the People's Representative Assembly, became 'Acting Premier' (*Keesing's*, 1978, p. 28805). In practice Pol Pot was back as prime minister within the month, though not officially so until September 1977 (Sagar, 1989, p. 30).

During those shadowy months, with the support of the south-western and northern military commanders, Pol Pot began an onslaught against other zonal armies on the pretext of *coup* attempts by 'traitorous forces which were

Vietnam's agents'.[1] Small clashes along the border with Vietnam occurred both in 1975 and 1976 but the Khmer army concentrated its attacks within Democratic Kampuchea until 1977 when fighting broke out on a larger scale, following attacks by the south-western zone Cambodian forces. From the start of 1977 purges began in the northern provinces, with officials replaced by loyalists from the south-west. From mid-1977, the attacks spread further afield, some areas being purged twice.

Pol Pot re-emerged as prime minister, his controlling position greatly strengthened, in September 1977. In a speech lasting five hours, he declared, for the first time, that the Communist Party of Cambodia had controlled the country since April 1975 and that he was the party general secretary. Before this, reference had only ever been made to Angkar, the Organization (*Keesing's*, 1978, p. 28806). In his speech he made reference to 'one or two per cent of the population' who continued to 'determinedly oppose the revolution'. At this point, So Phim, First Vice President of the State Praesidium and Party Secretary of the Eastern Zone, was refusing to start purges. In December 1977, Vietnam launched a counteroffensive, keeping troops in Cambodia for only a few weeks and initiating peace negotiations, which Pol Pot rejected. Fighting continued throughout 1978. In May 1978, the eastern zone was subjected to an onslaught from south-western troops. The attack was a success: thousands were massacred and others were forcibly removed to other zones for interrogation, torture and then execution (Sagar, 1989, p. 31).

These were the massacres that led to the start of the resistance movement, the Cambodian National United Front for National Socialism, which combined with the 100 000 Vietnamese troops (120 000 in all) and advanced on Cambodia in December 1978 to establish the People's Revolutionary Council, PRC, in Phnom Penh in January 1979. On 10 January, the PRC declared the 'dictatorial, fascist and genocidal regime of the reactionary Pol Pot – Ieng Sary clique' abolished and replaced by the People's Republic of Kampuchea (PRK) (Sagar, 1989, p. 31).

S-21, Tuol Sleng
At the centre of the purges was S-21, the Tuol Sleng school in Phnom Penh converted to Pol Pot's main centre for interrogation, torture and execution. Records were left behind as the Khmer Rouge fled in January 1979. The dossiers suggest that around 80 per cent of the prisoners held there were Khmer Rouge supporters (see Hawk, 1989, p. 209 and Quinn, 1989, p. 198). Elsewhere, evidence has to be pieced together through fragments in archives and the testimonies of refugees and survivors. These testimonies suggest that such 'prison–torture–execution centres' existed at regional, district and commune levels, some of them converted Buddhist temples (Hawk, 1989, p. 21). Quinn (1989, p. 198) notes that *Newsweek* (1980, vol. 42) refers to 'Brother'

Duch, the head of Tuol Sleng, as the head of Norkorbal, the secret police system. Outside of Phnom Penh, victims mainly met their deaths in mass executions carried out away from the population, by Khmer Rouge soldiers (Quinn, 1989, p. 186). A significant proportion of these victims were those who failed to achieve their work quotas or bemoaned conditions in the cooperatives (see *Keesing's*, 1979, p. 29582).

The records at Tuol Sleng showed that 14 499 people had been held there between April 1975 and the end of 1978. Of these, only four survived. Mass graves and evidence of atrocities were unearthed continually through the early 1980s. In the provinces of Kampot, Takeo and Kandal, a total of 66 000 bodies were found in 1981. In June 1982, over 1400 mass graves were found in Kandal province with a total of 16 000 bodies in 386 of the graves. In the Svay Rieng province, 650 mass graves contained a total of 38 000 bodies. In 1938, 20 mass graves containing nearly 10 000 bodies were found in Battambang province. (See *Keesing's*, 1981, p. 30671; 1982, p. 31418; 1984, p. 32672.)

Angkar
Angkar, or as Barron and Paul (1977) prefer, Angka Loeu, literally means 'Higher Organization', but is better translated as 'Organization on High'. From day one, 17 April 1975, the Organization on High was given as justification to commandeer vehicles, to order people out of hospitals, or later to order people to their death; 'Angka Loeu wants to re-educate you' was a euphemism for the death sentence (ibid., p. 12). As Barron and Paul (1977, p. 40) explain:

> The Organization on High was not interested in merely improving or even radically modifying existing Cambodian society. Rather Angka Loeu was determined to shatter it to bits and start completely anew. For Angka Loeu had resolved to annul the past and obliterate the present so as to fashion a future uncontaminated by the influences of either.

The purpose, Barron and Paul argue, was to reduce the population to 'one disoriented, malleable mass' (ibid., p. 41). Justification was offered by officers in terms of Angka Loeu's goal being the true communist classless society of true equality. Ponchaud (1978) similarly draws attention to the significance of the choice of 'organization' over 'party', though he stresses the receptiveness of the culture to such deified commands. 'Angkar', as Ponchaud prefers, is the object of adoration, which organized everything; 'the anonymous Angkar is the incarnation of the people's will'.[2] In support of their position, Barron and Paul (1977, pp. 49–60) quote from a report by Kenneth M. Quinn in 1974 on the actions taken in the areas occupied by the Khmer Rouge 'to psychologically reconstruct individual members of society':

...this process entails stripping away, through terror and other means, the traditional bases, structures and forces which have shaped and guided an individual's
life until he is left as an atomised isolated individual unit: and then rebuilding him
according to party doctrine by substituting a series of new values, organisations
and ethical norms for the ones taken away.

Barron and Paul point out, drawing on comparisons both with Aristotle's
analyses of tyranny and with the history of the Soviet Union and 'other
totalitarian states', that this process was not original to Angka Loeu. Chomsky
and Herman (1979), however, have taken particularly strong objection to the
comparison of Cambodia with Nazi Germany. They have also questioned the
assertion that Cambodia was ruled by 'nine men at the centre', the term they
prefer to 'Angka Loeu', 'the standard media picture: a centrally-controlled
genocidal policy of mass execution' (ibid., p. 159).

Ideology and its uses
The zero years, April 1975–January 1979, are most commonly described as
'communist'. (See, for example, Rummel, 1990, and Ponchaud, 1978 and
1989.) The dominance of 'Angkar' until September 1977, however, somewhat undermines this claim and though the Communist Party of Cambodia
was suddenly claimed to have been in power all along, Deputy Premier Ieng
Sary was reported as explaining in December 1977 that the Khmer Rouge
was following neither the Chinese nor Vietnamese lines: 'What we want is to
create something that never was before in history. No model exists for what
we are building. We are not imitating either the Chinese or the Vietnamese
model.' (Ieng Sary, quoted in *Keesing's*, 1978, p. 28807.) What had never
existed before in history was the total abolition of money and the use of land
for any form of private production in a claimed classless society of 'perfect
harmony'.

The 'Pol Pot – Ieng Sary clique' differed from the Vietnamese model in
another important way. In contrast to Hanoi-style internationalism, the Khmer
Rouge were ultra-nationalist. Jackson (1989b, p. 249) explains, 'The Khmer
Rouge's concept of total national independence sprang primarily from the
centuries old Khmer fear of foreign invasion', By mid 1978, anti-Vietnamese
rhetoric formed a major part of both government and party propaganda, as
made clear in their 'Black Book'. Pol Pot and his associates made endless
references to Cambodia's former glory during the Angkor Empire (800–
1444) and promised frequently to 'liberate' the ethnic Khmers of Kampuchea
Krom (the Mekong delta region in Vietnam) and of Surin and Buriram (provinces of Thailand) (Sagar, 1989, p. 35).

Racially distinct and ethnically different groups and nationalities of all
kinds were singled out for persecution (Hawk, 1989, p. 212). It was alleged,
for example, that these minorities were forced to speak Kampuchean and join

'people's communes' under threat of death, and of 20 000 people of Thai origin in the south-westerly Koh Kong province, only 8000 remained alive (*Keesing's*, 1981, p. 30670). It was also reported that 20 000 of the 30 000 Moslem Chans were massacred, that the Vietnamese minority suffered a similar fate and that Buddhists and Catholics were also persecuted (*Keesing's*, 1981, pp. 30670–71). These nationalities provided useful scapegoats.

Comparison with China also falters. Vickery, arguing against the classification of the zero years as a Marxist revolution, has pointed out that in all other cases of communist revolutions, the cities, urban workers and technology have been crucial, but in Cambodia they were not (Vickery, 1985, p. 280). In Cambodia the cities and towns were emptied and agricultural improvements were made not through improvements in technology but by concentrating all labour on the land. In drawing particular comparison with the Cultural Revolution in China Vickery contrasts the importance of workers and soldiers in the Chinese case and the critical nature of the relationship between rural areas and the cities where workers held power. Commenting on the mobilization against existing organizations in China, Vickery (1985, p. 272) remarks, 'nothing like this outburst of student and worker rage against bureaucracy and party ever occurred in Cambodia, where the party directed the poorest peasants against everyone else and where students and urban workers were class enemies'.[3]

Forced labour and substantive irrationality

Of key importance to an understanding of 'Democratic Kampuchea' is the fact that increased agricultural production was to be made, not through technological improvements, but through the use of increased labour to work on the land. This had been the whole thrust of Khieu Samphan's economic position which had been revealed in his doctoral thesis. Agricultural production was to be increased through the extra use of labour. As in Stalin's Russia and Nazi Germany economic policy was labour-extensive. On day one, 17 April 1975, the Khmer Rouge made it quite clear that they intended to use force to achieve their aims. Given the economic circumstances drastic measures were certainly required but, again as in Germany and Russia, what was involved was not planning but wild schemes. In Cambodia these schemes, which involved racialism and laying claim to territories of the past, resembled more those of Nazi Germany than Stalinist Russia, but in subjecting the population as a whole to a system of forced labour, rather than concentrating primarily on racial groups as in Germany, Cambodia under Pol Pot came closer to the USSR. In its universality, however, Cambodia also greatly surpassed Stalinist Russia.

The people forced to evacuate the cities and towns by the Khmer Rouge in April 1975 were set to work in the fields. The rice crop, harvested in Novem-

ber, was claimed at the time to have been exceptionally good, yielding
2 200 000 tons, twice the amount needed to feed the population for a year
(*Keesing's*, 1976, p. 27758). Over the summer, repairs took place on the
roads and bridges damaged in the war and transport was made possible for the
'second migration' which began in September 1975 (ibid.). The rural population was also made to move; for example, the inhabitants of the south-eastern
provinces were sent to the western provinces (*Keesing's*, 1981, p. 30670).

Belief in an extensive forced-labour system lay at the centre of the Khmer
Rouge's economic policy. This was why money was not needed in the system. Members of the cooperatives were paid in food and were given one set
of clothing a year. Conditions were most severe in the 'new economic zones'
where the one-time inhabitants of the cites were sent to work on virgin lands.
There thousands of families lived in make-shift barracks (*Keesing's*, 1979,
p. 29581). In these places conditions were closest to the labour camps in the
Soviet Union and in the Reich. The indictment against Pol Pot and Ieng Sary
by the recently installed People's Republic of Kampuchea, PRK, government
in August 1979 listed the following amongst their crimes:[4]

> 3) *Establishment of a System of Repression and Coercion*. People had been forced
> to work for 12 to 16 hours a day, or even longer, irrespective of their age or health,
> had been fed a scanty allowance of rice and stems from banana trees, had been
> dressed in rags and had lived in miserable huts. A network of secret informers had
> been set up to discourage any idea of opposition, and any violation of rules had
> been punished by forcing the offender to fulfil two or three times the normal work
> quota or by reducing or cutting off his food ration for a first offence, and by death
> for a second.

In Cambodia under the 'Pol Pot – Ieng Sary clique' the market had been
suspended completely and forced labour had become the central plank of
policy. As in Nazi Germany and Stalin's Russia the economy in Cambodia
was based on substantive irrationality and the economic crisis which resulted
was concealed by lies.

Systematic lying and economic crisis
In the five-hour speech which Pol Pot delivered in September 1977, in which
he claimed wonderful successes for the regime in all things, he declared the
following: 'The collective co-operatives of the peasants have transformed the
arid, impoverished Cambodian countryside of old into an increasingly beauti-
ful countryside equipped with extensive networks of reservoirs, trenches and
canals and freshened by verdant farmland' (*Keesing's*, 1978, p. 28806).

In March 1978 Pol Pot declared to a Yugoslav journalist that 'we have
succeeded in solving the agricultural problem' (Sagar, 1989, p. 33). While
some foreign visitors supported this view, others argued that the food short-

ages remained critical throughout the zero years (ibid.). The proclaimed good harvest of 1975 was declared poor by refugees escaping to Thailand and Vietnam. Famine conditions were reported in 1976 and although good harvests followed in both 1976 and 1977, the ordinary cooperative members had only two bowls of rice a day with much of the rice exported or put in storage. It was also reported that whilst the ordinary peasants managed on two bowls of rice, the officials ate 'meat, fish and vegetables'. In 1978, freak weather conditions brought the worst floods for 70 years to the Mekong delta while elsewhere there was drought; 10 per cent of the crop was lost. (For the above see Sagar, 1989, p. 33.)

The evidence, such as it is, contradicts Pol Pot's claims and rather supports the claim for the disastrous effects of the Khmer Rouge policies. Before the Lon Nol *coup* in 1970 approximately 2.4 million hectares were producing rice. In 1979, rice production covered only 700 000 hectares. Levels of rice yielded per hectare also dropped over the same period, from 62.5 per cent to 40.7 per cent. By 1979, rice production, at 280 000 tonnes was no more than the equivalent of the food aid received by the Lon Nol government in the year before the Khmer Rouge overthrew it. (For the above see D'Souza, 1989, pp. 86–7.)

With the devastating effects of the war between 1970 and 1975 and war with Vietnam from 1978 plus the freak bad harvest of 1978, comparisons between years are difficult to make.[5] The certain knowledge of torture centres, massacres and deaths on so large a scale not only from executions but from disease, malnutrition and overwork, along with the wholesale migrations obviously belies the rural idyll portrayed by Pol Pot! (See *Keesing's*, 1978, p. 28805.)[6] Perhaps the best evidence for the disastrous failure of Khmer Rouge economic policies has been the level of recovery achieved since, with rice production by 1989 at 2.7 million tonnes (D'Souza, 1989, p. 87) and improvements already evident by 1980 (*Keesing's*, 1981, p. 30676).

Problems with totalitarianism in Cambodia
The system of terror in Cambodia, though it had 'prison–torture–execution centres' and the equivalent of labour camps, stopped short of a sophisticated police system with concentration camps, so crucial to Arendt's view of the totalitarian regime.[7] Terror in Democratic Kampuchea was perpetrated through the guerrilla army. The Khmer Rouge army was divided into three sections: the 'regular' army which was used to put down uprisings and protect borders; the 'regional' troops, which were responsible for security and worked alongside the local political organization, usually itself appointed by Angkar; and the 'spy troops' who were unarmed and acted as informers (Ponchaud, 1978, pp. 122–3).

The army was not, however, used in 'totalitarian dictatorship' in Friedrich and Brzezinski's sense. There is neither claim nor evidence in the literature for a state bureaucracy having played an important part. There were neither decrees nor laws other than the January constitution. The party (in fact an 'organization' to September 1977) was not a modern, mass political party. Equally, the army was not used in 'dictatorship'. An argument could be made for the appropriateness of the description 'totalitarian dictatorship' for the period April 1975–76, when the Sihanoukists still had titular power at least and when army directives could be argued to have been more concerned with the emergency of economic collapse following the war. There is insufficient evidence to be sure. Pol Pot's secret operations from April 1976 and the lack of decrees and laws undermines any claim for the Khmer Rouge ever to have acted through the state at all. On balance it makes sense to view the zero years April 1975–January 1976 as a whole.

In view of the backward nature of the country and the importance of the army, and the country's lack of a separate and sophisticated secret police organization with specially built concentration camps, Democratic Kampuchea cannot, though, be properly fitted into the classification of a totalitarian regime.

Comparison with the Zulu state, 1816–40
States where terror rules have existed in pre-industrial societies. Walter (1972) analyses the terroristic despotism of the Zulu state under Shaka, 1816–28 and Dingane, 1828–40, and discusses Shaka's rule in the following terms:

> Notwithstanding the limitations of a primitive technology, Shaka was able to utilize violence on such a scale as to create what some social scientists have called a proto-totalitarian system. Without gas chambers, machine guns, or a guillotine, Shaka managed to establish one of the most effective regimes of terror on record. He modified the traditional assegai, which was a long throwing spear, by reducing the length of the shaft and turning it into a short, thrusting weapon. With this material instrument he constructed a pattern of terroristic controls more efficient, although smaller in scale, than the techniques of totalitarian states with all their deadly apparatus. (Walter, 1972, p. 110)

Under Shaka's terroristic despotism, it has been estimated that deaths, including those killed in war and reprisals at the end of wars, reached nearly 2 million (Walter, 1972, pp. 111–2). From the example of the Zulu state, and in particular under the rule of Shaka to 1828, Walter (1972, p. 110) determines that 'a system of terror' depends on the 'technique of social control'. He argues against contrary interpretations of Shaka's rule as the erratic behaviour of a madman as follows: 'It is important to correct statements that fail to admit Shaka's intent, because they lend support to the prejudice that primitive rulers are not capable of sophisticated policy and to the false theory that systematic terrorism is exclusively a function of advanced technology' (ibid., p. 132).

According to Walter (1972, p. 255) terror was used in the Zulu state to achieve an 'atmosphere of total submission'. The system of terror, Walter contends, was a policy to destroy resistance and bind the submissive people to the despot of 'infinitive resource, omnipotence, omniscience, and irresistibility' (ibid., pp. 253–4). Arbitrary violence, he argues, was fundamental to the system of rule; it was the very means by which the system was bound together, political order maintained by the use of terror.

As in Cambodia, the Zulu despot used soldiers (warriors) – *impi* – acting as police to maintain control over the wide area of the state, and relied on a 'network of spies and informers'. Fear of what the despot would do to those who did not act in accordance with his wishes ensured that bonds between families and groups were destroyed. In a large, peaceful gathering, Shaka, at the flick of his finger, could be sure that the innocent victim would be killed:

> No sooner is the signal given, and the object pointed out, than those sitting around him scramble to kill him, although they have good reason to expect the next moment the same fate themselves, but such apprehensions are far from their thoughts; the will of the King being uppermost. (Extract from the Diary of Henry Francis Fynn, quoted in Walter, 1972, p. 35.)

The Zulu state was also divided into military regions in a way similar to Democratic Kampuchea. Within each Zulu region military *induna*, commoners who owed their appointment and, therefore, 'their futures' to the despot, were in charge of both military and administrative operations. These *induna* shared authority with chiefs who were often kinsmen of Shaka.

Contrasting the system of terror in the Zulu state with views held in western political thought, Walter (1972, p. 257) argues that contrary to the conventional view, which looks for order and structures to hold systems together, it was irrationality, caprice and violence which were the 'organising principles of the Zulu State'. As in Arendt's view of totalitarianism, Shaka's total domination was used, as part of a deliberate policy, to destroy spontaneity.[8] Shaka's system of terror achieved total reach and total submission to the regime; indeed the state was perceived as being bound together by the process of terror itself. The Zulu state, like Germany under Hitler and the USSR under Stalin, was a 'vast predatory organism directed by a single will' in which 'there was no place for conventional resistance, opposition, or even different identities' (ibid., p. 249).

Certainly there are important similarities between the Zulu state and the zero years in Cambodia, but there are also too many important differences for them to share the classification of a proto-totalitarian system. Pol Pot was too shadowy and too much part of 'nine men at the centre' to be classed as a despot. The Zulu state was also too primitive. In it a system of terror was developed with the purpose of achieving the total submission of a whole nation, and others conquered besides, to the will of one man, Shaka. Terror-was a system for social control, its aim the destruction of resistance, the despot's total control, an end in itself. In Cambodia, in contrast, the system had important socioeconomic effects. As has been shown, in a country devastated by war, the system aimed to increase output in agricultural production with early success, turned peasants against urban-dwellers and utilized the nationalist 'ancient hatred'.

Rudimentary totalitarian regime and war
Democratic Kampuchea did not last long enough to perfect its system. It is useful to view Cambodia as a rudimentary form of totalitarian regime: at a stage before the system has been perfected and fully functional concentration camps and secret police system, separate from the army, have been achieved.[9] Whether, in Cambodia, totalitarianism could have 'been brought to perfection, as in concentration camps' (Arendt, 1958, p. 344) is uncertain, for more sophisticated technology would have been required. In the twentieth century, the necessary technology can, of course, by imported. A rudimentary form need not necessarily, however, go on to achieve the highest stage of development.

Assessment of the extent to which war was a deliberate policy, secrecy being acceptable to the public in wartime in order to develop this concealment, must be weighed against alternative possible explanations. War may have been a policy designed to correct or to cover economic disaster brought by a government's wild economic schemes. Indeed war may straightforwardly have been a wild scheme in itself, whether reflecting in part the ideology of racial discrimination, as in Germany, or, simply, the desire to rebuild an empire, as in Ancient Angkor. War also provides concealment for the terror system while victories confirm the leadership's infallibility, and can be used as a means to overcome economic crisis, the inevitable consequence of substantive irrationality. A war economy, even though it adds to crisis, conceals economic shortages brought about by mismanagement; victories permit the plunder of lands, resources and people. But 'wild schemes', plans not worked through, are an inherent part of terror regimes. Terror as government does not move logically, rationally towards an ideological goal; their leaders have 'infallible' immovable positions in which 'ideology' is used as proof of infallibility, rather than actual performance being compared against plans.

In terror regimes ideas and schemes are picked up and tossed around. The attractiveness of such schemes is their ambiguity, their two-facedness, so that whatever happens the outcome can be used as proof of infallibility. The 'infallible' leadership lacks the normal rational restraint provided by the recognition that victory is not assured.

The fall of Democratic Kampuchea
As in Nazi Germany, defeat in war was the means by which the terror government was brought to an end. Events after the Vietnamese invasion of 1979 have differed sharply from those in Germany after 1945. As Pedler (1989, p. 98) remarks, 'like the Allies in Germany when they set up a Western-style democracy in place of the Nazi Government, the Vietnamese created a government in their own image – in their case a government mirroring their communist regime in Hanoi'. In this sense, the new PRK government in Phnom Penh resembled more the changes after de-Stalinization, where the worst excesses of Stalinism were destroyed but a communist system remained, than the German case where the old system was completely eradicated in one sweep. Whereas Hitler was totally defeated and Stalin's death was soon followed by the end of Beria and then de-Stalinization under Khrushchev, in Cambodia the Pol Pot clique remained alive and, with bases on the Thai border, never entirely eradicated. From these bases counter-attacks were launched and the Khmers Rouges were eventually joined by other forces opposed to the PRK.

The task which Vietnam, a poor country, undertook in Cambodia, a country decimated by war, atrocities and destruction as the Khmers Rouges fled, was made more burdensome by international reactions. Not yet aware of Pol Pot's atrocities, carried out as they were in a secret society, and opposed to communist Vietnam, the West and members of ASEAN would not recognize the PRK government, refused aid and imposed an economic blockade (Pedler, 1989, p. 98). Only as the evidence of the atrocities emerged did international opinion begin to shift, by which time the civil war had grown and the Coalition Government of Democratic Kampuchea (CGDK) had been formed in Kuala Lumpur, in June 1982, from the three rebel factions – Khmer Rouge, Khmer Serei and forces loyal to Sihanouk. To improve their image, in 1986 Pol Pot was replaced as head of the Khmer Rouge by Khieu Samphan.

Through a long and halting series of negotiations and Vietnamese troop withdrawals, a peace plan, first initiated by Vietnam, was signed in Paris in 1991. Elections were held in May 1993, the first since 1981, for the 120-member Constituent Assembly. With 20 parties contesting the election and the Cambodian People's Party (a former communist party) and Funcinpec (the nationalist grouping headed by Sihanouk and supported by the rebel Khmer Rouge) each receiving less than 50 per cent of the votes (at around 37 and 42 per cent respectively) the election clearly showed a country divided (*Keesing's*, 1993, p. 39461). The lessons of Yugoslavia demonstrate the arrogance of the belief that democratic politics can solve everything. In drawing attention to Cambodia's rudimentary system of totalitarian terror, with crucial similarities shared with Nazi Germany and Stalin's USSR alike, the lessons here suggest that an international division of reactions along communist and non-communist lines has been and remains entirely detrimental to Cambodia's recovery. Such concentration on ideology rests, as has now become clear, on a mistaken understanding of both the nature and causes of terror regimes.

Notes

1. Quoted from a Cambodian statement of December 1977. See *Keesing's* (1978, p. 29270), where it is pointed out that information about the claimed September 1975 and April and September 1976 *coups* was never given but that these dates coincide with changes in the Cambodian government.
2. Ponchaud (1978, p. 127). For a discussion of 'organization' over 'party' see ibid. (p. 107). See also Ponchaud (1989). Pilger (1989, p. 388) has drawn attention to the 'medievalism' of the Khmer Rouge 'which their principally Marxist pretensions barely concealed'. Angkor was the capital of the Khmer empire which was at its peak between the tenth and thirteenth centuries. The kingdom was ruled by an oriental despot. See Melotti (1977) for expansion on oriental despotism and the Asiatic mode of production.
3. Quinn (1989) explains the terror through a combination of ideas modified from Mao Tse Tung's writings (in particular his Great Leap Forward) in combination with Stalinist methods (as employed in collectivization in the 1930s) and the use of poor, uneducated, young peasants. He admits, however, (p. 219) that there was acknowledgement of the influence of Stalin neither in Pol Pot's writings nor in his speeches. This is confirmed by Jackson (1989b, p. 249) where he also notes (p. 243) that 'the Third Reich's policies prove that Marxist regimes hold no monopoly on the utilization of violence to achieve rapid social change'.
4. For the full list see *Keesing's* (1981, p. 30670). Of particular note is point 6 which reads as follows: '*Ill-treatment of Children.* Children over six had not been allowed to live with their parents, and those over 10 had been forced to do very hard work just like the adults.'
5. See *Keesing's* (1981, p. 30672) for details of land taken out of production in 1978.
6. For evidence confirming the lies in the speech about medical improvements, see D'Souza (1989, pp. 87–8).
7. Tuol Sleng has been compared with Auschwitz by Pilger (1989, p. 393) and Carney (1989, p. 95) refers to it, once, as a 'concentration camp'. Descriptions used generally are a mixture of prison and centre of interrogation, for torture and execution.
8. For example, massacres when carried out were always total; no child or woman was ever left alive, for they might later produce more children to become enemies. So too the Khmer Rouge acted to minimize witnesses to their atrocities by conducting massacres in distant regions.
9. For a development of this argument elsewhere see O'Kane (1993).

Conclusion   Terror and modernity

In analysing Cambodia in the zero years as a terror regime, crucially similar to Nazi Germany from 1938 and Stalin's Russia from 1930, but as a case of a rudimentary totalitarian regime, what is at issue is the relationship between totalitarianism, as modern genocide, and modernity. For Arendt, totalitarianism was the product of a modern world with nation-states, universal suffrage, political parties and an industrial class system. For Friedrich and Brzezinski modern science and technology are absolutely essential to totalitarianism. For Bauman modern rational bureaucracy holds the key to understanding modern genocide. Fixing, rather, on societies dislocated by foreign and civil war, and on economies based on 'substantive irrationality', with the anchor to market mechanisms severed and with forced labour central to the system, connections to past societies are more easily made. Systems of forced labour have a long history, from the ancient world of slavery through to slave plantation systems and serfdom. Terror has been employed in both ancient and medieval empires and wars have ravaged societies and destroyed economies since written history.

Totalitarianism, however, is new and what is novel about it can be gleaned exactly from comparison of the cases of Cambodia, Russia and Germany. Concealment of terror in secret societies was important to all three cases. Massacres occurred in remote areas in Cambodia, in Germany the true nature of conditions, experiments and events in concentration camps were kept from public knowledge. Even the existence of camps was covered up and the closer to Germany terror operated the more careful concealment became. The open slaughter of Poles and Russian soldiers in distant eastern territories was one thing; the extermination of Jews on German soil quite another. In Russia concealment was eased by the vast expansion of Russian territory: camps could be kept to underpopulated, distant regions.

The relationship between 'modern civilization' and totalitarian regimes lies not in the existence of science and technology nor party states nor popular politics nor bureaucratic organization, though all these are connected to it, but in the need to conceal the actual barbarity of terror from the public eye. In modern civilizations witness to torture and systematic brutality is not acceptable to the wider public. The secret society, terror operating behind the state, is fundamental to totalitarian regimes. It is this very concealment which is new. Modern science and technology aid concealment but do not cause it. Modern democratic experiences render unacceptable behaviour which Shaka could employ openly, namely the public execution of the ostensibly innocent.

Social dislocation and economic devastation provide the conditions in which terror can occur but schemes based on substantive irrationality, with their integral use of coercion and then absolute terror, are the key to totalitarian regimes. In Cambodia, rudimentary totalitarianism was appropriate because it was a backward country suffering extremes of social and economic dislocation. In Russia and even more so in Germany, concealment was of the utmost importance. This very concealment, this secrecy so essential to the totalitarian regime, is exactly what makes it modern. To the extent that the history of modern society has been accompanied by the growth of institutions where people are kept from the public gaze – prisons as places of corrective punishment, mental institutions and hospitals for the permanently ill, and workhouses for the destitute – modernity has provided the basis upon which the secret system could be built, concealment in the very midst of increasing openness. But this does not make modernity its cause. Rather, the causes of terror regimes cannot be separated from wild schemes based on the immovable belief that the extensive use of forced labour is the key to success – schemes based, that is, on a conviction which is itself both pre-modern and the antithesis of modernity.

Bibliography

Almond, G.A. and G.B. Powell (1967), *Comparative Politics: A Developmental Approach*, Boston: Little Brown and Company.

Andics, H. (1969), *Rule of Terror*, London: Constable.

Arendt, H. (1958), *The Origins of Totalitarianism*, London: Allen and Unwin.

Arendt, H. (1963), *On Revolution*, New York: Viking Press.

Arendt, H. (1970), *On Violence*, London: Allen and Unwin, The Penguin Press.

Arendt, H. (1986), 'Communicative Power', taken from 'On Violence' (1970) in Lukes (ed.) (1986), pp. 59–74.

Aron, R. (1968), *Democracy and Totalitarianism*, London: Weidenfeld and Nicolson.

Bachrach, P. and M.S. Baratz (1970), *Power and Poverty: Theory and Practice*, New York: Oxford University Press.

Bacon, E. (1994), *The Gulag at War: Stalin's Forced Labour System in the Light of the Archives*, London: Macmillan.

Balfour, M. (1992), *Germany: The Tides of Power*, London: Routledge.

Barber, B.R. (1969), 'Conceptual Foundations of Totalitarianism' in Friedrich et al. (1969), pp. 3–52.

Barron, J. and A. Paul (1977), *Peace with Horror*, London: Hodder and Stoughton.

Bauman, Z. (1989), *Modernity and the Holocaust*, Cambridge: Polity Press.

Beetham, D. (1985), *Max Weber and the Theory of Modern Politics*, Cambridge: Polity Press.

Beetham, D. (1987), *Bureaucracy*, Milton Keynes: Open University Press.

Bierstedt, R. (1950), 'The Analysis of Social Power', *American Sociological Review*, **15**, 730–38.

Blinkhorn, M. (ed.) (1990), *Fascists and Conservatives: The Radical Right and the Establishment in Twentieth-Century Europe*, London: Unwin Hyman.

Bradley, J. F. N. (1975), *Civil War in Russia 1917–20*, London: Batsford.

Breitman, R. (1992), 'The Final Solution' in Martel (ed.) (1992), pp. 197–210.

Bright, C. and S. Harding (eds) (1984), *Statemaking and Social Movements*, Ann Arbor: University of Michigan Press.

Broszat, M. (1966), *German National Socialism. 1919–1945*, Santa Barbara, California: Clio Press.

Broszat, M. (1968), 'The Concentration Camps, 1933–45' in H. Krausnick et al. (1968), pp. 395–504.

Broszat, M. (1981), *The Hitler State: The Foundation and Development of the Internal Structure of the Third Reich*, London: Longman.

Brower, D.R. (1989), '"The City in Danger": The Civil War and the Russian Population' in D.P. Koenker, W.G. Rosenberg and R.G. Suny (1989), *Party, State and Society in the Russian Civil War: Explorations in Social History*, Bloomington and Indianapolis: Indiana University Press, pp. 58–80.

Browning, C.R. (1985), *Fateful Months: Essays on the Emergence of the Final Solution*, New York: Holmes and Meier.

Browning, C.R. (1992), *The Path to Genocide: Essays on Launching the Final Solution*, New York: Cambridge University Press.

Buchheim, H. (1968), *Totalitarian Rule: Its Nature and Characteristics*, Middletown, Connecticut: Wesleyan University Press.

Bullock, A. (1993), *Hitler and Stalin: Parallel Lives*, London: Fontana.

Burleigh, M. and W. Wippermann (1991), *The Racial State: Germany 1933–1945*, Cambridge: Cambridge University Press.

Burrowes, R. (1969), 'Totalitarianism: The Revised Standard Version', *World Politics*, **21**, 272–94.

Canovan, M. (1983), 'A Case of Distorted Communication: A Note on Habermas and Arendt', *Political Theory*, **11**, 105–16.

Canovan, M, (1992), *Hannah Arendt: A Reinterpretation of her Political Thought*, Cambridge: Cambridge University Press.

Carney, T. (1989), 'The Organization of Power' in Jackson (ed.) (1989a), pp. 79–107.

Carr, E.H. (1966), *The Bolshevik Revolution 1917–23, Vol. 2*, Harmondsworth: Penguin.

Chapman, B. (1970), *Police State*, London: Pall Mall.

Chomsky, N. and E.S. Herman (1979), *After the Cataclysm*, Nottingham: Spokesman.

Clegg, S.R. (1989), *Frameworks of Power*, London: Sage Publications.

Conquest, R. (1971), *The Great Terror: Stalin's Purge of the Thirties*, Harmondsworth: Penguin.

Conquest, R. (1990), *The Great Terror: A Reassessment*, London: Hutchinson.

Coraggio, J.L. (1986), *Nicaragua: Revolution and Democracy*, Boston: Allen and Unwin,

Crew, D.F. (ed.) (1994), *Nazism and German Society, 1933–1945*, London: Routledge.

Curtis, M. (1969), 'Retreat from Totalitarianism' in Friedrich et al. (1969), pp. 53–121.

Curtis, M. (1979), *Totalitarianism*, New Brunswick, New Jersey: Transaction Books.

Dahl, R.A. (1957), 'The Concept of Power', *Behavioural Science*, **2**, 201–15.

Dahl, R.A. (1989), *Democracy and its Critics*, New Haven: Yale University Press.

Dallin, D.J. and B.I. Nicolaevsky (1948), *Forced Labour in Soviet Russia*, London: Hollis and Carter.

Daniels, R.V. (1993), *The End of Communist Revolution*, London: Routledge.

Davies, R.W. (1993), 'Economic Aspects of Stalinism' in Nove (1993b), pp. 39–74.

Deutscher, I. (1968), *Stalin: A Political Biography*, Harmondsworth: Penguin.

D'Souza, F. (1989), 'Economics, Development and Aid', in Wright (ed.) (1989), pp. 85–94.

Easton, D. (1985), *A Systems Analysis of Political Life*, New York: Wiley.

Ebenstein, W. (1958), 'The Study of Totalitarianism', *World Politics*, **10**, 274–88.

Ellman, M. (1989), *Socialist Planning*, Cambridge: Cambridge University Press.

Engels, F. (1969), 'On Authority' in Feuer (1969), pp. 518–23.

Evans, P. R., D. Rueschemeyer and T. Skocpol (1985), *Bringing The State Back In*, New York: Cambridge University Press.

Fein, H. (1993), *Genocide: A Sociological Perspective*, London: Sage Publications.

Feuer, L.S. (ed.) (1969), *Marx and Engels: Basic Writings on Politics and Philosophy*, London: Fontana/Collins.

Finegold, K. and T. Skocpol (1984), 'State Party and Industry: From Business Recovery to the Wagner Act in America's New Deal' in Bright and Harding (eds) (1984), pp. 159–92.

Fitzpatrick, S. (1993), 'The Impact of the Great Purges on Soviet Elites: A Case Study from Moscow and Leningrad telephone directories of the 1930s' in Getty and Manning (eds) (1993), pp. 247–60.

Fleming, G. (1986), *Hitler and The Final Solution*, Oxford: Oxford University Press.

Foucault, M. (1979), *Power, Truth, Strategy*, Sydney: Feral Publications.

Frei, N. (1993), *National Socialist Rule in Germany: The Führer State, 1933–1945*, Oxford: Blackwell.

Friedrich, C.J. (1969), 'The Evolving Theory and Practice of Totalitarian Regimes', in Friedrich et al. (1969), pp. 123–64.

Friedrich, C.J. and Z.K. Brzezinski (1965), *Totalitarian Dictatorship and Autocracy*, Cambridge, Massachusetts: Harvard University Press.

Friedrich, C.J., M. Curtis and B.R. Barber (1969), *Totalitarianism in Perspective: Three Views*, New York: Praeger.

Gerth, H.H. and C.W. Mills (1970), *From Max Weber: Essays in Sociology*, London: Routledge and Kegan Paul.

Getty, J.A. (1993), 'The Politics of Repression Revisited', in Getty and Manning (eds) (1993), pp. 40–62.

Getty, J.A. and W. Chase (1993), 'Patterns of Repression among the Soviet Elite in the late 1930s: A Biographical Approach' in Getty and Manning (eds) (1993), pp. 225–46.

Getty, J.A. and R.T. Manning (eds) (1993), *Stalinist Terror: New Perspectives*, Cambridge: Cambridge University Press.

Geyer, M. (1984), 'The State in National Socialist Germany' in Bright and Harding (eds) (1984), pp. 193–232.

Giddens, A. (1968), 'Power in the Recent Writings of Talcott Parsons', *Sociology*, **2**, 257–72.

Giddens, A. (1981), *A Contemporary Critique of Historical Materialism, Vol. 1, Power Property and The State*, London: Macmillan.

Giddens, A. (1985), *The Nation-State and Violence: Volume Two of a Contemporary Critique of Historical Materialism*, Berkeley and Los Angeles: University of California Press.

Gill, G. (1990), *The Origins of the Stalinist Political System*, Cambridge: Cambridge University Press.

Goldman, A.I. (1986), 'Toward a Theory of Social Power' in Lukes (ed.) (1986), pp. 156–202.

Gordon, S. (1984), *Hitler, Germans and the 'Jewish Question'*, Princeton, New Jersey: Princeton University Press.

Gregor, A.J. (1974), *Interpretations of Fascism*, Morristown, New Jersey: General Learning Press.

Gregor, A. J (1982), 'Fascism's Philosophy of Violence and The Concept of Terror' in D.C. Rapoport and Y. Alexander (eds) (1982), *The Morality of Terrorism*, New York, Pergamon, pp. 152–68.

Groth, A. (1964), 'The "isms" in Totalitarianism', *American Political Science Review*, **58**, 881–901.

Habermas, J. (1986), 'Hannah Arendt's Communicative Concept of Power' in Lukes (ed.) (1986), pp. 75–93.

Harrison, M. (1993), 'Soviet Economic Growth Since 1928: The Alternative Statistics of G.I. Khanin', *Europe–Asia Studies*, **45** (1), 141–67.

Hawk, D. (1989), 'The Photographic Record' in Jackson (1989a), pp. 209–14.

Herbert, U. (1994), 'Labor as Spoils of Conquest, 1933–1945', in D.F. Crew (ed.) (1994), pp. 219–73.

Hiden, J. and Farquharson (1983), *Explaining Hitler's Germany: Historians and the Third Reich*, London: Batsford.

Hilberg, R. (1983), *The Destruction of European Jews*, New York; Holmes and Meier.

Homze, E.L. (1967), *Foreign Labor in Nazi Germany*, Princeton, New Jersey: Princeton University Press,

Jackson, K.D. (ed.) (1989a), *Cambodia 1975–1978: Rendezvous with Death*, Princeton, New Jersey: Princeton University Press.

Jackson, K.D. (1989b), 'The Intellectual Origins of the Khmer Rouge' in Jackson (ed.) (1989a), pp. 241–50.

Jacobsen, H.-A. (1968), 'The *Kommissarbefehl* and mass executions of Soviet Russian Prisoners of War' in Krausnick et al. (1968), pp. 503–35.

James, H.J. (1987), *The German Slump: Politics and Economics 1924–1936*, Oxford: Clarendon Press.

Jasny, N. (1961), *Soviet Industrialization, 1928–1952*, Chicago: Chicago University Press.

Kaiser, D.E. (1992), 'Hitler and the Coming of War' in Martel (ed.) (1992), pp. 178–96.

Keesing's Contemporary Archives, 1975–93, London and Harlow: Longman.

Kershaw, I. (1989), *The Nazi Dictatorship: Problems and Perspectives of Interpretation*, London: Edward Arnold.

King, R. (1986), *The State in Modern Society: New Directions in Political Sociology*, Chatham, New Jersey: Chatham House.

Klein, B.H. (1959), *German's Economic Preparations for War*, Cambridge, Massachusetts: Harvard University Press.

Kraus, O. and E. Kulka (1966), *The Death Factory*, Oxford: Pergamon.

Krausnick, H.B., H. Buchheim, M. Broszat and H.A. Jacobsen (1968), *Anatomy of the SS State*, London: Collins.

Kuromiya, H. (1993), 'Stalinist Terror in the Donbas: A Note' in Getty and Manning (eds) (1993), pp. 215–22.

Landau, R.S. (1992), *The Nazi Holocaust*, London: I.B. Taurus.

Lane, J.-E. (1993), 'The Twilight of the Scandinavian Model', *Political Studies*, **41**, 315–24.

Lassmann, P. and R. Speirs (eds) (1994), *Weber: Political Writings*, Cambridge: Cambridge University Press.

Leggett, G. (1981), *The Cheka: Lenin's Political Police*, Oxford: Clarendon Press.

Levytsky, B. (1972), *The Uses of Terror: The Soviet Secret Police 1917–70*, New York: Coward, McCann and Geoghegan.

Lewin, M. (1968), *Russian Peasants and Soviet Power: A Study of Collectivization*, London: Allen and Unwin.

Lewin, M. (1985), *The Making of the Soviet System: Essays in the Social History of Interwar Russia*, New York: Pantheon.

Lorrell, M.A. (1976), 'The Politics of Economic Debate: Anglo-American Perceptions of Germany's Economic Preparations for War, 1937–1939', doctoral thesis, University of Washington.

Lukes, S. (1974), *Power: A Radical View*, London: Macmillan.

Lukes, S. (ed.) (1986), *Power*, Oxford: Blackwell.

MacIver, R.M. (1926), *The Modern State*, London: Oxford University Press.

Malle, S. (1985), *The Economic Organisation of War Communism, 1918–21*, Cambridge: Cambridge University Press.

Mann, M. (1984), 'The Autonomous Power of the State' *Archives Européennes de Sociologie*, **25** (2), 185–213.

Manning, R.T. (1992), 'The Soviet Economic Crisis of 1936–1940 and the Great Purges' in Getty and Manning (eds) (1993), pp. 116–41.

Marshall, G. (1982), *In Search of the Spirit of Capitalism: An Essay on Max Weber's Protestant Ethic Thesis*, London: Hutchinson.

Martel, G. (ed.) (1992), *Modern Germany Reconsidered*, London: Routledge.

Marx, K. (1973), *The Revolutions of 1848: Political Writings Vol. I*, Harmondsworth: Penguin.

Mason, T.W. (1968), 'The Primacy of Politics – Politics and Economics in National Socialist Germany' in S.J. Woolf (ed.), *The Nature of Fascism*, London: Weidenfeld and Nicolson, pp. 165–95.

Mayer, A. (1989), *Why Did The Heavens Not Darken? The 'Final Solution' in History*, New York: Pantheon.

McLellan, D. (ed.) (1986), *The Essential Left*, London: Counterpoint (Unwin).

Melotti, U. (1977), *Marx and the Third World*, London: Macmillan.

Michels, R. (1962), *Political Parties: A Sociological Study of the Oligarchical Tendencies of Modern Democracy*, New York: Free Press.

Milgram, S. (1974), *Obedience to Authority: An Experimental View*, London: Tavistock.

Mills, C.W. (1956), *The Power Elite*, New York: Oxford University Press.

Milner, H. (1990), *Sweden: Social Democracy in Practice*, New York: Oxford University Press.

Milward, A.S. (1965), *The German Economy at War*, London: The Athlone Press, University of London.

Mixon, D. (1989), *Obedience and Civilization*, London: Pluto Press.

Moore B. Jr (1978), *Injustice: The Social Bases of Obedience and Revolt*, London: Macmillan.

Morriss, P. (1987), *Power: A Philosophical Analysis*, Manchester: Manchester University Press.

Neumann, F. (1944), *Behemoth: The Structure and Practice of National Socialism, 1933–44*, New York: Oxford University Press.

Noakes, J. (1986), 'The Origins, Structure and Functions of Nazi Terror' in O'Sullivan (1986), pp. 67–87.

Nove, A. (1993a), 'Victims of Stalinism: How Many?' in Getty and Manning (eds) (1993), pp. 261–74.

Nove, A. (ed.) (1993b), *The Stalin Phenomenon*, London: Weidenfeld and Nicolson.

Nove, A. (1993c), 'Stalin and Stalinism – Some Introductory Thoughts' in Nove (1993b), pp. 1–38.

O'Kane, R.H.T. (1989), 'Military Regimes: Power and Force', *European Journal of Political Research*, **17**, 333–50,

O'Kane, R.H.T. (1991), *The Revolutionary Reign of Terror: The Role of Violence in Political Change*, Aldershot: Edward Elgar.

O'Kane, R.H.T. (1993), 'Cambodia in the Zero Years: Rudimentary Totalitarianism', *Third World Quarterly*, **14** (4), 735–48.

O'Sullivan, N. (ed.) (1986), *Terrorism, Ideology and Revolution*, Brighton: Harvester Wheatsheaf.

Parsons, T. (1963), 'On the Concept of Political Power', *Proceedings of the American Philosophical Society*, **107**, 232–62, reprinted in Lukes (ed.) (1986), pp. 94–143.

Parsons, T. (1986), 'Power and the Social System' in Lukes (ed.) (1986), pp. 94–143.

Pedler, J. (1989), 'War or Peace?' in Wright (ed.) (1989), pp. 95–121.

Pilger, J. (1989), *Heroes*, London: Pan.

Ponchaud, F. (1978), *Cambodia Year Zero*, London: Allen Lane.

Ponchaud, F. (1989), 'Social Change in the Vortex of Revolution' in Jackson (ed.) (1989a), pp. 151–77.

Poulantzas, N. (1986), 'Class Power' in Lukes (ed.) (1986), pp. 144–55.

Pulzer, P. (1992), *Jews and the German State: The Political History of a Minority, 1848–1933*, Oxford: Blackwell.

Quinn, K.M. (1989), 'Explaining the Terror', in Jackson (ed.) (1989a), pp. 215–40.

Reese, R.R. (1993), 'The Red Army and the Great Purges' in Getty and Manning (eds) (1993), pp. 198–214.

Reiman, M. (1987), *The Birth of Stalinism: The USSR on the Eve of the 'Second Revolution'*, London: I.B. Taurus.

Rigby, T.H. (1979), *Lenin's Government: Sovnarkom 1917–22*, Cambridge: Cambridge University Press.

Rittersporn, G.T. (1993), 'The Omnipresent Conspiracy: On Soviet Imagery of Politics and Social Relations in the 1930s', in Getty and Manning (eds) (1993), pp. 99–115.

Rummel, R.J. (1990), *Lethal Politics: Soviet Genocide and Mass Murder since 1917*, New Brunswick, New Jersey: Transaction Publishers.

Russell, B. (1986), 'The Forms of Power' in Lukes (ed.) (1986), pp. 19–27.

Sagar, D. (1989), ' Historical Survey' in Wright (1989), pp. 9–70.

Sakwa, R. (1988), *Soviet Communists in Power: A Study of Moscow During the Civil War, 1918–21*, London: Macmillan.

Sarti, R. (1990), 'Italian Fascism: Radical Politics and Conservative Goals' in Blinkhorn (ed.) (1990), pp. 14–30.

Sartori, G. (1970), 'Concept Misformation in Comparative Politics', *The American Political Science Review*, **64**, 1033–53.

Sartori, G. (1984), 'Guidelines for Concept Analysis' in G. Sartori (ed.), *Science Concepts*, Beverly Hills, California: Sage, pp. 15–85.

Sartori, G. (1991), 'Comparing and Miscomparing', *Journal of Theoretical Politics*, **3** (3), 243–57.

Sartori, G. (1993), 'Totalitarianism, Model Mania and Learning from Error', *Journal of Theoretical Politics*, **5**, 5–22,

Schapiro, L. (1972), *Totalitarianism*, London: Pall Mall.

Schoenbaum, D. (1967), *Hitler's Social Revolution: Class and Status in Nazi Germany 1933–1939*, London: Weidenfeld and Nicolson.

Siegelbaum, L.H. (1992), *Soviet State and Society Between Revolutions, 1918–1929*, Cambridge: Cambridge University Press.

Skocpol, T. (1979), *States and Social Revolutions: A Comparative Analysis of France, Russia and China*, New York: Cambridge University Press.

Skocpol, T. (1985), 'Bringing the State Back In: Strategies of Analysis in Current Research', in Evans et al. (eds) (1985), pp. 3–43.

Stampp, K.M. (1956), *The Peculiar Institution*, New York: Knopf.

Starkov, B.A. (1993), 'Narkom Ezhov' in Getty and Manning (eds) (1993), pp. 21–39.

Steinberg, J. (1991), *All or Nothing: The Axis and the Holocaust 1941–43*, London: Routledge.

Swianiewicz, S. (1965), *Forced Labour and Economic Development: An Enquiry into the Experience of Soviet Industrialization*, London: Oxford University Press.

Talmon, J.L. (1952), *The Origins of Totalitarian Democracy*, London: Secker and Warburg.

Thurston, R. (1993), 'The Stakhanovite Movement: The Background to the Great Terror in the Factories, 1935–1938' in Getty and Manning (eds) (1993), pp. 142–60.

Tilly, C. (1985), 'War Making and State Making as Organized Crime', in Evans et al. (1985), pp. 169–91.

Tsipko, A. (1989), 'The Roots of Stalinism', essay number 4, *Nauka: Zhizn*, February.

Twining, C.H. (1989), 'The Economy' in Jackson (1989a), pp. 109–50.

Unger, A.L. (1974), *The Totalitarian Party: Party and People in Nazi Germany and Soviet Russia*, Cambridge: Cambridge University Press.

Vaksberg, A. (1990), *The Prosecutor and the Prey: Vyshinsky and the 1930s Moscow Show Trials*, London: Weidenfeld and Nicolson.

Vickery, M. (1985), *Cambodia, 1975–1982*, London: Allen and Unwin.

Viola, L. (1993), 'The Second Coming: Class Enemies in the Soviet Countryside, 1927–1935' in Getty and Manning (eds) (1993), pp. 65–98.

Walter, E.V. (1972), *Terror and Resistance: A Study of Political Violence*, New York: Oxford University Press.

Ward, C. (1993), *Stalin's Russia*, London: Edward Arnold.

Weber, M. (1964), *The Theory of Social and Economic Organization* (ed. T Parsons), New York: The Free Press.

Wheatcroft, S.G. (1993), More Light on the Scale of Repression and Excess Mortality in the Soviet Union in the 1930s' in Getty and Manning (eds) (1993), pp. 275–90.

Wright, M. (ed.) (1989), *Cambodia: A Matter of Survival*, Harlow: Longman.

Zaleski, E. (1980), *Stalinist Planning for Economic Growth, 1933–1952*, Chapel Hill, North Carolina: North Carolina Press and London: Macmillan.

Index

Angkar 185–6, 189
Ankor Empire 186, 194*n.2*
anti-Semitism 21, 46, 70, 74, 135
    see also Jews; Nuremburg Laws
Arendt, Hannah 10–19, 22, 23, 24*n.5, 6,*
    35, 45, 46, 47, 50–51, 63–73, 76–7,
    79–95, 96, 97, 95*n.1*, 101, 102,
    112, 117–18, 120, 133, 189, 195
armaments production 146, 158, 170,
    171
army 6, 35
    and foreign office 152
    German 87, 138, 143
    and labour office 157
    Russian, purges in 89
    Vietnamese 180, 184
    see also Khmer Rouge; military
        expansion and expenditure
asocials 140, 149, 158, 170
Auschwitz 154, 161, 163, 169, 170–71,
    174
authoritarian state 5, 41
authority 9, 11, 30

Babi Yar massacre 159
Bachrach, P. and M. S. Baratz 7–9, 10,
    12, 15, 18, 19, 25*n.8*, 71
bankruptcy 91, 93
Bauman, Z. 26–7, 37, 39, 41, 45–7, 50,
    52, 54, 55–6, 68–9, 83, 98*n.1*,
    174*n.4*, 195
Beetham, D. 42–5, 69
Blitzkrieg 154, 158
Bolshevik Party 104
Brüning, Heinrich 137, 138, 143
Buchenwald 148, 152, 170
Bukharin, Nikolai I. 107, 108, 109, 133
bureaucracy 3, 4, 5, 26, 28–30, 34–5,
    37–40, 42–4, 46
    destruction of in Russia 80, 120
    as a method of rule 82
    and secrecy 42–5
    in totalitarianism 53–4, 69

bureaucratic culture 28–30, 32
byvshie liudi 113, 135

Cambodia 180–94, 195, 196
Cambodian National Front for National
    Socialism 180, 184
capitalist system 40–42, 45–6
    enterprises in 38
    state and society of 6
capitalists, relationship with Nazi
    government 150*n.3*
Central Planning Board 165, 167,
    174*n.10*
central planning *see* planned economy
centralization of coercion, state's 26, 27,
    32
    see also monopoly of coercion, state's
Charter of Labour 59
Cheka 57, 86, 87, 104
China 52, 58, 61–2, 78*n.7*, 97, 187
    communism in 186
Chinese Revolution 4, 16–17, 24*n.7*
citizenship 82
civil society 5
civil war 16, 85–6, 87, 103
    in Cambodia 180–81
    in Russia (RSFSR) 105, 115*n.1, 2*
class
    conflict 6, 101
    in definition of power 6
    in definition of state 5–6
    liquidation of 80, 88–90, 109
        see also dekulakization
    membership of 79
classless society 186
    see also mass society
coal production 124–5, 132
coercion 6, 8–9, 10, 18, 35, 133, 172
    justification for 9, 10, 13, 14
    legitimation for 9, 10, 14
    means of 13, 14, 18, 19
    structures of 6
    see also force; forced labour;